COMMUNITY NAMES OF ALBERTA

By the authors
By Austin Mardon A Conspectus of the Contribution of Herodotus to the Development of Geographical Thought 1990;
International Law and Space Rescue Systems 1991;
Kensington Stone and Other Essays 1991;
A Transient in Whirl 1991;
Alone Against the Revolution 1996;
Political Networks in Alberta 1905-1992 2002;
7 days in Moscow 2005;
The Contribution of Geography to the Recovery of Antarctic Meteorites 2005;
By Ernest Mardon Narrative Unity of the Cursor Mundi 1967;
The Founding Faculty of the University of Lethbridge 1968;
Place Names of Southern Alberta 1970;
The Conflict Between the Individual & Society in the Plays of James Bridie 1971;
Who's Who in Federal Politics from Alberta Ridings 1972;
English Studies at Canadian Universities 1972;
Community Names of Alberta 1975
By Austin Mardon & Ernest Mardon
Alberta Judicial Biographical Dictionary 1990;
Alberta Ethnic Mormon Politicians 1991;
Alberta Ethnic German Politicians 1991;
When Kitty Met the Ghost 1991;
Down & Out & On the Run in Moscow 1991;
The Girl Who Could Walk Through Walls 1991;
Alberta Mormon Politicians 1992;
Alberta General Election Returns & Subsequent Byelections 1882-1992 1993;
Edmonton Political Biography 1994;
Alberta Political Biographical Dictionary 1994;
Alberta Executive Council 1905-1990 1994;
Early Christian Saints 1997;
Later Christian Saints for Children 1997;
Many Christian Saints for Children 1997;
Childhood Memories & Legends of Christmas Past 1998;
Community Names of Alberta 1999;
Men of Dawn 1999;
United Farmers of Alberta 1999;
The Genealogy of the Mardon Family 2000;
Alberta Catholic Politicians 2000; Alberta Anglican Politicians 2001;
Liberal Politicians in Alberta 1905-1992 2002;
What's in a Name? 2002;
Edmonton Members of the Legislature 2004

Ernest G. Mardon and
Austin A. Mardon

COMMUNITY NAMES OF ALBERTA

Expanded Third Edition

Edited by Larry Erdos

Edmonton 2010

A Golden Meteorite Press Book.

Printed in Canada by Golden Meteorite Press.

Supported by grant from Antarctic Institute of Canada.

Cover design Lawrence Dommer, 2010
Published by Golden Meteorite Press.
Post Office Box 1223, Station Main,
Edmonton, Alberta, Canada. T5J 2M4
Telephone: 780-378-0063

ISBN 978-1-897472-17-0

Mardon, Ernest G., 1928-
    Community place names of Alberta / Ernest G.
Mardon, Austin A. Mardon. -- 3rd ed.

Includes index.
ISBN 978-1-897472-17-0

1. Names, Geographical--Alberta. 2. Alberta--History,
Local. 3. Cities and towns--Alberta. I. Mardon, Austin
A. (Austin Albert) II. Title.

FC3656.M37 2010   917.123'0014   C2010-904987-X

Contents

The Authors

Dr. Ernest G. Mardon

He was born December 21, 1928 at Houston Texas, U.S.A., son of Professor Austin Mardon, a British historian, and his wife Marie Dickey. On his maternal side, he is seventh generation. His Dickey ancestors settled in the New England Colonies in 1732.

He was educated at Gordonstown, Morayshire, Scotland, he attended Trinity College, Dublin University, Ireland, the University of Alberta, graduating with an education degree and did post graduate studies at the University of Ottawa.

He came to Alberta as a young man, and worked as the United Press International bureau manager at Edmonton. He interviewed Premier E. C. Manning weekly for four years and met most of the prominent Alberta politicians during the last forty-five years.

A retired University of Lethbridge professor he in partnership with his son, Austin A. Mardon is the author of several scholarly works.

In 1957, he married May G. Knowler, daughter of the late A. E. Knowler, an Edmonton businessman. They have one son and two daughters.

Austin A. Mardon

Born June 25, 1962 at Edmonton, Alberta, son of Dr. Ernest G. Mardon, a retired professor, and his wife May Knowler.

Educated at Lethbridge, he attended the South Dakota State University and Texas A&M University. He holds two Masters degrees. He is the only Canadian to go on a NASA sponsored meteorite recovery expedition to the southern polar plateau. He holds the United States Antarctic Medal.

For a decade, he has collaborated with his father in Alberta political biographical research that has resulted in the publication of this book. He is also a scientific author of numerous articles. This spring, he received a Canadian Governor General's Caring Award for his charity work.

Preface to the New Edition

This edition contains 1,977 main entries, a full hundred newly added since the 1973 edition, as well as many others fully rewritten and corrected.

This new edition has been carefully prepared to be useful for a wide variety of readers. Tourists will find it a fascinating companion to their experience of Alberta's hospitality, giving fascinating insights into the origins of the places and people that they visit.

Scholars in genealogy, sociology, history, politics and industry may utilize the text and thorough index to cross-reference many interesting dimensions of the patterns of settlement. And since it contains far more place names than appear on most readily available maps, this book can be used to easily locate those obscure communities that from time to time crop up in historical references and mailing addresses.

If community names are mentioned in a main entry, they appear in capitals. If that community has its own main entry, it appears bold. Entries containing just a cross-reference will not be indicated in bold type.

The map has been devised as an integrated tool for use with the text:

Each main entry contains the geographic coordinates for Township – Range – Meridian (unless unavailable) which can easily be located on the map.

Each entry contains a status line in italics giving the current status and vicinity of the community.

All cities and towns are named directly on the map.

A series of numbered dots, running roughly from top left to bottom right of the map, represent the other communities that are mentioned in the status lines. All vicinities mentioned are locatable on the map using the alphabetical listing of map references.

The map references are also listed numerically so that glancing around the map may be the point of departure for a curious investigator.

The index, though it may seem rather large, contains several special features that give the text many fascinating dimensions and ease of access to related information. In fact, the index itself can be a source of many wonderful browsing adventures. It contains numerous themes and relationships that otherwise might not come to light.

Main entries are indicated by a bolded page number in the index.

Where places are mentioned in the status lines as being nearby, they are sub-indexed under *vicinity*. This feature allows modern explorers to identify many neighboring localities in and around the same district.

The chronological listings under such index headings as *post office, hamlet, village, town, city, trading post* and *railway station* are given as the dates closest to the origins of the names of communities, often the dates of name changes rather than the dates of settlement. Many communities had multiple name changes.

Former post offices, and other former entities, are separately indexed, though not according to the year that they were closed, but consistently with the rest, by the year they opened.

The heroes of these stories, the bold explorers, pioneers, native leaders and industrialists are indexed along with their main professions.

The home country origins of settlers, and others who directly influenced the places and their names, are indexed. Canadian provinces and American states are entered separately, but cities and towns are listed only as sub-entries. Therefore, *Winnipeg* is to be found under *Manitoba*. England, Scotland, Ireland, and Wales, the original homes of so many Alberta settlers, are indexed by county or shire. It is to be hoped that this will aid those seeking clues to their personal genealogy and heritage.

One further value of this work, which is too rarely considered, but precious in its potential, is its possible function as a springboard for further literary works. By gathering the stories of the earliest hopes, dreams and achievements of those who set the shape of the province, the Mardons have provided a rich tapestry in which the strands of Alberta's history are woven. Future songwriters, poets, and storytellers, by following linked stories, discovering connections, or investigating neighboring districts, can find here a vast body of material to stimulate the imagination.

Larry Erdos
Editor

Foreword to the First Edition

The present publication supplements recent works on Canadian toponymy, in particular those referring to Western Canada, viz.: G.P.V. Akrigg and H.B. Akrigg: *1001 British Columbia Place Names* (Vancouver, 1969), and J.B. Rudnyckyi: *Manitoba Mosaic of Place Names* (Winnipeg, 1970). It appears that only Saskatchewan is lagging behind in this respect and leaves a gap which otherwise would cover the whole area of the Prairie Provinces and British Columbia.

Mardon's study is based primarily on the outdated book *Place-Names of Alberta* (Geographic Board of Canada, Ottawa, 1928); however, in many cases, the author brought new data, taken either from printed sources (including his own, *The History of Place Names in Southern Alberta*, Lethbridge-Winnipeg, 1972), or from questionnaires and field trip investigations, the latter being the most valuable contribution to the Albertan toponymic research.

As far as the 1928 publication of *Place-Names of Alberta* is concerned, in several instances corrections were made; thus, for example, the name COSSACK was explained as a toponym, named after "Southern Russian" Cossacks; in Mardon's text they were rightly designated as "Ukrainian" Cossacks. With regard to the place-name MAZEPPA, the author introduced some more relevant characteristics of this Cossack Hetman who "became a symbol of Ukrainian struggle for independence". The Post Office Slawa did not derive "from the Russian for 'praise' " as explained in 1928, but stems from the Ukrainian expression *Slawa (Bohu)*- "Glory (to God)." Shepenge, place-name left unexplained in 1928, is rightly interpreted as a transplanted name from Bukowyna: *Shypynci*. There are other persuasive additions and corrections of data which appeared in the 1928 publication.

All in all, Mardon's book is a welcome addition to the growing Canadian toponymic literature. Certainly it will render its services as a useful source of information on the history and meaning of place-names in this oil-rich province of Alberta.

J.B Rudnyckyi
University of Manitoba

Preface to the First Edition

The book is the result of years of intensive research backed by a lifetime interest in place names. There are scattered pieces of information about the names of Alberta communities and settlements in history books, town booklets, and newspaper articles. There has been only one major work on this fascinating subject, the Geographic Board of Canada's *Place-Names of Alberta*, published in 1928. This is the main source of my work, and I would like to publicly acknowledge my debt to it.

The study of place names is a valuable sidelight to history. The direct method of seeking information in written records often yields scanty returns or, in some cases, none at all. Efforts have been made to check each item, but we would advise caution as few sources are without errors. In some instances we may have been led astray by incorrect or incomplete information. One cannot be dogmatic in many cases and say that such-and-such is the one and only explanation for the name. All that we can vouch for in this work is that we have given our readers the best information that we could find. I am very conscious of the fact that without the labors of many writers of studies of regional histories, this book could not have been undertaken.

I have attempted to verify the factual material in each of the entries. This is especially true of the trading posts, communities, stations and post offices that have disappeared from the more recent maps of Alberta. The preservation of names, which have dropped out of current use, was one of the aims of this research project.

I would like to thank many libraries, institutions and individuals, such as Professor Yar Slavutych, that made the work possible. A special mention should be made to Mr. G. F. Delaney and his staff of the Toponymy Division of the Department of Energy, Mines and Resources. Without the assistance of the Library of the University of Lethbridge, this work could never have been completed. I am also most grateful to Miss Dorothy Phillips and Mrs. Anita Firth for typing the manuscript.

It is my hope that this book on the meaning of place names of Alberta communities, past and present, will be followed with another work on the names of the physical features of Alberta, and that these two works will preserve the history of place names in this province.

Ernest G. Mardon, Ph.D.
The University of Lethbridge
September 30, 1973

Introduction

This is a community study of the past and present settlements in the Province of Alberta. The region has been inhabited by man for some ten thousand years. However, recorded history only covers the last two hundred years. The place names of Alberta communities reveal the eloquent survival of a succession of races and peoples. The native Amerindians lived a nomadic existence, following the caribou, moose, or bison on their annual migrations. In the northern part of the province the Slave, the Beaver, the Chipewyan, and the Sarcee inhabited the woodland and their economy was based on the caribou and moose. To the south wandered the plains Indians; Cree, Blackfoot, Blood, Piegan, Stony and Gros Ventures. Their lives revolved around the buffalo, which were the basis of their economy. They have all contributed a heritage of names of physical features. It has been observed that names of rivers last the longest: "Their names are in our rivers and we cannot wash them out."

The first stratum of permanent settlements and onomastics was to be laid down in the last half of the eighteenth century by European explorers and fur-traders. The exploration of the interior of the continent was accomplished largely by water. This was true of Alberta which was approached by way of the Clearwater and the Athabasca Rivers. Within a generation there was a string of fur-trading posts across the northern portion of what is now Alberta. They included Fort of the Forks [1788], Fort George [1792], Fort Edmonton [1795], Fort Vermilion [1788], Rocky Mountain House [1798], Chesterfield House [1800], Fort Dunvegan [1805], Jasper House [1813], and Fort Assiniboine [1825].

These trading posts were fortified against the Indians. They had heavy outside walls so that the Indians could not climb over or set fire to them. These strong walls were usually made of tree trunks set as closely together as possible. At the corners, diagonally opposite each other, square blockhouses were built on top of the walls. The construction of these trading "forts" justified their name, and in several cases, the towns that grew up around these early fortified posts have kept the descriptive and historic word as part of their name.

The next stratum of permanent settlements owes its existence to Christian missionaries. In 1838, the first two missionaries ever to enter Alberta visited Fort Edmonton. Fathers Francois Blanchet and Modeste Demers, acting on orders from Bishop Provencher of St. Boniface, rested here on their way to open a mission at Fort Vancouver on the Columbia River. Two years later Rev. R.T. Rundle, representing the Wesleyan Society of London, commenced his missionary labors. At the same time Catholic missionaries such as Fr. Thibault, Fr. Lacombe, OMI, Fr. Leduc, OMI, and Fr. Petitot, OMI, commenced their work among the nomadic Indians. They established permanent missions at Lac Ste. Anne [1842], Fort Chipewyan [1847], Lac La Biche [1853], St. Albert [1861], and Lady of Peace, Calgary [1873]. Permanent Protestant missions were established at Rocky Mountain House [1841], Pigeon Lake [1847], Whitefish Lake [1859], Pakan [1863], and Morley [1873].

The American whiskey forts, which were established across Southern Alberta in the late 1860's, had a brief but turbulent life. They had colorful names such as Fort Whoop-up, Stand Off, Slide Out, Robber's Roost, and Whiskey Gap. Their main influence on the development of the region was that they led directly to the formation of the North West Mounted Police. In the summer of 1874, a detachment of North West Mounted Police arrived on the western prairie, bringing law and order in its wake. Communities grew up around military posts at Fort Macleod, Fort Calgary, Fort Saskatchewan and Fort Walsh

During the 1870's the buffalo, which had at one time roamed in their millions across the plains from the Missouri to the banks of the North Saskatchewan, disappeared. This and disease wiped out the Indian's nomadic way of life. But still a greater economic change was at hand. Through the coming of the railway, hunters and traders were replaced by ranchers and farmers. The building of the Canadian Pacific Railway opened up the prairies to homesteaders and settlers. Railway officials encouraged permanent settlement to pay for the vast construction costs. It has been said that the CPR should make a statue in honor of Louis Riel who lead the Metis and Indians to rebel in 1885 and forced Prime Minister John A. Macdonald to bail out the company financially.

The selection of town-sites every ten miles or so was apparently designed to accommodate an agricultural population dependent on horse-drawn vehicles. Railway or postal officials are responsible for the selection of the vast majority of the names of past and present Alberta communities.

In Alberta there are more than 1900 places that have, some time in their history, reached the status of a community. In the 1972 Highway Map of the province only a total of 770 communities appear. There are other "communities" such as railway stations and hamlets which are too small to be shown on current maps. Each one, however, no matter how humble or important its role in the history of the province, had a name, an identity, and a part to play. The object of this study has been to locate these places in time, space, and nomenclature and to preserve their identity for the future. It includes 1,878 entries exclusive of a list of 218 name changes. The origin and meaning of the name is given for some 1,700 places; it is unavailable for about 200.

If the names of communities referred to in this book were classified under the categories suggested by George R. Stewart, the percentage figures would be as shown below. However, it must be emphasized that categories and percentage figures used here are necessarily arbitrary because so many names can easily fit into two or more categories.

DESCRIPTIVE NAMES: It would appear the topography of the land has directly or indirectly been responsible for the naming of 12% of the communities in Alberta. Certainly a sampling of these names gives a picture of the province: *Grande Prairie, Picture Butte, Three Hills.*

SHIFT NAMES: These are names that are placed upon places by the mere shifting of the specific name of a geographical feature to a nearby community. Thus from *Chief Mountain* we get the name of the custom post, or from the *Red Deer River* we get the name of the city. This category contains 11% of the names of communities in the province. Many of the names in this category could be classified as descriptive.

INCIDENT NAMES: These identify the place by means of some incident which had occurred at or near it, such as *Grizzly Bear,*

Pincher Creek, or *Whiskey Gap.* Three percent of names are in this group.

MANUFACTURED NAMES: Neologisms account for about 4% of the names of Alberta communities. Often two names are combined such as *Carway, Scotford,* and *Ukalta,* or names are reversed such as *Niton* and *Retlaw.*

EUPHEMISTIC NAMES: Idealistic names often express the hopes of early settlers. Names such as *Success, Patience, Unity,* fall into this group. They make up about three percent of the names of communities.

POSSESSIVE NAMES: Though mountains, rivers and lakes are most often named for a natural feature, communities are often named for an early pioneer, the first postmaster, or, in the case of railway stations, for a minor official. Many names have been applied because of the feeling that some person owned that particular place. The individual may have owned the land on which the community was built or the place might have been referred to originally as, for example, *Halcro's* and in time the possessive "s" was dropped. Names in this group account for 21%.

COMMEMORATIVE NAMES: These arise by the process of taking an already established name and giving it a new application, for honorific ends.

Indian names account for 5%
French names account for 3%
Religious names account for 2%
Literary names account for 3%
Prominent Albertans names account for 4%
Prominent Canadians names account for 5%
Prominent Britishers names account for 4%
Transferred names from other parts of Canada account only for a few
Transferred names from the British Isles account for 12%
Transferred names from the United States account for 3%
Transferred names from other parts of the world account for 5%

There is an interesting ethnic pattern discernible through the names of communities across Alberta. There are three districts that are predominantly French. They are centered around Falher in the Peace River, Morinville north of Edmonton and St. Paul - Bonnyville in the northeastern part of the province. The Ukrainian settlement is centered in a wide belt east of Edmonton on both sides of the North Saskatchewan River based on Mundare and Smoky Lake. German and Scandinavian settlers homesteaded in the Camrose area, in a ring some twenty miles out of Edmonton, in the Beiseker - Rockyford district northeast of Calgary and in the Medicine Hat district. British settlers concentrated in the Lloydminster area, the Barr Colony, Red Deer Valley south to Calgary and on to Fort Macleod.

There is also a religious pattern discernible in Alberta. The French areas are mainly Catholic, the Ukrainian districts are either Orthodox or Catholic, the German-Scandinavian are Lutheran, the English in the Red Deer Valley are Presbyterian, while to the south are found large numbers of Anglicans. There is also a Mormon belt across the southern portion of the province based on Cardston, Raymond, Magrath and Taber. The Mormons introduced irrigated farming. The Metis are concentrated in the Lesser Slave Lake - Athabasca - Cold Lake region. Until recently they were employed in freighting and trapping. These generalizations are derived from the *Atlas of Alberta* (1969).

Some groups that have settled in the province, such as the Hutterites, have given no place names. This Anabaptist Christian sect rigorously insists on a communal frame of existence, which requires that all important property be shared by the entire community.

Several of the larger ranches that once covered most of southern Alberta are mentioned in this work. The "great days" of the ranchers passed away when large numbers of settlers arrived from eastern Canada, the United States and Europe at the turn of the century.

There was a ribbon of development along the railway line across the prairies. The CPR main line crossed the southern part of the province from Medicine Hat, which used to be in the postal district of Saskatchewan until 1905, to Calgary, on to Banff, to cross the continental divide via the Kicking Horse Pass which was completed in 1883. A branch line was then constructed to Lethbridge and on to the Crowsnest Pass. Branch lines from these were built into the more remote regions. The Grand Trunk and the Canadian Northern linked Edmonton with the east in 1905. They were continued side by side towards the mountains and eventually one line crossed the continental divide by way of the Yellowhead Pass. The main north-south route before the railway was the Fort Macleod - Calgary - Edmonton Trail.

Lethbridge was the cradle of the coal industry in Alberta. The first coal was mined by Nicholas Sheran in the 1880's and mining communities sprang up at Coalhurst, Hardieville, Diamond City, as well as Coalbanks, which name was later changed to Lethbridge. At one time 500,000 tons of coal were produced from the Lethbridge mines. All the mines in the area are now closed. The coal mines in the Nordegg region of Central Alberta were also closed down in the late 1950's with the development of the petroleum industry. This is also true of the mines in the Coal Branch District south of Edson. These mines in this remote region of the Rockies once employed close to 10,000 miners, but are now only ghost communities. The names of these once thriving mining settlements include Cadomin, Coal Valley, Coalspur, Foothills, Leyland, Luscar, Mercoal, Mountain Park, Reco, and Starco. They have disappeared from recent maps. The only district where coal is still being mined is in the Crowsnest and Drumheller areas.

The petroleum industry has given rise to a number of communities. Oil City in Waterton National Park was a thriving community in 1902, but has totally disappeared. Turner Valley and Black Diamond south of Calgary were the center of the oil industry in the 1920's.

Alberta's present prosperity dates from the boring in of the Leduc oil field in 1947. Other communities that are associated with the oil and natural gas industry include Medicine Hat (which, according to Kipling, has hell for its kitchen), Drayton Valley, Redwater, Rainbow Lake, Viking and Lloydminster.

It is interesting to note that the Dominion Census of 1941 revealed that in Alberta sixty percent of the population were rural dwellers and forty percent lived in urban areas. Twenty years later, the figures were reversed; the 1961 census shows that forty percent were rural and sixty percent urban. The trend is continuing as rural communities wither and die. The railways have closed down hundreds of stations on branch lines across the province and are discontinuing service. The service areas are increasing in size because people are more mobile with cars than they were in the old days with the horse and buggy. Rural and village schools are closing as the service areas increase in size. Now children are bussed to one central school from a fifty mile radius. Young children now often spend two hours a day on a bus. This means that towns are becoming villages and villages are becoming hamlets or merely localities. Some one hundred post offices in the Edmonton region were closed down last year. The place names of Alberta are starting to disappear.

We are witnessing a change in our way-of-life and our civilization. Without any history, without an understanding of the past, we lose our sense of value; everything becomes of equal importance. In Alberta today we are witnessing the growth of the two metropolitan areas of Edmonton and Calgary at a rate of close to two thousand a month while the countryside is being depopulated. Some ten farmers close their front door for the last time every week.

The land is being farmed in larger and larger units. It reminds one of the later Roman Empire when a few slaves worked vast estates. What will happen? Possibly new barbarians will again occupy the vast prairies. But let us understand our place names - let us understand our history. For the stories behind the place names of Alberta record history as colorful, picturesque and varied as any tale that has ever been told.

E.G.M.

Explanatory Notes

WHEN?

The date when the community was established is given whenever possible. Since origins imply dates, and the establishment of a post office is a firm date that can be obtained from official records, it is one of the most significant clues that can be obtained as to when a settlement was started, when it was active and when it declined, if it did. In many cases the postal records contain the only available dates.

WHY?

This is the heart of the research undertaken in this cultural and historical study of communities in Alberta. It seems of the utmost importance to know why a settlement was given such-and-such a name. The names given to communities reflect all the phases of the history of the province. They show the ever-changing and shifting interests of the inhabitants of the area, and often even give an indication of the attitudes of the early settlers.

WHO?

In many cases the ethnic or religious origins of the pioneer settlers of a community can be determined by reference to the name given to the first post office in the district. For example: CARDSTON was named after Charles Ora Card, the great Mormon pioneer and colonist. The Mormon Country covers a wide belt across the southern portion of the province. The Mormons were the first to introduce irrigation on a wide scale. Other predominantly Mormon settlements are Magrath, Raymond, Stirling, and Taber.

WHERE?

The location of the various communities is given in two ways. First, the township, range, and meridian of each settlement is given in brackets. For example: MANNYBERRIES [5-6-W4] indicates Township 5, Range 6, West of the Fourth Meridian. The Fifth Meridian [longitude 114° west] passes through Calgary.

A second method used to indicate the approximate location of settlement is by reference to a physical feature or community. For convenience the map of Alberta has been divided into the following nine regions:

1. Southern Alberta: - the region between US border and 50th parallel, across the province.

2. Calgary area: - the area between 50th and 52nd parallel from 113 to B.C. border.

3. Palliser Triangle: - the region between 50th and 52nd parallel from Saskatchewan border to 113

4. Central Alberta: - the region between 52nd and 53rd parallel, across the province.

5. East Edmonton: - the region between the 53rd and 54th parallel, east of the capital.

6. West Edmonton: - the region between the 53rd and 54th parallel, west of the capital.

7. Northeastern Alberta: - the region between the 54th and 55th parallel, from Saskatchewan border to 113 .

8. Peace River District: - the region between 55th and 57th parallel, from 116 to B.C. border.

9. Northern Alberta: - the region between 55th parallel and the Northwest Territories border, across the province, excluding Peace River District.

Glossary

(Gazetteer of Canada: Alberta)

Incorporated Entities

CITY: A community of more than 10,000 inhabitants, incorporated by Order in Council.

TOWN: A community of at least 1,000 inhabitants, incorporated by Order in Council.

VILLAGE: A community containing at least 75 occupied dwellings, incorporated by Order in Council

SUMMER VILLAGE: A community containing at least 50 seasonally occupied dwelling, incorporated by Order in Council.

Unincorporated Entities

HAMLET: A place usually containing eight or more occupied dwelling and at least one retail business outlet.

LOCALITY: A place with scattered population or less than eight occupied dwellings.

FORMER LOCALITY: A place usually uninhabited or with a small scattered population. [Names are not shown on current National Topographical Maps]

POST OFFICE: A Canada Post designation listed where the post office name differs from the name of the place where it is located.

FORMER POST OFFICE: Name retained for a post office now closed.

RAILWAY POINT: A named point of tracks, as designated by a railway company. Formerly approved names may indicate "Station" or "Junction".

Abbreviations

U.F.A. - United Farmers of Alberta (political party)

P.C. - Progressive Conservative (political party)

C.C.F. - Co-operative Commonwealth Federation (political party)

N.D.P. - New Democratic Party (political party)

MLA - Member of the Legislative Assembly

MP - Member of Parliament

D.S.O. - Distinguished Service Cross

M.C. - Military Cross

D.F.C. - Distinguished Flying Cross

O.M.I. - Oblates of Mary Immaculate

K.C. - King's Counsel

Q.C. - Queen's Counsel

CNR - Canadian National Railway

CPR - Canadian Pacific Railway

HBC - Hudson's Bay Company

NWC - North West Company

NWMP - North West Mounted Police RCMP – Royal Canadian Mounted Police

COMMUNITY NAMES OF
ALBERTA

A

(The) "A 7" Ranch
~ near Calgary.

This ranch was established by A. Ernest Cross (1861-1932), son of a Quebec Judge, in 1885. In time he became one of the most prominent ranchers in Southern Alberta and was one of the four founders of the Calgary Stampede. Besides being a rancher, he became a Calgary brewer.

A. Ernest Cross was returned as a member of the Northwest Territories Legislative Assembly in 1899 and represented ranches in the Assembly for three years. The ranch is still in the family. In 1909 he married Helen Rothney 'Nell' Macleod, eldest daughter of the late Justice James F. Macleod.

ABASAND
~ former post office near Fort McMurray.

The name is a contraction of Athabasca Tar Sands. It opened in 1937.

ABEE   [61-21-W4]
~ hamlet northwest of Smoky Lake.

It was named in 1914 after A. B. Donley, manager of the North West Lumber Company, Edmonton. The name is derived from the initials of his Christian names.

ABILENE   [59-10-W4]
~ former post office of St. Paul.

There are several places with this name in the United States called after the province of ancient Syria, lying east of the Antili-banus ("against Lebanon") mountains. The classic Abilene came under Roman domination with Pompey's conquest of Syria in 62 B.C.

The post office was opened in 1912 and has since been closed.

ACADIA VALLEY   [25-2-W4]
~ hamlet southeast of Oyen.

Settled in 1910 by Nova Scotians, this region was named after the first French colony in North America, established on the Bay of Fundy in 1604. The colony was ceded to Britain by the Treaty of Utrecht in 1713. The French settlers were deported by the British in 1755. Henry Longfellow derived the basis for his poem *Evangeline* from this historical event.

ACHESON   [53-26-W4]
~ former station west of Edmonton.

It was named after A. Acheson Tisdal, a Canadian National Railway official.

ACME   [29-25-W4]
It was so named in 1909 after the Greek word meaning "summit". When named, it was the most northerly point on the Canadian Pacific Railway branch. Previously the community was called **TAPSCOTT**.

ACTON HOUSE   [39-7-W5]
~ a trading post built by the Hudson's Bay Company.

This trading post was built beside the North West Company post at **ROCKY MOUNTAIN HOUSE** in about 1799. Samuel Wegg, Governor of the trading company from 1782 to 1799, lived in Acton, England. "Acton" is a less obvious form in Old English: oak-field.

ADAMS LANDING   [108-7-W5]
~ on the Peace River east of Fort Vermilion.

This was a settlement that has since been abandoned.

ADEN   [1-10-W4]
~ former post office southwest of Foremost.

It was named after an important seaport at the tip of the Arabian peninsula in 1913. The first postmaster was H. E. Anderson, a former sailor. ADEN was a custom post along the Canadian-United States border.

AERIAL   [28-19-W4]
~ former post office south of Drumheller.

For many years, an aerial tramway conveyed coal from the Star Mine here across the Red Deer River to **ROSEDALE** railway station. It was opened in 1916 and has since been closed.

AETNA   [2-25-W4]
~ hamlet south of Cardston.

It was named in 1900 after the Mormon ecclesiastical district of Aetna, which in turn was named after Mount Etna, the highest volcano in Europe, located in Sicily.

AGATHA   [14-10-W4]
~ former station north of Bow Island.

It was named after Agatha Lillian, Lady Hindlip, whose husband was the Unionist Whip in the House of Lords in 1914.

AGGIE   [74-18-W5]
~ former station north of High Prairie.

It was named after Aggie McArthur, a relative of W.R. Smith, a former General Manager of the Edmonton, Dunvegan and British Columbia Railway in 1915.

AIRDRIE   **[27-1-W5]**
~ city north of Calgary.

The railway reached here in 1893. Settlers named it after the Lanarkshire coal mining town of some 33,000 inhabitants in the Scottish Black Country. There is a total of four communities in Scotland with this name. It is the Gaelic for "high-king". It could also come from the Gaelic *ard reidh,* meaning "high flat ground". In 1928 it was a village. The population was 1,033 in 1972. By 2009 it was a city of approximately 38,091 residents.

AIRWAYS   **[37-8-W4]**
~ former post office near Coronation.

It was named when this part of the province was surveyed from the air.

AKENSIDE   **[53-23-W4]**
~ former station northwest of Edmonton.

The origin of this name is not known. (see: **AKENSTADT**)

AKENSTADT
~ former community near Lethbridge.

It was named after Rev. C. Van Aken, a Dutch pioneer pastor. At one time the settlement was called KENEX.

ALBERT PARK   **[24-29-W4]**
~ hamlet east of Calgary.

The post office was opened in 1913.

ALBERTA
~ most westerly of the three prairie provinces.

It has an area of some 255,000 square miles. Its average width from west to east is more than 300 miles, its length 800 miles from the 49th parallel to the border of the Northwest Territories. It owes its name to H. R. H. Princess Louise Caroline Alberta, fourth daughter of Queen Victoria and wife of the Marquis of Lorne (later Duke of Argyle), who served as Governor-General of the Dominion of Canada from 1878 to 1883. She died in 1939 at 91 years of age. He chose his wife's name for the new postal district created in the Northwest Territories in 1882. Northern Alberta was the postal district of Athabasca.

ALBERTA was established as a province in 1905, and is often referred to as the Princess Province.

ALBERTA BEACH   [54-3-W5]
~ summer village on Lac Ste Anne.

It was named after the name of the province in 1917.

ALBION RIDGE   [11-22-W4]
~ former post office north of Lethbridge.

This is an "English" settlement on a "ridge". Albion is the ancient name for Britain. The Romans derived the name from *albus*, "white", to identify England by the white cliffs of Dover. Albion Ridge was formerly the name of a post office in this district. It was opened in 1907 and has since been closed.

ALBRIGHT   [72-10-W6]
~ former post office north of Grande Prairie.

It was named after W. D. Albright, a pioneer settler, who had come west from Ontario as a young man. Later he served as the superintendent of the Dominion Experimental Farm.

ALCOMDALE   **[57-26-W4]**
~ *former village north of Edmonton.*

It was named after Dr. Alcombreck of Edmonton, who owned property in the neighborhood. "Dale", a north of England word for a valley, is used as a final syllable instead of "breck" (stream).

ALCURVE   **[52-1-W4]**
~ *post office north of Lloydminster.*

The origin of this name is not known.

ALDER FLATS   **[46-7-W5]**
This community is named after alders found in the vicinity. Alders are a group of deciduous trees and shrubs of the birch family, which flourish in swamps and beside streams. They were among the first woody plants to spring up in stony rubble left by retreating glaciers.

ALDERSON   **[15-10-W4]**
~ *hamlet west of Medicine Hat.*

It was named in 1915 in honor of General E. A. H. Alderson who was then Commander of the Canadian Expeditionary Force in France in World War I. Previously the post office had been called CARLSTADT and the station LANGEVIN.

ALDERSYDE   **[20-28-W4]**
~ *hamlet north of High River.*

The name of this community was suggested by an early Scottish settler who recalled a story entitled *Aldersyde*, written by Annie Swan in 1927:

"Nearly fifty years ago, when I was a young girl in my father's house in Medlothan, I wrote a story of the Border country dealing with Scottish life and character, and named it *Aldersyde*, a purely fictitious name, a combination of typical Border syllables. There are many 'sydes' in the Borders, notably Bemersyde, the ancestral estate of Earl Haig", (commander in the British Imperial Forces on the Western Front in World War I).

ALEXANDER   [56-27-W4]
~ Cree Indian reserve near Edmonton.

It was named after Chief Alexander Arcand (1845-1913). When the reserve was formed in 1882, he and his band moved to it from the Lac La Nonne district.

ALEXO   [40-13-W5]
~ former station north of Saunders.

It was named after the Alexo Coal Company, which in turn was called after Alex Kelso who discovered coal deposits in the district. It opened in 1923.

ALHAMBRA   [39-5-W5]
~ hamlet south of Rocky Mountain House.

It was named after the ancient palace and fortress of the Moorish King of Granada which King Ferdinand and Queen Isabella conquered in 1492. The post office here was known as **HORSEGUARDS** until 1916.

ALISKE   [48-4-W5]
~ former post office north of Breton.

It was opened prior to 1958.

ALIX   [39-23-W4]
~ village south of Buffalo Lake.

It was named In 1905 after Mrs. Alix Westhead, an early settler and rancher. Alix is an unusual version of the Christian name "Alice", which means "noble kind".

ALLERSTON   [2-14-W4]
~ former post office southwest of Foremost.

It was named after Jacob Allers, a pioneer settler in 1914. Previously it had been called DORAN after the name of the first postmaster's son.

ALLIANCE [40-13-W4]
~ *village north of Castor.*

It was named after Alliance in the State of Ohio in 1916. The American city was formed by the amalgamation of Freedom, a Quaker settlement, with Williamsport and Mount Union, in 1854. Previously the post office was called GALAHAD.

ALNESS [31-13-W4]
~ *former station east of Hanna.*

It was named after Alness, Ross-shire, Scotland. Probably from the Gaelic *ailean*, "green plain".

ALTARIO [34-2-W4]
~ *hamlet northeast of Grassy Island Lake.*

The name is a combination of Alberta and Ontario; probably the present and past homes of settlers.

ALTORADO [34-2-W4]
~ *former community south of Foremost.*

In 1913 it had a population of 100, many of whom were Mormons from Colorado. It declined when the railway was built a couple of years later to the north. Previously the post office was WILHELMINA.

ALYTH [24-1-W5]
~ *former station near Calgary.*

It was named after Alyth, Perthshire, Scotland. The name is the Gaelic word *eileach*, meaning a "rocky place".

AMBER VALLEY [66-20-W4]
~ *former post office east of Athabasca.*

Amber is the yellow fossil resin exuded by coniferous trees, now extinct, which has spent eons of time at the bottom of the sea. The chief source of amber is the Baltic. It is connected with many superstitions and is believed to be a preventative against disease and bad luck. This is one of the few prominently Afro-American communities in Alberta, established by Jim Edwards in 1916.

AMESBURY [70-17-W4]
~ *former post office near Wandering River.*

It is probably named after the English rivertown of Amesbury, Wiltshire. It is the place, according to legend, where King Arthur's wife Queen Guenevere is buried. It was opened in 1933 and has since been closed.

AMISK [41-8-W4]
~ *village south of Wainwright.*

It is the Cree word for "beaver".

AMUNDSON [63-3-W6]
~ *former railway station near Grande Prairie.*

It was named after Burgo Amundson, a Canadian soldier, killed in Italy in December 1943.

ANALTA [62-25-W4]
~ *former hamlet near Westlock.*

It would appear that this name is partly formed from the abbreviation for Alberta.

ANASTASIA [20-22-W4]
~ *former station south of Gleichen.*

This was the name of one of the daughters of Czar Nicholas II who, some claim, survived the murder of the royal family by the Bolsheviks in July 1918.

ANATOLE [31-3-W4]
~ *former station south of Grassy Lake.*

The origin of this name is not known.

ANCONA [40-12-W5]
~ *former station east of Saunders.*

It was named possibly after the Italian city of Ancona in 1914. Previously the community was called POLLOCK. There is also a town Ancona in Illinois.

ANDREW [56-16-W4]
~ village near Willingdon.

The post office was opened in 1902 and it was named after Andrew Whitford, a pioneer homesteader of the district. Whitford was the name of the Legislative Constituency for years. It's first member was Andrew Shandro, the first Ukrainian Canadian to sit in the Alberta Legislature.

ANGLE LAKE [55-7-W4]
~ former post office south of Elk Point.

It was opened in 1911. The name is descriptive, as the post office was located at the angle of a lake.

ANKERTON [43-17-W4]
~ former village south of Camrose.

It was named after Anker H. Lauritsen, a pioneer of the district. "Ton" is the Old English word for a "field", or "enclosure". Prior to 1915 it was called CAMPBELTON.

ANNING [58-11-W4]
~ former post office near St. Paul.

It was named after S. H. Anning, the first postmaster in 1911.

ANSELL [53-18-W5]
~ former station on the Grand Trunk Pacific Railway, near Jasper.

The next station to the west was Bickerdike, the turn-off point of the coal branch.

ANSELM [53-17-W5]
~ former station near Jasper.

It was opened in 1911.

ANSELMO [57-10-W5]
~ former post office southwest of Mayerthorpe.

It was named after Anselmo Nebraska, the first postmaster's former home, in 1913.

ANSHAW [61-6-W4]

It was named after Angus Shaw, an early voyageur and fur trader, who is said to have built the first house in what became Alberta in 1789.

ANSTEAD [12-5-W4]
(See: **BELLCOTT**)

ANTHRACITE [26-11-W5]
~ hamlet east of Banff.

This is now a ghost town. Semi-anthracite was mined in the neighborhood from 1885 by the Canadian Anthracite Company until the mines were closed in 1897.

ANTON LAKE [60-23-W4]
~ former post office east of Westlock.

There is a community in the State of Texas called ANTON. French for "Anthony".

ANTONIO [10-14-W4]
~ former station southwest of Bow Island.

It was named after "Antonio", one of the main characters in William Shakespeare's comedy, *The Merchant of Venice*.

ANTROSS [47-4-W5]
~ former station near Wetaskiwin.

The name is formed by combining the names of two saw-mills in the District, the Anthony Lumber Company and the Ross Board Lumber Company. It was opened in 1926, and has since been closed.

ANZAC [86-7-W4]
~ former station south of Fort McMurray.

It was named after the Australian-New Zealand Army Corps that served in Europe during the Great War. The name is derived from the initial letters of the corps. It opened in 1917. There was a post office there from 1955 to 1964.

ARCADIA   [74-14-W5]
~ former station south of High Prairie.

It was opened in 1914. It is a quiet rural district, thus the descriptive name. Arcadia relates to a mountainous district of Greece, celebrated as the abode of a simple, contented, pastoral people.

ARDENODE   [25-25-W4]
It was named in 1914 after Ardenode in Ireland. Prior to then the post office was called HARWICK.

ARDENVILLE   [7-26-W4]
It was named after Arden Simpson, an early pioneer homesteader who had come from Ontario in 1910.

ARDLEY   [38-23-W4]
~ hamlet north of Delburne.

It was named in 1913, possibly after the English parish of Ardley in Oxfordshire. The word *ardley* means "high pasture". Previously the community was called **COALBANKS** because coal was found in the vicinity.

ARDMORE   [62-4-W4]
~ hamlet north of Bonnyville.

It was named after the school district in 1913. There are five Ardmore's in Scotland, and two in Ireland. "Ard" means "high", so the names were given to high moorelands.

ARDROSSAN   [53-22-W4]
~ hamlet east of Edmonton.

It was named after Ardrossan, Ayrshire, Scotland, where originally it was spelt as two separate words - *ard rosain* - meaning "the height of the little headland". It was named in 1910.

ARMADA [17-21-W4]
~ former post office east of Claresholm.

The word armada is Spanish for "fleet". Sir Francis Drake defeated the Spanish Armada in 1588. The post office was opened in 1914.

ARMELGRA [13-13-W4]
~ former station northwest of Bow Island.

It was named in 1917 after Arthur Melville Grace, engineer for the Canadian Pacific Railway, by combining the letters of his names.

ARMENA [48-21-W4]
~ former village northwest of Camrose.

A railway station was opened here in 1915. (See: THORENSKJOLD)

ARMISTICE [57-7-W4]
~ former post office south of St. Paul.

The armistice that brought the Great War to a close came into effect at the eleventh hour of the eleventh day of the eleventh month of 1918.

ARNESON [26-1-W4]
~ hamlet southeast of Oyen.

The origin of this name is not known.

ARROWWOOD [20-23-W4]
~ village on East Arrowwood Creek.

It was named from its location, near a tributary of the Bow River, which was a favored district for nomadic natives to get wood to make their bows and arrows.

ARVILLA [58-1-W5]
~ former post office northwest of Morinville.

It was opened in 1911.

ASHMONT   [59-11-W4]
~ former village west of Therien.

It was named in 1911 on the suggestion of L. W. Babcock, the postmaster, after a suburb of Boston, Massachusetts, where he had formerly resided. The municipal district was also named ASHMONT in 1919.

ASPEN BEACH   [40-28-W4]
~ post office west of Lacombe.

The reference in this name is to the aspen, or poplar, trees found along the shore of Gull Lake. Prior to 1916 the post office was called **WIESVILLE**.

ASPLUND   [68-22-W5]
~ former post office near Valleyview.

It was named after the "aspen" tree, a variety of poplar and the last part of A. Werklund, the first postmaster's surname. He was a Scandinavian. It opened in 1940.

ASSINEAU   [73-8-W5]
~ former station south of Lesser Slave Lake.

The name is derived from the Cree word meaning "stony" There is an Assineau river nearby. It was opened in 1914.

ASSUMPTION   [112-5-W6]
~ former post office southeast of Hay Lake.

The feast of the Assumption of the Blessed Virgin Mary is celebrated on August 15. It took its name after Our Lady of Assumption native missionary school in 1953. Later the name was changed to **CHATEH**.

ATHABASCA   [66-22-W4]
~ town north of Edmonton.

Known also as ATHABASCA LANDING, it is located on the Athabasca River where the Hudson's Bay Company established a post in 1884, for transshipping supplies by flatboats to the far north via Lake Athabasca. The Cree name means "where there are reeds". It increased to 2,300 in 1998.

ATIKAMEG   [80-11-W5]
~ former post office west of Utikuma Lake.

The Cree word for "caribou" is *atik*, while *ameg* means "water". The Cree called the whitefish "white caribou". It was opened in 1927.

ATLEE   [22-7-W4]
~ former village south of Empress.

It was named after W. Atlee James, an official of the Canadian Pacific Railway. Originally this English surname was given to someone who lived "at the clearing in the wood".

ATMORE   [67-17-W4]
~ former post office west of Lac La Biche.

There is an Atmore in the State of Alabama.

AUBURNDALE   [47-6-W4]
~ former post office near Vermilion.

It was named after a town in Massachusetts where L. W. Crowe, the first postmaster, originally resided. It opened in 1907.

AURORA   [91-23-W5]
(See: **MANNING**)

AVALON   [3-9-W4]
~ former post office west of Pakowki Lake.

It was named in 1911 after Avalon where, according to legend, King Arthur is said to have held his court.

AVENIR   [70-15-W4]
~ former post office north of Lac La Biche.

It was named after the French word *avenir*: "future". It was opened in 1949.

AZURE   **[18-29-W4]**
~ former station south of High River.

It received its name after the blue skies prevalent in this locality most of the year. It is the sunniest place in Canada.

B

BAD HEART [75-2-W6]
~ former post office east of Manning.

It was named after the nearby Bad Heart River. This name is a translation of the Cree word *missipi*. It opened in 1929 and closed in 1968.

BADGER LAKE [16-18-W4]
~ former post office near Travers.

It was named after a small lake of the same name situated north of the post office where badgers were plentiful. It was opened in 1913, but has since been closed.

BAILEY
~ railway point east of Edmonton.

It was named after John Bailey, a pioneer settler.

BAIN [4-3-W4]
It was named after James Bain, a CPR section foreman of Bredenbury, Saskatchewan, who had won the Military Medal during the Great War.

BAINTREE [25-24-W4]
~ hamlet north of Calgary.

It ranked as a village in 1928.

BALKAN [49-21-W5]
(See: **ROBB; COAL BRANCH**)

BALLANTINE [57-4-W5]
~ former post office near Sangudo.

Prior to 1914 the post office was called WILD HORSE.

BALLATER [76-21-W5]
~ *former post office southwest of Kimiwan Lake.*

It was named after Ballater, Deeside, Aberdeenshire, in Scotland. The name is probably from the Gaelic *bealaidh tir*, meaning 'broom land." The post office was opened in 1937.

BALLINA [23-24-W4]
~ *former station near Calgary.*

It was so named in 1912 after the village of Ballina, county of Mayo, Ireland. It has since been closed.

BALM [57-9-W5]
~ *former post office near Mayerthorpe.*

Balsam (balm of Gilead) trees are plentiful in the district. It was opened in 1914 and closed in 1952.

BALZAC [26-1-W5]
~ *hamlet north of Calgary.*

This hamlet derives its name from Honoré de Balzac (1799-1850), noted nineteenth century French novelist. While yet a young man, he resolved to present a complete picture of modern civilization entitled "La Comédie Humaine." All ranks, professions, arts, trades, all phases of manners in town and country were to be portrayed. In attempting to carry out this impossible mission, Balzac produced almost a literature in itself. In twenty years he wrote a total of eighty-five novels.

BANFF [25-12-W5]
~ *town site in Banff National Park.*

This community was named by Lord Strathcona after a town near his birthplace in Scotland. The Scottish namesake is the capital of the county of the same name, and was the site of a royal castle which on three occasions was the headquarters of King Edward I of England during his attempts to conquer Scotland in the thirteenth century. The Gaelic word *bunaimb*, "the mouth of the river", has been corrupted into "Banff". According to Mrs. C. M. Matthews, its original form was *banba*, a term of endearment meaning literally "little pig".

The population was 2,896 in 1972 and increased to 8,721 in 2007.

BANKHEAD [26-12-W5]
~ ghost town near Banff.

It was named by Lord Strathcona in 1905 after Bankhead in Banffshire, Scotland. All that remains of this ghost town is the war memorial to the men of Bankhead who served and died in the First World War. The Canadian Pacific Railway opened Bankhead as a mining town in 1905. At one time the population was close to 2,000 persons. The community became a ghost town about 1923.

BANTRY [18-13-W4]
~ former station southeast of Brooks.

It was named in 1884 after Bantry Bay, Ireland. There is also a Bantry in the State of North Dakota. *Bantry* is the Gaelic for "peaks by the sea shore".

BAPTISTE RIVER [43-8-W5]
~ former post office near Rocky Mountain House.

It was named after a tributary of the North Saskatchewan River.

(The) BAR S RANCH
~ on Mosquito Creek, West of Calgary.

The proprietor was Walter de Vere Skrine, a wealthy Englishman who had obtained property on Mosquito Creek. He was a pioneer rancher. He was also a member of the world champion Calgary polo team. In 1902 he sold the Bar S Ranch and returned to the United Kingdom.

(The) BAR U RANCH [17-2-W5]
~ east of Calgary.

For several years in the early 1880's this ranch of the North West Cattle Company had George Lane (1856-1925) as its foreman. By 1905 he owned the Bar U Ranch. Lane was one of the four founders of the Calgary Stampede in 1912. In 1913 he was elected to the Legislature but resigned his seat before being sworn in.

BARACA   [27-11-W4]
~ former post office near Brooks.

The name was derived from the Biblical word "berachah" (baracha), meaning "blessing" or the "blessed." it was suggested by Mrs. E. E. Boggess, a Lutheran preacher. Prior to 1913 the community was called WHARRANTON.

BARDO   [50-19-W4]
From 1898 to 1904 the post office in this community was called NORTHERN. The name Bardo was given to the station by Norwegian settlers after their original home in northern Norway.

BARGRAVE   [30-25-W4]
~ station south of Three Hills.

The origin is unknown.

BARICH   [60-18-W4]
~ post office northwest of Smoky Lake.

The origin is unknown.

BARKER'S STOPPING HOUSE   [43-25-W4]
(See: **CALGARY-EDMONTON TRAIL STAGING POSTS; PONOKA**)

BARLOW   [23-29-W4]
~ former station east of Calgary.

Probably named after Dr. A. E. Barlow, geologist, who was on the staff at McGill University. He lost his life in a marine disaster connected with the sinking of *The Empire of Ireland* in the St. Lawrence River near Quebec City in May 1914.

BARNEGAT   [67-12-W4]
~ post office northeast of Lac La Biche.

This name is derived from the Dutch, *barende gat*, meaning "breakers inlet." There is a Barnegat Bay in New Jersey which was so named by Henry Hudson, the seventeenth century English navigator and explorer.

BARNETT'S STOPPING HOUSE
(See: **CALGARY-EDMONTON TRAIL STAGING POSTS;**
LACOMBE)

BARNEY   **[13-17-W4]**
(See: **RETLAW**)

BARNWELL   **[9-17-W4]**
~ hamlet southeast of Taber.

It was so named after R. Barnwell, general tie agent for the Canadian Pacific Railway in 1909. Previously this Mormon community was called WOODPECKER, some say because the railway telegraph, operating out of a railway carriage, made the same sound as the bird. An island in the Oldman River nearby is called Woodpecker Island.

BARONS   **[12-23-W4]**
~ village northwest of Lethbridge.

It was named after a Canadian Pacific Railway official called Baron in 1909. It was not until several years later that the "s" was added. This was necessitated when the Union Bank called itself Baron's Bank. Prior to 1909 the post office was called BLAYNEY.

BARRHEAD   **[59-3-W5]**
~ town northwest of Edmonton.

This community was named after Barrhead, Scotland, the birthplace of James McGuire, an early pioneer. The name was suggested by the directors of the Paddle River and District Co-operative. *Barr* is the Gaelic word for "top" or "height". Barrhead is a tautology.

The population was 2,718 in 1972 and increased to 4,209 in 2006.

BARSTOW   **[22-23-W4]**
~ former station west of Gleichen.

The name is a transposition of the surname of F. W. Stobart, a Winnipeg merchant.

BASHAW   [42-21-W4]
~ town north of Buffalo Lake.

This community was named after Eugene Bashaw, who purchased the land from a Metis in the early days before the coming of the railway. Prior to 1910 the post office was called FORSTER.

The population was 772 in 1972 and it had topped 868 by 2007.

BASING   [47-20-W5]
(See: **STERCO; COAL BRANCH**)

BASSANO   [21-18-W4]
~ town east of Calgary.

Eighty miles east of Calgary, this town is named after the Italian nobleman, the Marquis of Bassano, one of the CPR's major shareholders in 1884. Armstrong states in *The Origin and Meaning of Place Names in Canada* (1930):

"At Bassano is the great Horseshoe Bend Dam where the level of the Bow River has been raised forty feet. This dam is the second largest in the world, being exceeded in size only by the one a Assuan or Aswan, Egypt, which holds back the waters of the Nile. Horseshoe Bend Dam has been the means by which the semi-arid lands of Southern Alberta have been irrigated into thousands of fertile farms."

The population in 1972 was 855. It increased to 1,390 by 2007.

BATHGATE   [51-17-W4]
~ former post office near Mundare.

It was named after Bathgate in the State of North Dakota, which was the former home of J.C. Morrison, the first postmaster in 1906.

BATTENBURG   [56-23-W4]
Name was changed during World War I because of anti-German sentiment. It had been named after Prince Louis of Battenburg. (See: **GIBBONS**)

BATTLE [46-20-W4]

Probably named after Battle River, a tributary of the North Saskatchewan. The Crees and Blackfoot used to fight along its banks in the old days.

BATTLE BEND [40-10-W4]
~ former post office near Hardisty.

It was located near a bend in the Battle River. The post office was opened in 1910 and closed in 1944. It also was the name of the school district.

BATTLE LAKE [46-1-W5]
~ former post office near Pigeon Lake.

It was named in 1908 after a small lake. The name "battle" appears eight times on the map of Alberta, reflecting the Cree-Blackfoot wars.

BATTLE RIDGE [39-9-W4]
~ former post office near Hardisty.

It is located near the Battle River. It was opened in 1914 and closed in 1947.

BATTLE RIVER CROSSING [45-21-W4]

A settlement of five French Canadian Laboucan brothers, was established in 1880. This was the only ford on the river for many miles either upstream or downstream. It was on the Calgary-Edmonton Trail. Later the name was changed to **DUHAMEL** .

BATTLE RIVER PRAIRIE [93-23-W5]
~ former post office north of Manning.

The post office was opened in 1919 and named after the nearby Notikewin river.
(See: **NOTIKEWIN**)

BATTLEVIEW   **[47-6-W4]**
~ former post office near Wainwright.

It was opened in 1908 and closed in 1928. It was located in the valley of Battle River.

BAWLF   **[45-17-W4]**
~ village southeast of Camrose.

It was named in 1907 after Nicholas Bawlf, the president of the North Elevator Company. Formerly the post office was called MOLSTAD after O. Molstad, the first postmaster.

BAY TREE   **[79-13-W6]**
~ post office west of Blueberry Hill.

Possibly named after bay trees, a variety of ash tree in the district. It also was the name of a school district.

BAYROCK
~ formerly an Indian encampment, now an archaeological site near Taber.

The earliest demonstrable evidence for early man in Alberta was found here by L. A. Bayrock, a geologist of the Research Council of Alberta. Here, while excavating the bones of a now extinct bison, he found a cobblestone inside its crushed skull. Since these bones came from a deposit of pure sand laid down by a stream which at that time had been draining the nearby icesheet, the geologist inferred that the bison had probably been killed by a hunter. Later, archaeologists recognized the cobble as having been made by man because several flakes had been chipped from one end of it. Radio carbon dating established the date of the kill at approximately 9,000 B.C.

BEACH CORNER   **[53-1-W4]**
~ former post office north of Stony Plain.

It was situated where the road to Edmonton Beach, a summer village, left the Jasper Highway.

BEACON CORNER [60-8-W4]
~ former post office south of St. Paul.

This name may be descriptive.

BEAR CANYON [83-12-W6]
~ former post office north of Spirit River.

At one time there were a number of grizzly bears in the vicinity. It was opened in 1959.

BEAR LAKE [82-24-W5]
(See: **BERWYN**)

BEARBERRY [33-7-W5]
~ former post office northeast of Parker Ridge.

It was named after a nearby stream along whose banks bearberries grow. It was opened in 1909 and closed in 1969.

BEARSPAW [25-3-W5]
~ former hamlet north of Calgary.

It was named after Chief Masgwaahsid, or "Bear's Paw", who was one of the Indian chiefs to sign the historic Treaty Number Seven at Blackfoot Crossing on September 22, 1877.

BEAUMONT [50-24-W4]
~ town south of Edmonton.

It was named by early French Canadian pioneer settlers in 1895 because of the beauty of the locality. It is located on a hill with a view of the North Saskatchewan River. The name is the French for "beautiful mountain".

The population was 234 in 1972 and increased to 11,794 in 2009. It is now a city dormitory community.

BEAUVALLON [54-10-W4]
~ hamlet west of Myrnam.

This community received its descriptive name because of the great beauty of the valley. It is situated on the bank of the North Saskatchewan River. The name is the French for "beautiful vale". The post office was opened in 1909.

The population was 70 in 1972 and increased to 6,000 in 1998.

BEAVER CROSSING   [62-2-W4]
~ hamlet north of Bonnyville.

It is situated on the Beaver River. The post office was called **COLD LAKE** and then BEAVER CROSSING. It was open from 1910 to 1970.

BEAVER MINES   [6-2-W5]
~ hamlet southwest of Pincher Creek

The Beaver coal mines are located here. The post office was opened in 1912.

BEAVER RIVER   [62-2-W4]
~ former station northeast of Bonnyville.

It is named after a nearby river. The post office is now called **LE GOFF.**

BEAVERDAM   [60-3-W4]
~ former post office south of Bonnyville.

The name of this small animal appears twenty-eight times on the map of Alberta.

BEAVERHILL   [55-20-W4]
~ former station north of Beaverhill Lake.

The name for the nearby hills was first used on the Thompson Map in 1814.

BEAVERLODGE   [72-10-W6]
~ town west of Bear Lake.

This Peace River District town is named after the nearby Beaver River, with the word "lodge" (a temporary dwelling) added. From 1910 to 1928 the post office was called BELLOW. At one time it was called REDLOW.

The population was 1,138 in 1972 and increased to 2,264 in 2006. (See also: **LAKE SASKATOON**)

BEAZER   **[2-27-W4]**
~ hamlet southwest of Cardston.

The name is derived from the Beazer Ward, organized by Charles Card in 1900 who named Mark E. Beazer its first Mormon bishop.

BEDDINGTON   **[25-1-W5]**
~ former station, now part of Calgary.

The CPR tracks reached here in July 1893, and the station was named after Beddington in Surrey, England. The name Beddington is mentioned in the Domesday Book (1086) census of William the Conqueror as "Beddingstone."

BEDSON   **[49-27-W5]**
(See: **MIETTE**)

BEHAN   **[72-10-W4]**
~ former station north of Philomena.

It was named in 1912 after Brother Behan, a Catholic missionary, who served as a cook.

BEISEKER   **[28-26-W4]**
~ village northeast of Calgary.

It was named after Thomas L. Beiseker, a banker from Fessenden, North Dakota, who lived here for about ten years and was largely instrumental in the settlement of the region with successful American farmers about 1910.

The population in 2008 was 837.

BELLCAMP   **[52-2-W4]**
~ former post office near Lloydminster.

It was named after George Campbell, an early pioneer settler. The order of the syllables of his surname was reversed. The post office was opened in 1915 and closed in 1927.

BELLCOTT   [12-5-W4]
~ former station near Medicine Hat.

It was named after Belle Cotterell, wife of an important official of the Canadian Pacific Railway. Prior to 1914 it was called ANSTEAD.

BELLE ROCK
~ settlement on the border of the Northwest Territories.

The word *belle* means "beautiful" in French.

BELLEVUE   [7-3-W5]
~ ghost mining town in the Crowsnest Pass.

Its beautiful mountain setting suggested its name (*belle vue* "pretty view"). It has two large bituminous coal mines, opened in 1907.
(See: **CROWSNEST PASS**)

BELLIS   [59-15-W4]
~ hamlet north of Smoky Lake.

The post office was opened in 1914 and the community ranked as a village in 1928. *Bellis* is the Ukrainian word for white popular.

BELLOW   [72-10-W6]
(See: **BEAVERLODGE**)

BELLOY   [78-2-W6]
~ former station north of Spirit River.

This former railway station was so named in 1916 to honor Madame Belloy, a Belgian operatic singer who sang during the Great War for the Belgian Relief Fund.

BELLSHILL   [42-11-W4]
~ former post office near Hardisty.

It was named by Archibald Brown, the first postmaster, after his wife Isobel (Bell). It was opened in 1907 but has since been closed. It was located on a hill.

BELVEDERE   [58-3-W5]
~ former post office near Barrhead.

It was named by Robert Telfer, the first postmaster in 1905, because of the fine view. Previously the community had been called **PEMBINA CROSSING**, and then MacDONALD CROSSING. (The latter name is a reference to an early settler, George MacDonald.)

BENALTO   [38-2-W5]
~ hamlet west of Red Deer.

The name is a hybrid meaning "high hill". *Ben* is the Gaelic word for "mountain" and *altus* is the Latin word for "high". A station was opened here in 1914.

BENBOW   [59-18-W5]
~ railway junction near Edson.

It was named after Private William N. Benbow, a Canadian soldier killed in action in 1945.

BENNETT   [23-28-W4]
~ former station west of Langdon.

Canadian Pacific Railway officials named this station in 1911 to honor its then legal advisor, Richard Bedford Bennett (1870-1947), who later became the Prime Minister of Canada.

Born at Hopewell, New Brunswick, he was educated in the public school there and qualified as a teacher. He only taught long enough to collect sufficient funds to take law at Dalhousie University. He was called to the New Brunswick Bar in 1893 and practiced for a couple years in Chatham before coming west to Calgary. His political career began in 1898 when he was elected a Conservative member in the Legislature of the Northwest Territories, in which he sat until Alberta was created a separate province in 1905. He failed in his first attempt to be elected to the provincial House, but was successful in 1909. He resigned his seat in the Legislature when he was elected to the Commons two years later.

When he became Prime Minister of Canada after defeating Mackenzie King in 1930, his only experience in office had been in Meighan's pre-election Cabinets in 1921 and 1926 in which he had held respectively the portfolios of Justice and Finance. In 1935 the Liberals pushed him out of office. After leading the opposition for three years, Bennett retired to England where he was created a Viscount in 1941.

BENTLEY   [40-1-W5]
~ village west of Lacombe.

It was named after George Bentley, the first postmaster and pioneer settler in the district in 1900.

BENTON STATION   [27-3-W4]
~ hamlet east of Oyen.

It was named after Benton Trail, from Fort Benton, Montana, to Lethbridge. In its hey-day, the American town was an important fur-trading post at the head of navigation on the Missouri, and the whiskey traders obtained their "fire-water" here to trade with the Blackfoot Indians.

BENVILLE   [73-6-W6]
~ former village at Sexsmith.

It was named after J. Bernard 'Ben' Foster, a pioneer settler and owner of the town site. It was unofficially so named until Ottawa officially stated its name would be **SEXSMITH**.

BEREN'S HOUSE
~ an abandoned fur-trading post on the west bank of the Athabasca River at the mouth of Calumet Creek.

This was an early fur-trading post, sixty miles from Chipewyan near the present Fort MacKay. It was built in 1815 by Thomas of the Hudson's Bay Company. The Arctic explorer, Franklin, stopped here in 1825. It was named after Joseph Berens, one-time Governor of the Hudson's Bay Company.

BERGEN [32-5-W5]
~ post office north of Cremona.

Probably named after Bergen, the ancient capital of Norway, situated on the west coast. It was opened in 1907. It was a Norwegian settlement.

BERNY [66-16-W4]
~ former post office southwest of Lac La Biche.

It was opened in 1914. The origin of the name is unknown.

BERRY CREEK [31-14-W4]
~ former post office near Hanna.

It was named after a nearby stream which flows into the Red Deer River. It was opened in 1910 but has since been closed.

BERRYMOOR [50-6-W5]
~ former post office near Wabamun Lake.

The name is descriptive, there being large quantities of wild berries in the vicinity. It was opened in 1910 and closed in 1985.

BERWYN [82-24-W5]

It was named after Berwyn in Denbigshire, Wales, by early settlers from that part of the British Isles. Prior to 1912 it was called BEAR LAKE.

BETULA BEACH [53-5-W5]
~ summer village near Drayton Valley.

This name was chosen for the new community in 1960 because of the birch trees in the vicinity. *Betula* is the Latin word for "birch".

BEVERLY   [53-24-W4]
~ former town, now a suburb of Edmonton.

It was named in 1904 after Beverly township in Wentworth County, Ontario, which was the former home of R. R. Jamieson, general superintendent of the Canadian Pacific Railway in Calgary. The Ontario township in turn, was named after a town in Yorkshire, England. Beverly became part of Edmonton in 1961 when its population was about 10,000.

BEYNON   [27-20-W4]
~ former post office south of Drumheller.

It was named after H. Beynon Briggs, the first postmaster in 1914.

BEZANSON   [72-3-W6]
~ former post office north of Grande Prairie.

It was named after A. M. Bezanson, a pioneer settler in 1915.

BICKERDALE   [53-18-W5]
~ former station west of Edson.

It was named in 1911 after Robert Bickerdike (1843-1928). Born at Kingston, Canada West, he became a successful Montreal businessman. After spending one term in the Quebec legislature, he was elected to the House of Commons in 1900 as the Liberal member for St. Lawrence, Montreal. Bickerdike, who was an early advocate of prison reform and the abolition of the death penalty, sat in the federal House for seventeen years.

The population: nil.

BIG COULEE   [68-22-W4]
~ former post office north of Athabasca.

This name is descriptive of the location of the post office. It took its name from the school district.

BIG PRAIRIE   **[30-5-W5]**
~ former post office west of Cremona.

The name is descriptive. It opened in 1909 and closed in 1960.

BIG SLOUGH   **[113-19-W4]**
~ hamlet east of High Level

It is a translation of a Cree word. Rev. Vantroys , OMI, a Catholic missionary, says "A small settlement of six cabins ... but it has a very old name." The name was approved in 1963.

BIG STONE   **[26-9-W4]**
~ former post office southwest of Oyen.

It was named in 1911 after a nearby stream. In 1930 it ranked as a village but has since been on a decline.

BIG VALLEY   **[32-20-W4]**
~ village south of Stettler.

The name is descriptive, the community being situated in a wide open valley. In the 1920's this coal mining community was ranked as a town with a population of 3,500 persons. In 2006 its population was only 351.

BILBY   **[54-1-W5]**
~ former post office north of Stony Plain.

In 1928 this community ranked as a village. It is said that the name is a corrupted form of "Wilby" to "Bilby". It was open from 1918 to 1961. There is an English village called Wilby in Suffolk.

BILLOS   **[66-15-W4]**
~ former station near Lac La Biche.

It was named after J. O. Billos, a pioneer Italian settler who arrived in the district in 1902. It was changed to **VENICE** in 1916.

BINDLOSS   [22-2-W4]
~ hamlet south of Empress.

It was named in 1914 after Harold Bindloss (1866-1945), the author of several western novels which were popular at the time.

BINGEN   [6-10-W4]
~ former community near Foremost.

Probably named after the German Rhineland town of Bingen -- many of the original settlers in the district were German. It had a post office for a brief time after 1911. The graveyard, containing the bodies of plague victims, is all that remains today. Later it was resettled (see: **NEMISKAM**)

BINGLEY   [40-6-W5]
~ former post office north of Rocky Mountain House.

It was named in 1910 after Bingley in Yorkshire, England, the birthplace of the first postmaster.

BINGVILLE   [17-7-W4]
~ former post office near Redcliff.

It is said that this name was taken from the comic section of the *Spokane Review*. It was opened in 1914 but has since been closed.

BIRCHAM   [29-25-W4]
~ hamlet near Drumheller.

Presumably named after Bircham, King's Lynn, England. The post office was in operation from 1925 to 1966.

BIRDSHOLM   [4-11-W4]
~ former post office near Foremost.

It was named after A. W. Bird, the first postmaster. It was opened in 1914 but has since been closed.

BISMARK [43-27-W4]
~ former settlement near Ponoka.

It was named after the great "Iron Chancellor" of Germany, Prince Otto von Bismark. It was originally a German settlement.

BISSELL [53-25-W4]
~ former station west of Edmonton.

It was named after American judge H. P. Bissell (1856-1919) of Buffalo, New York. It was in operation by 1874.

BITTERN LAKE [46-21-W4]
~ village west of Camrose.

It was named after the nearby Bittern Lake. A bittern is a tawny brown heron that inhabits reedy marshes. Prior to 1910 the station was called **ROSENROLL** in honor of Anthony Sigwart de Rosenroll, who was elected to the first Alberta legislature as the Liberal member for Wetaskiwin.

BITUMOUNT [97-11-W4]
~ former post office near Fort McMurray.

It was named after the International Bitumount Company that was attempting to extract petroleum from tar sands. It opened in 1934.

BLACK DIAMOND [20-2-W5]
~ town northwest of High River.

It owes its name to nearby coal mines and its growth to the adjacent Turner Valley oil and gas fields. The name was suggested in 1907 by Addison McPherson, an early pioneer of the district.

The population was 955 in 1972, and increased to 2,308 by 2009.

BLACKFALDS   [39-27-W4]
~ town north of Red Deer.

The first name of the community in 1891 was WAGHORN. Since it was the eleventh siding north of Calgary, the railway called it just the **ELEVENTH SIDING**. In 1902 the name was changed to BLACKFALDS after a place with the same name in Scotland:. The Old English word *fald* means a fold or a pen for keeping animals

The population was 877 in 1972 and it increased to 5,610 by 2009.

BLACKFOOT   [50-2-W4]
~ hamlet south of Lloydminster.

It was named after the Blackfoot Confederation, the loosely allied nomadic tribes of Indians that wandered over the western prairies, following the mighty buffalo herds. The name is commonly believed to have reference to the discoloration of the moccasins by the ashes of the prairie fires. Their own name for themselves is *Siksika*.

BLACKIE   [19-27-W4]
~ former village northeast of High River.

It was named after John Stuart Blackie, a nineteenth century novelist and publisher, by one of his admirers. He founded the firm of Blackie and Sons which still exists. The village voted itself out of existence in 1997.

BLACKTAIL   [13-29-W4]
~ former post office near Claresholm.

It was named in 1913 because it was situated on the Blacktail coulee which, possibly was in turn named after the black tailed deer. Originally the post office was called WILLOWS but the name was changed to avoid duplication.

BLAIRMORE [7-4-W5]

According to the Geographic Board of Canada, it is named for Andrew G. Blair, Liberal Premier of New Brunswick (1883-1896) and federal Minister of Railways and Canals (1896-1903) and a railway contractor named More (or Moore). It is the largest center in the **CROWSNEST PASS** area at an altitude of 4,226 feet.

The population in 2009 was 2,088.

BLAYNEY [12-23-W4]

(See: **BARONS**)

BLISS

~ former station near Edson.

This name may have been chosen because it expressed the sentiments of the early settlers that they had arrived at their destination.

BLOOMING PRAIRIE [31-20-W4]

(See: **MORRIN**)

BLOOMSBURY [60-4-W5]

~ former post office northwest of Westlock.

This name was suggested in 1921 by former residents of the Bloomsbury school district in Manitoba. This, in turn, was named after the residential district in central London (England), in which is located the British Museum.

BLUE JAY [68-17-W4]

~ former post office west of Lac La Biche.

It is named after the bird.

BLUE RIDGE [59-10-W5]

~ hamlet east of Whitecourt.

This descriptive name was given in 1923. It is said that there is a blue haze on the ridge when seen from a distance in summer.

BLUEBERRY MOUNTAIN   [80-8-W6]
~ former post office north of Blueberry Hill.

The name is descriptive, there being a large number of shrubs in the neighborhood. It opened in 1925 and closed in 1945.

BLUESKY   [82-2-W6]
~ hamlet east of Fairview.

This name is descriptive of the cloudless skies which are characteristic of the Peace River Country.

BLUFFTON   [43-2-W5]
~ hamlet north of Gull Lake.

It was so named in 1922 when it ranked as a village. "Bluff" is a word used on the Canadian prairies for "a grove of trees." Previously the post office was called BLUFF CENTRE.

BLUMENAE   [39-19-W4]
(See: STETTLER)

BLUMENFORT   [107-14-W5]
~ a Mennonite settlement south of High Level.

It was one of several Mexican Mennonite settlements near La Crete. It was established in 1930.

BODO   [37-1-W4]
~ hamlet southwest of Provost.

There is an inlet of the sea called Bodo in northern Norway.

BOGGY HALL   [46-9-W5]
~ former fur trading post near Drayton Valley.

This Northwest Company fur trading fort was flourishing when it was visited by David Thompson in 1810. The name is probably descriptive.

BOIAN   [56-14-W4]
~ former post office near Vegreville.

It was named after a village in the Ukraine where many of the original settlers were from. It was opened in 1913 but has since been closed.

BON ACCORD   [56-23-W4]
~ town north of Edmonton.

"Bon Accord" is the motto of the city of Aberdeen, Scotland. It is said to have been the password used by the Aberdonians when they took the castle from the English. Later, Robert the Bruce authorized the use of the word as the city's motto. The phrase means, "Happy to meet, sorry to part, happy to meet again." It was the name adopted for a new school in 1896 and was carried over to the post office and village.

The population in 1972 was 322. It increased to 1,534 by 2006.

BONANZA   [80-12-W6]
~ former post office west of Blueberry Hill.

Probably named after Bonanza Creek, a stream of the Yukon that flows into the Klondike River at Dawson. It was famous for placer mining in the days of the gold rush of 1898. The literal meaning of this Spanish word is "smooth sea", hence "good luck", or a rich vein of ore.

BONAR   [31-13-W4]
~ former station east of Hanna.

It is most probably named after Andrew Bonar Law (1858-1923), the Canadian-born Prime Minister of Britain in the 1920's. Born at Rexton, New Brunswick, Bonar Law spent his early years in his father's manse before being sent to Scotland. He became a successful Glasgow merchant and entered British politics in 1900 when he was elected as a Conservative member for a Glasgow constituency. When Balfour resigned as the leader of the Conservative Party in 1911, Bonar Law was elected his successor. He served as Chancellor of the Exchequer in Lloyd George's war-time coalition cabinet, and then as Lord Privy Seal after the war. When the Coalition government was brought down in October, 1922, Bonar Law became Prime Minister. He was victorious in the held later that year, but was forced to retire in May, 1923, because of failing health.

BONDISS   [65-18-W4]
~ former post office south of Athabasca.

BONLEA   [45-14-W4]
~ former post office near Hardisty.

The name is probably descriptive. The post office was opened in 1914 but has since been closed.

BONNIE GLEN   [47-27-W4]
~ former post office near Wetaskiwin.

This name was descriptive of the locality. The post office was opened in 1905 but has since been closed.

BONNYVILLE   [61-5-W4]
~ town northeast of St. Paul.

It was named in honor of Rev. Francois Bonny, a White Father of Africa, who established the first Catholic church in the district. Prior to its incorporation as a village in 1929, Bonnyville was known as ST. LOUIS DE MOOSE LAKE. In the vicinity are ruins of GREENWICH HOUSE, a trading post that was flourishing when Peter Fidler wintered here in 1799.

The population in 1972 was 2,529. It increased to 6,470 by 2009.

BONNYVILLE BEACH   [60-6-W4]
~ summer village.

It was named after the nearby town of Bonnyville. It is situated on the shore of Moose Lake.

BORDENAVE   [61-9-W4]
~ former post office near Therien.

It was named after F. H. Bordenave, the first postmaster, in 1914. It closed prior to 1970.

BORRADAILE   [50-5-W4]
~ hamlet east of Vermilion.

BOSCOMBE   [60-10-W4]
~ former post office southwest of Therien.

It was named after Boscombe in Wiltshire, England. This name means "box-tree" in a combe or valley.
(See: **DEAVER**)

BOTHA   [38-18-W4]
~ village east of Stettler.

It was named after General Louis Botha (1862-1919), the famous Boer military leader during the South African War (1899-1902), and later the first Prime Minister of the Union of South Africa. *Veldt*, the Boer word for "plain", is a station in the same railway subdivision.
(See: **VELDT**)

BOTTREL   [28-4-W5]
~ former post office south of Cremona.

It was named after Edward Botterel, a pioneer settler. The change in spelling was due to an error of an official in Ottawa.

BOUNDARY CREEK   [1-26-W4]
~ former post office south of Cardston.

It obtained its name from a nearby stream that crosses the international border into the United States. The post office was opened in 1907 but has since been closed.

BOUVIER   [67-15-W4]
~ former post office near Lac La Biche.

It was named after its first postmaster, Xavier Bouvier when the post office was established in 1924. Later the name was changed to Egg Lake. The post office closed in 1970.

Bouvier's grandson was Dr. Damas David Bouvier, member of the Legislature from 1968 to 1975.

BOW CITY   [17-17-W4]
~ hamlet south of Brooks.

It is situated on the Bow River. The hopes of the early settlers were never realized; the community does not yet rank in size as a "city".

BOW FORT
~ abandoned trading post on the east bank of the Old Fort Creek near its junction with the Bow River.

This early fur-trading post was occupied by John E. Harriot as the factor. Official records of the Hudson's Bay Company in 1833 refer to it as PEIGAN POST. It was later abandoned.

BOW ISLAND   [10-11-W4]
~ town west of Medicine Hat.

It was named after the Bow River. It was part of a ranching area before the start of homesteading and the arrival of the railway in 1907. There is a story in the district that Bow Island should have been called **GRASSY LAKE**, and Grassy Lake - Bow Island, but some official in Ottawa switched the names in error. It is said that the travelers from eastern Canada used to claim in their expense accounts for ferry transportation from Grassy Lake to Bow Island!

The population in 1972 was 1,165. It increased to 1,868 by 2007.

BOWDEN **[34-1-W5]**
~ town north of Olds.

It was named after Bowden in Chestershire, England. Arrival of the railway in 1891 brought an influx of English settlers who changed the name from LONEPINE, a stopping place, on the Calgary-Edmonton stage route.

The population in 1972 was 554. It increased to 1,236 in 2009. (See: **CALGARY-EDMONTON TRAIL STAGING POSTS**)

BOWELL **[14-7-W4]**
~ hamlet northwest of Medicine Hat.

It was named in 1884 after Sir Mackenzie Bowell Conservative Prime Minister from 1894 -1896. He was the federal Minister of Customs when this community on the Edmonton-Calgary Trail was named. Bowell (1823-1917) became Prime Minister on the death of Sir John Thompson, but he was unable to exercise his leadership. In January, 1896, half the ministers -Bowel's "nest of traitors" - resigned *en masse* and forced him to retire. He was succeeded as Prime Minister by Sir Charles Tupper.

BOWMANTON **[15-14-W4]**
~ former post office near Medicine Hat.

It was named in 1913 after Mrs. Whitson, nee Bowman, the wife of a local farmer.

BOWNESS **[24-1-W5]**
~ now a suburb of Calgary.

It was named after E.W. Bowness of Canadian Utilities. Prior to 1942 the community was called CRITCHLEY. The it took the name of Bowness and was incorporated as a village in 1948. Four years later it became a town, but lost its identity in the mid-1960's when it was incorporated into the city of **CALGARY**.

BOYLE   **[65-19-W4]**
~ village north of Edmonton.

It was named after John Robert Boyle (1871 -1936), an Alberta Liberal politician. Born in Ontario in 1871, he moved west as a young man after teaching school in Lambton County, Ontario, and became a lawyer in Edmonton. Boyle represented the rural constituency of Sturgeon from 1905 to 1923. In 1912 he replaced C. R. Mitchell as the Minister of Education and six years later was also named the Attorney General. Charles Stewart's Liberal administration was defeated by the United Farmers of Alberta in 1921 and Boyle became the leader of the opposition. He was later appointed a Judge of the Supreme Court of Alberta.

The population in 1972 was 498. The population increased to 918 in 2009.

BOYNE LAKE   **[61-12-W4]**
~ former post office west of Therien.

It was named in 1905 after the river in Ireland which was the site of Dutch William's great victory over King James II on July 12, 1690. This date is remembered annually by Orangemen all over the world.

BRAATEN   **[67-5-W6]**
~ railway point near Grande Prairie.

It was named after Private Lester L. Braaten who was killed in action in August 1944. It was established in 1969.

BRADSHAW   **[5-22-W4]**
~ former station southwest of Magrath.

It was named in 1912 after a wealthy rancher, William Bradshaw.

BRAEBURN   **[75-5-W6]**
~ former station east of Saddle Hills.

Originally this station was called SURBITON.

BRAGG CREEK [23-5-W5]
~ hamlet southwest of Calgary.

It was named in 1911 after an early settler of the district, George Bragg. The population in 1972 was 83.

BRAINARD [74-12-W6]
~ former post office northwest of Hythe

It was named in 1919 after the first postmaster, W. L. Brainard.

BRANT [18-26-W4]
~ hamlet southeast of High River.

It was named by its founder, E. E. Thompson of High River, in 1905 for brant geese which were very plentiful that season on the lakes in the vicinity.

BRAZEAU [40-15-W5]
~ former station west of Rocky Mountain House.

It was named after Joseph E. Brazeau, an employee of the Hudson's Bay Company for many years who helped the Palliser Expedition. Palliser said of him, "Brazeau had been for many years in the American Indian fur trade, was a wonderful linguist and spoke Stony, Sioux, Salteau, Cree, Blackfoot and Crow. Being of an old Spanish family and educated in the United States, he also spoke English, French and Spanish fluently."

BREAGE [50-6-W4]
~ former post office, west of Lloydminster.

It was named after a Cornish village by a Barr Colonist. Later it was changed. (See: **VERMILION**)

BREDIN [72-7-W6]
~ former post office near Sexsmith.

It was named after Mrs. W. Fletcher Bredin, the postmistress from 1915 to the time it closed in 1930. Her husband, W. Fletcher (1857-1942) had arrived in the postal district of Athabasca to trade in 1882 and for decades was a partner of 'Peace River Jim' Cornwal, D.S.O. Fletcher sat in the Legislature from 1909 to 1913.

BREMNER   **[53-22-W4]**
~ hamlet east of Edmonton.

Probably named after Colonel James John Bremner, one time commander of the 66ᵗʰ Regiment, Prince of Wales Fusiliers, who saw active service during the Northwest Rebellion of 1885. Prior to 1912 it was called HORTONBURG.

BRETON   **[48-4-W5]**
~ village northwest of Pigeon Lake.

It was named after Douglas C. Breton, the United Farmer MLA for Leduc from 1926 -1930., who was a pioneer settler in the district. From 1912 to 1926 the post office was called **KEYSTONE**.
The population in 1972 was 447.

BRETONA   **[51-23-W4]**
~ former station southeast of Edmonton.

At one time the post office in this community was called **HERCULES**.

BREYNAT   **[71-17-W4]**
It was named in 1949 in honor of Mgr. Gabriel Breynat (1867-1954), a French-born Oblate missionary who was the bishop of the Mackenzie district from 1902 to 1943.

BRICKBURN   **[24-2-W5]**
~ former station west of Calgary.

It was so named because there were brick kilns in operation in the vicinity in 1914.

BRIDGEVIEW   **[77-6-W6]**
~ former post office near Spirit River.

This is a descriptive name. It was opened in 1930, but has since been closed.

BRIEREVILLE   **[63-12-W4]**
~ former post office northeast of Whitefish Lake.

It was named after the J.C.O. Brière, the first postmaster in 1917.

BRIGGS [39-28-W4]
~ former station northwest of Red Deer.

It was given this name in 1922. Previously it was called TANNIS.

BRIGHTBANK [51-2-W5]
~ former post office near Wabamun Lake.

The name is descriptive. It was opened in 1908 but has since been closed.

BRIGHTVIEW [46-25-W4]
This was the name of the first postmaster's farm and is probably descriptive.

BRITANNIA COLONY [50-1-W4]
(See: LLOYDMINSTER)

BROCKET [7-28-W4]
~ former post office north of Pincher Creek.

It was named after the English estate of Sir George Stephen (1829-1921), president of the Canadian Pacific Railway (1881-1888). He later received a title and was known as Lord Mount Stephen. Brocket Hall is situated near Hatfield in Hertfordshire.

BROOK [40-24-W4]
(See: TEES)

BROOKFIELD [38-26-W4]
(See: BROOKSLEY)

BROOKS [18-14-W4]
~ town southeast of Calgary.

It was named after N. E. Brooks, divisional engineer of the Canadian Pacific Railway at Calgary. His name was selected from a postal department list of suggested community names by Ernest M. Crooker who opened the first store in the community.

The population in 1972 was 3,858. It increased to 13,581 by 2007.

BROOKSLEY   [38-26-W4]
~ *former post office near Red Deer.*

Originally this community was called BROOKFIELD, which is still the name of the school district. But when the post office was opened its name was changed to Brooksley to avoid duplication. It has since been closed.

BROSSEAU   [56-12-W4]
~ *hamlet northeast of Two Hills.*

It was named after Edmond Brousseau who was a successful farmer and merchant in the district. There was formerly a Catholic mission called St. Paul des Cris in the vicinity that was founded by Fr. Lacombe. Nothing remains of it save some traces in the cemetery.

BROWNFIELD   [39-10-W4]
~ *former post office southeast of Alliance.*

It was named in 1907 after the first postmaster, C.D. Brownfield.

BROWNVALE   [82-25-W5]
~ *hamlet southwest of Peace River.*

It was named after John H. Brown a pioneer settler who homesteaded in the district from Ontario. It opened in 1926.

BROXBURN   [9-20-W4]
~ *former station near Lethbridge.*

Probably named after Broxburn in Linlithgowshire, Scotland. There is also a Broxbourne in Hertfordshire, England. The station was in operation in 1911.

BRUCE   [48-14-W4]
~ *hamlet south of Vegreville.*

It was named after A. Bruce Smith, a telegraph company official. Prior to 1909 the post office was called HURRY. But some one in Ottawa apparently did not like this name and so it was changed.

BRUDERHEIM [55-20-W4]
~ town northeast of Edmonton.

This name is German for "brethren's home.". It was a Moravian settlement. The Moravian Church is often called the Brethren's Church. A colony of brethren came to western Canada from Volnyia in Russia and settled in Alberta in 1893. Twenty families took up homesteads and called their community BRUDERHEIM. The post office was opened in 1895.

The population in 1972 was 358. It increased to 1215 in 2006.

BRÛLÉ [50-27-W5]
~ former station west of Brûlé Lake.

It is located on the Canadian National Railway main line near the Alberta Resource railway line. The name presumably comes from the French word meaning "burnt".

This name was recorded first as POINT BRÛLÉ in 1892.

BRÛLÉ MINES [50-27-W5]
~ former post office near Brûlé Lake.

A coal mine was opened here in 1917.

BRUNTON [4-17-W4]
(See: **WARNER**)

BRUTUS [17-8-W4]
~ former post office near Medicine Hat.

It was named after Brutus in the State of Michigan, which was the former home of the first postmaster, Jonas Brubacher. It was opened in 1913 but has since been closed.

BUCK CREEK [47-7-W5]
~ former post office northwest of Buck Lake.

It was named after a nearby stream that flows into Buck Lake. Game used to be plentiful in the vicinity.

BUCK LAKE [46-6-W5]
~ hamlet on the shore of Buck Lake.

A male deer is often referred to as a "buck".

BUCK LAKE HOUSE   [50-5-W5]
~ abandoned trading post near Vermilion.

The Hudson's Bay Company built a fur-trading post here in 1800. It was situated on the south side of the North Saskatchewan River above the mouth of Buck Lake Creek. It was soon abandoned for a more suitable location.

BUCKHORN
~ former post office near Red Deer.

It is believed that the name was suggested by the first postmaster, Abraham Davidson, who was a keen hunter. For many years a pair of deer horns adorned the post office gateway. It was opened in 1908 but has since been closed.

BUCKINGHAM HOUSE
~ abandoned trading post on the North Saskatchewan River near Fort George.

It was built by William Tomison of the Hudson's Bay Company in 1792 to compete with the North West Company's nearby Fort George for Indian trade, and was visited in 1793 by David Thompson. In 1801 it was moved to Fort Island and was abandoned in 1802. It was named after Buckingham Palace, the London residence of the British monarch.

BUFFALO   [21-5-W4]
~ hamlet southeast of Empress.

This community is named after the largest hoofed animal native to North America. The buffalo originally ranged across most of the continent, feeding on the almost inexhaustible supply of wild grasses. They were very important in the economy of the nomadic tribes of Indians. Firearms introduced by Europeans decimated these large wild animals in their millions. By the 1880's the herds of buffalo had disappeared forever from the western prairies.

BUFFALO HEAD PRAIRIE   [104-15-W5]
~ hamlet near High Level.

It is located near the Bear River and was settled by Mennonites. A post office was opened in 1976.

BUFFALO LAKE   [74-7-W6]
~ former post office north of Bear Lake.

It was named after a nearby lake. The bison often used to go into the water during the hot summer to get rid of flies. They also used to roll in buffalo wallows, covering themselves with mud for the same reason. It was previously called SPITEFIRE LAKE.

BUFFALO VIEW   [42-6-W4]
~ former post office near Wainwright.

It was located near the south boundary of the federal government buffalo park. It was opened in 1912 but has since been closed.

BUFORD   [49-27-W4]
~ hamlet southwest of Edmonton.

Many of the first homesteaders in the district were Americans who had come from Buford in the State of North Dakota.

BULLOCKSVILLE   [39-23-W4]
(See: HEATBURG)

BULLPOUND   [24-15-W4]
~ former station south of Hanna.

A number of bull buffalo were once said to have been killed in a pound here.

BULLSHEAD   [11-6-W4]
~ former station south of Medicine Hat.

A butte in the vicinity has a shape that is not unlike the head of a bison.

BULWARK   [38-12-W4]
~ hamlet northwest of Coronation.

It received its present name in 1916. Previously the community was called LINDSVILLE.

BUOYANT   [29-25-W4]
~ former station west of Drumheller.

This name may have expressed the optimism of the early settlers.

BURBANK   [39-27-W4]
~ former station north of Red Deer.

It was probably named after Luther Burbank (1849-1926), the American horticulturist. He is noted for originating and introducing 618 new varieties of flowers, fruits, grains, grasses, trees, forage plants, nuts, vegetables and ornamental shrubs.

BURDETT   [10-12-W4]
~ village southwest of Medicine Hat.

It was named in honor of Baroness Georgina Burdett-Coutts, who was born in 1814 and inherited a vast fortune from her step-grandmother, the Duchess of St. Albans. Miss Burdett-Coutts was "the richest heiress in all England," enjoying a fame throughout the country second only to Queen Victoria. Suitors were numerous. No young man of good family is said to have abstained from a proposal, and an exaggerated rumor included the aged Duke of Wellington and Prince Louis Napoleon. She received a peerage from the Queen in 1871. Finally she married a young American who was an Oxford graduate (see **COUTTS**), and thirty-seven years younger than herself. By royal license he assumed her name. Her wealth opened up and developed coal mining in southern Alberta where she was a major shareholder in the North West Coal and Navigation Company. The baroness died in 1906.

BURFIELD [26-15-W4]
~ former post office near Hanna.

It was named after the first postmaster, H. E. Burfield. It was opened in 1914 but has since been closed.

BURMIS [7-3-W5]
~ hamlet southeast of Blairmore.

It was named in 1901 after two early residents whose surnames were Burns and Kemmis.

BURTONSVILLE [50-4-W5]
~ former post office south of Wabamun Lake.

It was named in 1909 after the first postmaster, C. Burton.

BUSBY [57-27-W4]
~ hamlet northwest of Morinville

This community was probably named after Edward S. Busby, the inspector of customs in the Yukon during the time of the Klondike gold rush. Prior to 1915 the post office was called INDEPENDENCE.

BUTTE [37-6-W5]
~ former post office north of Caroline.

It was so named because of a butte of hill in the vicinity.

BUTZE [43-1-W4]
~ former station northeast of Provost.

It was named after A. Butze, a purchasing agent for the Grand Trunk Pacific Railway. It is second in a series of stations of the Grand Trunk Pacific Railway that are in alphabetical order — Artland (just inside Saskatchewan), Butze, Chauvin and Dunn.

BYE [39-6-W5]
~ former station near Hardisty.

It was named in 1924 after S. Bye, D.C.M., who had formerly been a trucker in Vancouver.

BYEMOOR   **[35-16-W4]**
~ hamlet northeast of Drumheller.

The Norse word for a village is *by*. Thus, this name could mean a "village on a moor".

C

CABIN LAKE   [24-9-W4]
~ former post office south of Oyen.

It was named in 1923 after a lake with an old log cabin on its shore. The name is descriptive.

CACHE LAKE   [59-12-W4]
(See: **SPEDDEN**)

CADOGAN   [39-4-W4]
~ former village southwest of Provost.

It was named in 1909 possibly after George Henry, the fifth Earl of Cadogan (1840-1915), the British statesman who was secretary to the colonies from 1886 to 1892. It used to rank as a village.

The population in 1972 was 81.

CADOMIN   [47-23-W5]
~ ghost mining town in the Coal Branch.

The word is a contraction of Canadian Dominion Mine, invented by the first president of the Cadomin Coal Company, F. L. Hammond, in 1913. (See: **COAL BRANCH**)

CADOTTE LAKE   [86-16-W5]
~ early settlement north of Peace River.

It was named after nearby Cadotte River is mentioned in Archibald McDonald's Journal under the date 25 August 1828. It in turn was named after Rev. Jean Baptiste Cadotte, an early Catholic missionary.

CADRON   [58-16-W4]
~ former post office south of Smoky Lake.

CAIRNS   [39-4-W4]
~ former village near Provost.

The Gaelic word *cairn* means "a rounded heap of stones". It was named in 1909.

CALAHOO   [54-27-W4]
~ former village northwest of Edmonton.

It was named after William Calahoo, a Metis of Iroquoian origin, who came west with the early bateaux brigades. So named in 1915.

CALAIS   [70-24-W5]
~ former post office south of Sturgeon Lake.

It was named in 1911 in honor of Rev. Calais OMI, a Catholic missionary who worked for years among the inhabitants of Northern Alberta.

CALBECK   [27-5-W5]
~ former post office west of Calgary.

It was named after the English town of Calbeck, Cumberland. The name means "cold stream".

CALDWELL   [2-28-W4]
~ former post office south of Cardston.

It was named after D. H. Caldwell , the first postmaster in 1900. He was a Mormon settler from Utah who arrived in the 1880's.

CALENDULA   [29-2-W4]
~ post office near Medicine Hat.

It was named after the orange or yellow marigold found in abundance in the district. "Calendula" is the genus name of the flower. It was opened in 1913.

CALGARY [24-1-W5]
~ the largest city in the province, situated at the junction of the Bow and Elbow Rivers within sight of the Rocky Mountains.

It is believed to be on or near the site of FORT LA JONQUIERRE which was built by La Vérendrye in 1757 and abandoned the next year. **FORT BRISEBOIS,** a North West Mounted Police outpost from **FORT MACLEOD,** was erected in 1875, and renamed FORT CALGARY in 1876. That year Assistant Commissioner A. G. Irvine wrote to Ottawa as follows: "As we now have a post of Fort at Bow River, it would be well if it was known by some name .... Colonel Macleod has suggested the name of Calgary, which I believe, in Scotch, means clear running water, a very appropriate name, I think".

Mrs. C.M. Mathews in *Place Names of the English-Speaking World* (1972) says: "It was probably given by Norsemen, for all those islands (Hebridean) were once part of a Viking Kingdom, and it may have meant an enclosure for calves."

Calgary also happened to be the name of the ancestral estate of Colonel Macleod's cousins , the Mackenzies of the Isle of Mull, Scotland, which he had visited shortly before coming to western Canada. Irvine's suggestion concerning the name of the future city was approved of by the then federal Minister of Justice, Edward Blake The Hudson's Bay Company opened a trading station here in 1876 with Angus Fraser in charge.

In 1883, a post office was opened and that same year the Canadian Pacific Railway came to town, with a population of 500. It became a city in 1893. The famous Calgary Stampede was inaugurated in 1912.

The population was 398,034 in 1972 and increased to 1,065,455 in 2009. (See: **BOWNESS; FOREST LAWN; GLENBOW; PRIDDIS**)

CALGARY-EDMONTON TRAIL

STAGING POSTS (1883-1891)

When the Canadian Pacific Railway tracks reached Calgary in the autumn of 1883, the Edmonton mail route changed from the 1,000 mile Winnipeg-Fort Carlton-Edmonton to the 200 mile Calgary-Edmonton Trail. A one-way ticket cost twenty-five dollars and the journey took approximately seven days. The stage had to be ferried across the Bow River to the Nose Hill side. During fall freeze-up and the spring thaw, there was no stage coach. This was the means of travel for eight years until the Calgary-Edmonton railway tracks reached Strathcona, across the river from Edmonton in 1891. When the railway became operational, the time for the journey was cut to 12 hours.

DICKENSON STOPPING HOUSE *on McPherson Creek at mile 187 of the trail north of Calgary.*

The proprietor was Captain Francis J. Dickens, former member of the N.W.M.P. He was a son of Charles Dickens, the British novelist and author of "A Tale of Two Cities."

SCARLET'S STOPPING HOUSE *at Service Berry Creek Crossing mile 35 of the trail*

. The proprietor was Samuel T. Scarlet, an American squatter who had arrived in 1872. In 1909, he was an unsuccessful Legislature candidate.

LONE PINE STOPPING HOUSE [14-7-W4] *at mile 63 of the trail.*

For several years the proprietor was "Paddy", a French Canadian Metis. Travelers referred to his establishment as "Hotel Rustle". The visitors were required to rustle up their own lay beds, look after the stage coach's four horses, and to cook their own meals.

RED DEER CROSSING *at mile 93 of the trail.*

The proprietor was William Bannerman, a Scot and former member of Parliament. He opened a post office and obtained an "official ferrying license. He operated a large scow to transport the coach across the wide river. (See: **RED DEER**)

WHITFORD STOPPING HOUSE *at Blindman's River crossing at mile 100 on the trail.*

The proprietor was Charles Whitford, a prominent pioneer settler. A constituency was named after him. (See: **WHITFORD**)

BARNETT'S STOPPING HOUSE *at mile 115 on the trail.*
The proprietor was Edward Barnett, former member of the N.W.M.P. who was one of the original homesteaders on the Strawberry Plain. (See: **LACOMBE**)

BARKER'S STOPPING HOUSE *at Battle River Crossing, mile 125 on the trail* (See: **PONOKA**).

TELFORD'S STOPPING HOUSE *at mile 187 on the trail.* (See: **LEDUC**)
The proprietor was Robert T. Telford, former member of the N.W.M.P. Later he sat in the Alberta Legislature from 1905 to 1913. It was a steamboat landing below Strathcona in the south side of the valley of the North Saskatchewan River where the trail ended. Edmonton was located on the north bank.

CALLING LAKE   [72-21-W4]
~ former post office east of Calling Lake.

It was named after the nearby lake of the same name in 1920. The lake makes a loud noise when its deep water commences freezing up each year. It is a translation of the Indian name.

CALMAR   [49-27-W4]
~ town east of Edmonton.

It was named on the suggestion of the first postmaster, C. J. Blomquist, after his old home at Kalmar, Sweden in 1900.

The population was 797 in 1972 and increased to 2,033 in 2009.

CALTHORPE   [31-2-W4]
~ former station east of Grassy Lake.

It was named after Calthorpe in Norfolk, England. The name means "the village of Kali".

CAMBRIA   [28-19-W4]
~ hamlet near Drumheller.

It was named after the word *Cambria*, the old Latin name for Wales, by early miners. It had a post office from 1942 to 1969.

The population in 1972 was 88.

CAMP CREEK   [61-4-W5]
~ post office near Fort Vermilion.

It was named after a nearby stream. In ancient times this was a campsite for nomadic natives.

CAMPBELL   [54-25-W4]
~ former station north of Edmonton.

The Gaelic words, *can beul*, mean "crooked mouth" or cambel, "wry mouthed". The Duke of Argyll is the head of the Clan Campbell.

CAMPBELL HILL   [32-8-W4]
~ former post office.

It was named after R. J. Campbell, a Scot, the first postmaster in 1913.

CAMPBELL SIDING   [17-13-W4]
~ near Medicine Hat.

It was named after Sir Keith Campbell, a railway official in 1979.

CAMPBELLTON   [43-17-W4]
(See: ANKERTON)

CAMPBELLTOWN   [52-23-W4]
~ former dormatory town east of Edmonton.

It was named after Campbelltown in Scotland. It is also called **SHERWOOD PARK**.

CAMPSIE   [59-5-W5]
~ former post office west of Westlock.

It was named in 1909 on the suggestion of the first postmaster, William Wallace, a Scot, after Campsie near Glasgow, Scotland. The Gaelic word *campsie* means "crooked hill" or "hill range".

CAMROSE [47-20-W4]
~ city and center of Scandinavian settlements.

This city is named after Camrose in Wales. It is said the name was selected from a British Postal Guide, when officials could not decide on a name. The first settlers were mostly Scandinavians. It was formerly called **SPARLING**.

The population in 1972 was 8,903 and increased to 16,543 in 2008.

CANMORE [24-10-W5]
~ town east of Banff.

It may have been named after Malcolm Canmore, the son of King Duncan, murdered by Macbeth, who finally, with the aid of English troops, defeated the Thane of Castor and became the King of Scotland in 1060.

The population in 1972 was 1,604. It increased to 12,226 souls by 2009.

CANNELL [53-25-W4]
~ former village near Edmonton.

It was named after William Cannell, an Edmonton contractor.

CANYON CREEK [73-8-W5]
~ former post office south of Lesser Slave Lake.

The name is descriptive of its location near a stream with the same name. In 1925 the post office opened.

CAPPON [25-5-W4]
~ former post office south of Oyen.

It was named in 1912 on the suggestion of J.W. Jake, after Professor Cappon of Queen's University. Jake was a graduate of Queen's.

CAPRONA [36-20-W4]
~ former station south of Stettler.

It was opened in 1921.

CARBON   [29-23-W4]
~ *village west of Drumheller.*

There are coal mines in the vicinity. The post office was opened in 1904. And the railway arrived in 1920.

CARBONDALE   [55-24-W4]
~ *former station north of Edmonton.*

It was named after coal deposits found in the district with the name word Dale added.

CARCAJOU   [101-19-W5]
~ *former post office east of Keg River, Northern Alberta.*

It was named in 1923 after a *carcajou*, the French word for "wolverine". It appears on David Thompson's map of 1814.

CARDIFF   [55-25-W4]
~ *former village north of Edmonton.*

It was named after the southern Welsh mining center of Cardiff in 1907. The name was suggested because of the coal mines in the district.

CARDSTON   [3-25-W4]
~ *town south of Lethbridge.*

This community is the center of Mormonism in Canada, and was named after Charles Ora Card, son-in-law of the great Mormon leader Brigham Young, of Salt Lake City. It was under Card's guidance that members of the Latter-Day Saints Church of Jesus Christ moved north into Canada in the late 1880's.

The population in 1972 was 2,721. It increased to 3,578 by 2007.

CARLOS   [41-5-W5]
~ *former post office northeast of Rocky Mountain House.*

The applicant for a post office in the district was J. Sleeper, son of Carlos Sleeper of Minnesota. *Carlos* is the Spanish form of "Charles".

CARLSON LANDING   [115-11-W4]
~ hamlet north of Fort McMurray.

It was named after Mr. Carlson, a Wood Buffalo National Park official in 1959. Previously called POINT PROVIDENCE.

CARLSTADT   [15-10-W4]
(See: **ALDERSON**)

CARLTON HILL   [59-4-W5]
~ former post office near Barrhead.

It was opened in 1917, but has since been closed.

CARMANGAY   [13-23-W4]
~ village north of Lethbridge.

The name is quite romantic, combining the surnames of two early residents who were married in 1907, Mr. C. W. Carman and the beautiful Mill Gay. Carman owned the land the community was built on.

The population was 270 in 1972 and decreased to 261 in 2007.

CARNWOOD   [48-5-W5]
~ former post office north of Breton.

It was named in error for Cornwood, the name of an English parish in Devon.

CAROLINE   [36-6-W5]
~ village south of Rocky Mountain House.

It was named in 1908 after the only child of the first postmaster, H. A. Langley.

The population was 342 in 1972 and increased to 515 in 2006.

CAROLSIDE   [26-12-W4]
~ former post office southeast of Hanna.

It received its present name in 1920 after the English home of a local rancher, George Purvis, who was killed in the Great War. Previously the community was called JETHSON.

CARROT CREEK   [53-13-W5]
~ former post office south of Niton.

The name is descriptive, since wild carrots grow in the vicinity. It was opened in 1910.

CARSELAND   [22-25-W4]
~ former village south of Strathmore.

The name is descriptive, meaning "rich valley land". Before 1910 the community was called **GRIESBACH** in honor of General William Antrobus Griesbach (1878-1945). Born at Fort Qu'Appelle, Northwest Territories, he was the son of one of the original officers of the North West Mounted Police. Educated at St. John's Winnipeg, he was called to the Bar in 1901 and practiced law in Edmonton. He was appointed to the Senate in 1921.

Griesbach had served in the Boer War as a private, and rose to the rank of general while serving in France during the Great War.

CARSTAIRS   [31-1-W5]
~ town north of Calgary.

It was named after a Scottish town of Carstairs in Lanarkshire in 1893. The name comes from the Old English *castel tarres*, meaning "castle of Turres". Terras or Turres is still a Scandinavian name.

The population in 1972 was 904. It increased to 2,656 in 2006.

CARUSO   [24-25-W4]
~ locality near Strathmore.

It was named in 1917 after the famous Italian tenor, Enrico Caruso (1873-1921). Previously this one-time village was called **CHEADLE** after physician and explorer, Dr. Walter Butler Cheadle (1835-1910), co-author with Lord Milton of *The Northwest Passage by Land* (1865).

CARVEL   [52-2-W5]
~ former post office west of Edmonton.

It was named after the title of a romance *Richard Carvel* written by Winston Churchill, nineteenth century American novelist—not to be confused with the famous twentieth century British statesman Sir Winston Spencer Churchill. It opened in 1911.

CARWAY   [1-26-W4]
~ hamlet, custom station south of Cardston.

Originally the office was classified as a preventive station. It was opened in 1926. William Roberts, the first officer in charge, says this about the name: "Originally the road (trail) from Babb, Montana, to Cardston, was called 'Cardston Highway.' I took the 'car' from Cardston and the 'way' from highway and coined the name 'Carway'".

CASAVANT   [58-25-W4]
~ former post office near Barrhead.

It was named after Emile Casavant, the first postmaster in 1914.

CASLAN   [65-17-W4]
~ former post office southwest of Lac La Biche.

It was opened in 1914.

CASSILS   [19-15-W4]
~ former village west of Brooks.

It was named after Charles Cassils of the Montreal firm of Cassils and Cochrane in 1884. He was an early rancher.

CASTLE MOUNTAIN   [26-14-W5]
~ former station northwest of Banff.

It was named in 1883 after nearby Castle Mountain. The name of this mountain was changed in 1946 to Mount Eisenhower to honor General Dwight Eisenhower, Allied Commander-in-Chief in Europe during the final years of the Second World War. But more and more people are referring to this mountain by its original name.

CASTOR   [37-14-W4]
~ town east of Red Deer.

The Latin word castor means "beaver". This name was probably suggested by the name of Beaverdam River which runs through the community. Beavers were still plentiful in the area as late as 1921. The post office was opened in 1909.

The population in 1972 was 1,103. It declined to 931 by 2006.

CAVENDISH   [21-4-W4]
~ former post office northwest of Medicine Hat.

It was named after Victor Christian William Cavendish, the 9th Duke of Devonshire (1869-1938), who was the Governor General of Canada from 1916 to 1921. The Dukes of Devonshire have been a powerful political family for more than three centuries in Britain. Two of the Duke's ADC's became later prominent in their own right: George Vanier, Governor General of Canada in the 1960's, and Harold Macmillan (who married one of the 9th Duke's daughters) British Prime Minister in the 1950's and 1960's.

The former name of the community was **PANCRAS**.

CAYLEY   [17-28-W4]
~ village south of Calgary.

It was named in 1893 after Hugh St. Quentin Cayley (1857-1934), member of the Council of the Northwest Territories from 1886 to 1896. He was a Calgary newspaper publisher and later became a British Columbia judge.

CECIL [13-12-W4]
~ former station northwest of Bow Island.

It was named in 1924 after Mrs. J. M. Cameron, wife of an official of the Canadian Pacific Railway. Previously it had been known as TERRACE.

CEREAL [28-6-W4]
~ village northwest of Oyen.

The district is remarkable for the quality of the grain it produces and the growing potential when it rains. The district was called the Bread Basket of the west until the droughts of the 1930's.

The population was 219 in 1972 and it decreased to 126 in 2006.

CESSFORD [23-12-W4]
~ former post office southeast of Coleman Lake.

It was named in 1910 after 'Cess Ford' the farm of the first postmistress, Mrs. Anderson. The early homesteaders in this district had come from Sweden.

CHAILEY [52-9-W4]
~ post office northwest of Mannville.

It was named in 1907 on the suggestion of the first postmaster C. H. Brown, after his former English home at Chailey in Sussex. This name means "the field of chag".

CHAMPION [15-23-W4]
~ village north of Carmangay.

It was named after H. T. Champion, a Winnipeg banker. Originally the community was called CLEVERHILL because it was built up around the farm of Martin Clever. It was moved a short distance to the railway line in 1910.

The population in 1972 was 380, and increased to 384 in 2007.

CHANCELLOR   [24-21-W4]
~ former post office southwest of Drumheller.

It was named for Theobald von Bethmann-Hollweg, the Chancellor (i.e. Prime Minister) of Germany when this German community was settled in 1913. The post office was closed in 1970.

CHAPEL ROCK   [24-21-W4]
~ former post office near Blairmore.

The name is descriptive. It was opened in 1921, and closed a few years later.

CHARD   [79-6-W4]
~ former station east of Fort McMurray.

It was named after Alfred Chard, an Alberta Government railway official. A post office was opened in 1925.

CHARITY   [6-11-W4]
(See: CHARLES)

CHARLES   [6-11-W4]
~ former community near Foremost.

The residents demanded that the name CHARITY be changed to CHARLES.

CHARRON   [68-16-W4]
~ former post office west of Lac La Biche.

It was named after a French Canadian fur trader who lived in the district for many years. There was a post office there from 1917 to 1968.

CHATEH   [112-5-W6]
~ isolated community near Zama Lake.

It was named after Chief Chateh. Previously called ASSUMPTION.

CHAUVIN [43-1-W4]
~ village north of Provost.

It was named after George Von Chauvin, director of the Grand Trunk Railway in 1908.

CHEADLE [24-26-W4]
~ former hamlet east of Calgary.

It was named in 1884 after Dr. Walter Cheadle (1835 -1910) who accompanied Viscount Milton on a journey for holiday across the Canadian Prairies and through the Rocky Mountains via the Yellowhead Pass to the Pacific coast in 1862-63. He is the author of *Cheadle's Journal of Trip Across Canada*.
(See: **CARUSO**)

CHEECHAM [84-6-W4]
~ former station southwest of Gordon Lake.

It was named after the Cheecham family.

CHENEKA [25-6-W5]
~ former station west of Cochrane.

It was named after the Stony chief who signed Treaty Number Seven in 1877 at Blackfoot Crossing for his tribe.

CHERHILL [56-5-W5]
~ former village southeast of Sangudo.

It was named after A. P. Stecher, the first postmaster, with the word "hill" added to the final syllable of his surname in 1911.

CHERRY GROVE [62-1-W4]
~ former post office northeast of Bonnyville.

The name is descriptive, there being a number of wild cherry trees in the vicinity.

CHERRY POINT [83-13-W6]
~ former post office west of Fairview.

The name is descriptive, there being many wild cherry trees growing in the vicinity. The cherries are choke-cherries.

CHESTERFIELD
~ *an abandoned fur trading post near the Saskatchewan border.*

Established in 1800 by Peter Fidler of the Hudson's Bay Company in the hope the Blackfoot would come there with their valuable furs. It was abandoned in 1805.

CHESTERMERE   [24-28-W4]
~ *town east of Calgary.*

The word "Chester" originally comes from the Latin *castra*, meaning a military camp, while "mere" refers to a pool in a river.
The population in 2009 was 13,760.

CHESTERWOLD   [44-27-W4]
~ *former post office near Ponoka.*

It was named in 1903 after the former home of the first postmaster, Peter A. Cooper, who came from Chesterville in the State of Nebraska.

CHEVIOT   [45-24-W5]
~ *approved open coal development near Jasper National Park.*

The mining community itself has not yet been named.
It was named after the Mountain Cheviot which, in turn was named after the hills on the English-Scottish border which are known as the Cheviots.

CHIEF MOUNTAIN   [1-28-W4]
~ *custom post near Waterton.*

It was named after a mountain a few miles away in the State of Montana. It was opened in 1936. The mountain is a geological oddity, standing as it does on the plains east of the main range. It has attracted the attention of explorers and map makers form the earliest times. Its existence was first noted on Arrowsmith's maps of 1795, upon which it was called "King Mountain". Captain Meriwether Lewis called it "Tower Mountain" when he saw it in 1806. James Doty, who explored the eastern front of the Rockies in 1854, referred to it as "The Chief or King Mountain".

There are many legends regarding this mountain, the most popular being that of the young Flathead brave who spent several days upon the top of the peak searching for his "medicine vision", and using a bison skull for a pillow.

CHIGWELL [40-25-W4]
~ former station east of Lacombe.

It was named in 1905 after a suburb of London, England. The post office was closed in 1970. Chigwell, like many other prairie communities is now a ghost town.

CHILMARK [24-7-W4]
~ former post office near Hanna.

It was probably named after the English village of Chilmark in Wiltshire. It was opened in 1915 and closed in 1928.

CHIN [9-19-W4]
~ hamlet southwest of Taber.

The name is derived from the Blackfoot *mistoame*, meaning "beard". A nearby hill seen from a distance has a shape like a beard.

CHINIKI
~ former station near Brooks.

It was named after the Stony Chief who signed Treaty Number Seven of September, 1877 at the Blackfoot Crossing.

CHINOOK [29-7-W4]
~ former village southeast of Hanna.

The name Chinook has been given to a warm, dry wind that blows into Alberta from the Pacific Ocean at irregular intervals during the winter months. It is most striking when it breaks a cold wave that has been accompanied by snow. A clear "Chinook Arch" is formed on the western horizon and temperatures may rise as much as 60 degrees F. in a relatively short time. When the Chinook blows in Southern Alberta winter turns to spring — for a few hours or days until the wind dies. There is a lovely Indian legend or myth of a princess being lost in the mountains, who is saved by this warm wind from the west. Sociologists find that extreme variations of temperature and suicidal rates correlate.

CHINOOK VALLEY [86-24-W5]
~ former post office northwest of Peace River.

It opened in 1931 and later was closed. (See: **CHINOOK**)

CHIP LAKE [53-10-W5]
~ former station west of Edmonton.

"Chip" is a shortened form of "buffalo chip". Palliser's Map of 1865 so referred to it. "Buffalo chips" were the traders' name for the primary source of fuel in regions that did not have a plentiful supply of wood. The post office was closed in 1970.
(See: **LEAMAN**)

CHIPEWYAN [112-7-W4]
(See: **FORT CHIPEWYAN**)

CHIPEWYAN LAKE [91-22-W4]
~ an abandoned fur trading post south of Chipewyan Lake in northern Alberta.

It was named after a Déné tribe. It is a Cree name and means "pointed skins", or "tassels" which the tribe was wont to wear. (See: **FORT CHIPEWYAN**)

CHIPMAN   [54-18-W4]
~ village east of Edmonton.

It was named in 1905 after Clarence Campbell Chipman, private secretary to Sir Charles Tupper, who was federal Minister of Railways and Canals in the Conservative administration of 1882. Chipman became Chief Commissioner of the Hudson's Bay Company.

CHISHOLM   [28-2-W5]
~ former station south of Lesser Slave Lake.

It was named after Thomas Chisholm, a former Klondike gold seeker and pioneer, who later became a railway contractor in 1914.

CHISHOLM MILLS   [28-2-W5]
~ former post office south of Lesser Slave Lake.

It was named for the sawmill. It opened in 1923.

CHOKIO   [7-28-W4]
~ former station north of Pincher Creek.

"Chokio", is said to be a corruption of *chok-ieo*, the way Indians pronounced "choke-cherries", which they sold to the construction workers on the Crowsnest Pass railway, built in 1904.

CLAIRMONT   [72-6-W6]
~ former village north of Grande Prairie.

It was named after Claremont, Ontario, which was the birthplace of Walter McFarlane, who surveyed the town-site in 1916. The spelling is erroneous.

CLANDONALD   [53-5-W4]
~ former village northeast of Vermilion.

It was named in 1927 after the prominent Scottish clan who were strong in the Hebrides. Previously the community was called **WELLSDALE**.

The population in 1972 was 185.

CLARESHOLM   [12-27-W4]
~ *former village northeast of Vermilion.*

It was named after the home ("holm") of Superintendent Niblock, where he lived in Medicine Hat. His wife's Christian name was Clare. The Canadian Pacific Railway reached this point in 1893.

The population in 1972 was 3,350. It had increased to 3,700 by 2006.

CLARINDA   [1-13-W4]
~ *former post office near Foremost.*

It was named after Mrs. Clarinda Clark, mother of Miss F. Clark, the first postmistress in 1911.

CLARK MANOR   [46-8-W4]
~ *former post office near Wainwright.*

It was named after J. G. Clark, the first postmaster in 1911.

CLARKSON VALLEY   [71-25-W5]
~ *former post office west of Sturgeon Lake.*

It was in operation by 1958.

CLAYSMORE   [50-7-W4]
~ *hamlet east of Mannville.*

Possibly named after the English village of Claysmore, Middlesex, in 1905.

CLEAR HILLS   [87-25-W5]
~ *former post office near Peace River.*

The name is derived from the nearby Clear Hills. It opened in 1921.

CLEAR PRAIRIE   [87-10-W6]
~ *former post office south of Clear Hills.*

The name is descriptive of the open terrain.

CLEARVIEW [72-11-W6]
~ *former post office near Grande Prairie.*

The name was descriptive. It was opened in 1920 but has since been closed.

CLEVERHILL [15-23-W4]
(See: **CHAMPION**)

CLIVALE [26-16-W4]
~ *former post office near Hanna.*

It was said to be named after a place in England. It was opened in 1916 and closed in 1932.

CLIVE [40-24-W4]
~ *village east of Red Deer.*

It was named in 1909 after Robert Clive (1725-1774), who established British rule in the sub-continent of India. Prior to 1909 the community was called **VALLEY CITY**.

CLOVER BAR [53-23-W4]
~ *former post office east of Edmonton.*

It was named for Thomas H. Clover (1809-1897), an American gold-seeker. As a young man, Clover went to California as a "forty-niner". In the late 1850's he was panning for placer gold on the Fraser River in what is now British Columbia. He then crossed the Rockies to pan for gold in the North Saskatchewan River near **EDMONTON** in the early 1860's before he returned to the States. The post office was moved to Edmonton in 1970. It is also the name of a provincial constituency.

CLUNY [22-21-W4]
~ *village south of Gleichen.*

It was named in 1884 after the parish of Cluny in Aberdeenshire.

CLYDE   **[59-25-W4]**
~ *village north of Edmonton.*

It was named after George Clyde, the first postmaster in 1906. He was a Scot.

CLYMONT   **[51-26-W4]**
~ *former post office near Edmonton.*

It was named after E. B. McClymont, the first postmaster. It was opened in 1914 but has since been closed.

COAL BRANCH

The mines in this remote region of the Rockies, south of Edson, once employed close to 10,000 miners. Now only ghost communities, these once thriving mining settlements included: **CADOMIN, COAL VALLEY, COALSPUR, FOOTHILLS, LEYLAND, LOVETTVILLE, LUSCAR, MERCOAL, MOUNTAIN PARK, RECO, SHAW** and **STERCO.**

COAL VALLEY   **[47-20-W5]**
~ *former station in the Coal Branch district.*

The name is descriptive. It was opened in 1923, but is now a ghost town. (See: **COAL BRANCH**)

COALBANKS, Red Deer River   **[38-23-W4]**
It was named after a coal mine in operation for many years. Later the name was changed in 1912. (See: **ARDLEY**)

COALBANKS   **[10-26-W4]**
~ *former mining settlement on the bank of the Oldman River.*

It was named by Nicholas Sheran, a former whiskey trader and veteran of the American Civil War. The coal mine was located in the coulee bottom of the Oldman River. Sheran sent the empty freight wagons that came to **FORT WHOOP-UP** back the 200 miles to Fort Benton, Montana Territory, loaded with coal in the early 1870's.
(See: **LETHBRIDGE;**)

COALDALE   [9-20-W4]
~ town east of Lethbridge.

It was named after the residence which E. T. Galt, General Manager of the Alberta Railway and Irrigation Company first had in the coulee near **COALBANKS (LETHBRIDGE)**. However, he moved when he became unhappy about some of his neighbors. Some of the other houses in the coulee were part of the red light district.

The population in 1972 was 2,739. It increased to 6,943 by 2009.

COALHURST   [9-22-W4]
~ town west of Lethbridge.

Coal was still being mined here until the mid-1930's. **COLLIERY** was the former name of the railway station, now the official site of The University of Lethbridge.

COALHURST was also the official name of the present city of **LETHBRIDGE** prior to 1885. In 1872 Nicholas Sheran opened a coal mine on the east bank of the Oldman River. The local inhabitants called the settlement that began to develop on the flat prairie nearby **COALBANKS**, even though the officials in far-away Ottawa insisted on referring to it as COALHURST. In 1885, both names were dropped in favor of LETHBRIDGE (q.v.)

The population in 2009 was 1,810.

COALSPUR   [48-21-W5]
~ ghost town in the Coal Branch district.

At one time there were a dozen coal mining communities in the **COAL BRANCH** district with a combined population of about 15,000. Now they are all ghost towns.

COCHRANE   [26-4-W5]
~ village west of Calgary.

It was named in 1884 after Senator M. H. Cochrane (1823-1903), president of the British American Ranch Company of the Foothills.

It increased to 6,800 by 1998.

COCHRANE RANCH
~ west of Calgary.

It was the first large ranch to be established by Senator Cochrane in Alberta. It received a federal charter in May 1881, giving it rights to 109,000 acres of grassland. It was sold to the Mormon Church in 1906.

CODESA   [78-1-W6]
~ former post office near Spirit River.

It was named after three railway officials E. Collins, J. Desa, and W. Saunders. It was in operation by 1958. It was formerly called RAHAB.

CODNER   [39-6-W5]
~ former station north of Rocky Mountain House.

It was opened in 1914 and has since been closed.

COGHILL   [39-23-W4]
~ former station south of Alix.

It was opened in 1914.

COLD LAKE   [63-2-W4]
~ town northeast of St. Paul.

It was named after a nearby cold lake. (The name is descriptive as personal experience can verify!) This lake is referred to as COLDWATER LAKE on Turnor's Map of 1790.

The population in 1972 was 1,242. It increased to 13,924 by 2009. In the 1990's, there were discussions that COLD LAKE and **GRAND CENTER** be joined to form one large town of more than 8,000 residents.

(See: **BEAVER CROSSING**)

COLD LAKE HOUSE
~ abandoned fur trading post in northeastern Alberta.

Peter Fidler's journal for September 18, 1799, states: "Put up at 4 p.m. at Cold Lake House . . . deserted a few years since . . . now all in ruins within—all the outer walls still standing." it had been established in 1781.

COLERIDGE   [12-5-W4]
(See: DUNMORE)

COLEMAN   [8-4-W5]
~ former town northwest of Blairmore.

According to the Geographic Board of Canada, it was named in 1904 by A. C. Flumerfelt, president of the International Coal and Coke Company, after his youngest daughter. (See: CROWSNEST)

COLINTON   [65-22-W4]
~ hamlet east of Athabasca.

t was named in 1912 after Colinton near Edinburgh, Scotland, the former home of J. M. Milne, who had an interest in the town-site. Previously it was called KINNOULL.

COLLEGE HEIGHTS   [40-26-W4]
~ post office north of Lacombe.

It was named for the Seventh Day Adventist College near LACOMB.

COLLES   [1-24-W4]
(See: KIMBALL)

COLLICUTT   [28-1-W5]
~ junction south of Crossfield.

It was named after Dr. Frank Collicutt, a pioneer rancher of the district.

COLLIERY   [9-22-W5]
~ former station west of Lethbridge.

It was close to the coal pits. The post office was called COALHURST.

COLUMBINE   [61-8-W4]
~ former post office near St. Paul.

It was named in 1915 after the flower. It has since been closed.

COMMERCE   [10-22-W4]
~ hamlet north of Lethbridge.

This descriptive name was given in 1913.

COMPEER   [33-1-W4]
~ hamlet east of Grassy Lake.

The name was changed to this in 1915 on the request of local residents. Previously it was called SLEEPY HOLLOW.

COMREY   [2-6-W4]
~ former post office southeast of Pakowki Lake.

It is formed from the initial letters of the names of six early settlers in the district—Columbus Larson, Ole Roen, Mons Roen, R. Rolfson, J. J. Evenson, and E. Yager.

CONDOR   [39-4-W5]
~ former village southeast of Leslieville.

It was named in 1914 after the British gun boat Condor which took part in the bombardment of Alexandria, Egypt, in July 1882.

CONJURING CREEK   [49-27-W4]
~ former post office near Edmonton.

It was named in 1900 after the nearby stream, a tributary of the North Saskatchewan, which flows from Wizard Lake. The Cree name for this stream means literally "to vomit".

CONKLIN   [76-7-W5]
~ former station near Lac La Biche.

It was named after John Conklin, a railway official. A post office opened in 1924.

CONNELLY   [49-6-W4]
~ former post office near Wainwright.

It was named after the first postmaster, W. A. Connolly in 1913. The spelling was an official error.

CONNEMARA   [16-28-W4]
~ former station near Claresholm.

It was named after county Connemara, Ireland.

CONNOR CREEK   [59-8-W5]
~ former post office southeast of Whitecourt.

It was named after James Connor, a pioneer settler in 1913.

CONRAD   [6-15-W4]
~ former station south of Taber.

It was named in 1914 probably after Joseph Conrad, the Polish-born British novelist who wrote *Lord Jim* and *The Heart of Darkness*.

CONRICH   [25-28-W4]
~ former post office northeast of Calgary.

The name is derived from the surnames of two real estate promoters named <u>Con</u>nacher and <u>Rich</u>ardson in 1925. It closed in 1960.

CONSORT   [35-6-W4]
~ village southwest of Provost.

It received its present name in 1911 when King George V came to the throne. Previously the post office was called **SANDERVILLE**.
(See: **CORONATION, LOYALIST, THRONE** and **VETERAN**)

CONTENT   [38-22-W4]
~ former post office near Red Deer.

It was named after A. A. Content, the first postmaster in 1904. It closed in 1913.

CONTROL   [24-14-W4]
~ former station south of Coleman Lake.

It may have got its name from being a control point on the railway.

COOKING LAKE   **[51-22-W4]**
~ summer village southeast of Edmonton.

In the days of the Red River carts, it was on one of the major trails across the western prairies. Wagon trains used to stop here to cook a last meal before pushing on to Edmonton. It was also a favorite Indian camping ground in the old days.

COOKING LAKE   **[51-21-W4]**
~ former station east of Edmonton.

It is now a summer village.

COOLIDGE   **[65-24-W4]**
~ former post office southwest of Athabasca.

It was named after Calvin Coolidge (1872-1933), the President of the United States from 1923 to 1929.

COOPERVILLE   **[31-14-W4]**
(See: HANNA)

COPEVILLE   **[30-14-W4]**
~ former post office near Hanna.

It was named after G. R. Cope, the first postmaster. It has since been closed.

COPPICE HILL   **[53-21-W4]**
~ former post office near Edmonton.

It was named in 1906 because the post office building was situated on hilly ground covered with poplar brush. It has since been closed.

CORBETT CREEK   **[61-8-W5]**
~ former post office north of Whitecourt.

It was named after W. E. Corbett, the first postmaster.

CORK [58-11-W4]
~ former post office south of Therien.

It was named after the southern Irish city of Cork in 1910. The name is derived from an Irish word meaning "a swamp".

CORNUCOPIA [36-16-W4]
~ former post office near Stettler.

It was named because of the fertile soil in the district in 1910. The name means in Latin "horn of plenty". It has since been closed.

CORONADO [56-23-W4]
~ former post office northeast of Edmonton.

It was named after Coronado in the State of California in 1921.

CORONATION [36-11-W4]
~ town northeast of Calgary.

It was so named in Coronation Year of 1911-the year George V came to the throne on the death of his father, Edward VII. Other communities in the vicinity are **CONSORT, LOYALIST, THRONE** and **VETERAN**.

The population in 2006 was 1,015.

COSMO [57-6-W5]
~ former post office near Whitecourt.

The Greek word *cosmo* means "the universe". It was opened in 1911 but has since been closed.

COSSACK [60-17-W4]
~ post office north of Smoky Lake.

Originally the name *Cossack* referred to restless souls and escaped serfs who formed fortified villages on the Ukrainian steppes in the fifteenth century. There were a large number of Ukrainian homesteaders in the district.

COSWAY   [29-25-W4]
~ station southwest of Three Hills.

The origin is unknown.

COUNTESS   [21-17-W4]
~ hamlet east of Bassano.

It was named after the Countess of Bassano in 1914.

COUSINS   [13-6-W4]
~ former station north of Medicine Hat.

It was named after William Cousins, a one-time prominent
MEDICINE HAT businessman.

COUTTS   [1-15-W4]
~ custom post south of Lethbridge.

It was named after Sir William Lehman Ashmead Bartlett
Burdett-Coutts, the husband of Baroness Angela Burdett-Coutts of
Highgate and Brookfield Middlesex (see **BURDETT**). Sir William
was born in the United States in 1851 and came to England as a
student. He married the wealthy baroness, 37 years his senior, in
1881 and assumed her name. He was elected Member of
Parliament for Westminster in 1885 and was one of the directors of
the Alberta Railway and Irrigation Company with headquarters at
COALBANKS, which later became **LETHBRIDGE**. The custom
station was established in 1889.

COWLEY   [7-1-W5]
~ village northwest of Pincher Creek.

It was named by a rancher, F. W. Godsal, who, while
watching his cattle (cows) wandering across the prairie (lex) was
reminded of Thomas Gray's "Elegy Written in a Country
Churchyard", and especially of the opening lines:
The curfew tolls the knell of parting day,
The lowing herd winds slowly o'er the lea,

CRADDOCK   **[6-19-W4]**
~ former station east of Raymond.

It was named after Sir Christopher Craddock (1862-1914), who was an Admiral in the Royal Navy. He was killed when his flag-ship, the cruiser Good Hope, sank with all on board during the battle of Coronel off the South American coast on November 1, 1914.

CRAIGDHU   **[27-26-W4]**
~ former station northeast of Calgary.

The Gaelic word *craigdhu* means "black rock". It was opened in 1912.

CRAIGEND   **[65-13-W4]**
~ former post office south of Lac La Biche.

This was originally the name of the school district. It was opened in 1925.

CRAIGMILLAR   **[38-7-W4]**
~ former post office near Coronation.

It was named in 1913 after Craigmillar near Edinburgh, Scotland, which was the former home of the first postmaster, William Penman. The Gaelic word *craigmillar* means "rock of the bare height.

CRAIGOWER   **[4-4-W4]**
~ former station east of Pakowki Lake.

It was opened in 1914.

CRAMMOND   **[35-5-W5]**
~ former post office southeast of Caroline.

The origin of this name is not known it opened in 1937 and closed in 1948.

CRANFORD   [9-18-W4]
~ hamlet south of Taber.

It was possibly named after Cransford in Suffolk, England. The name means ford of the "cranes" or "herons".

CREMONA   [30-4-W5]
~ former village south of Didsbury.

The post office opened in 1906. It is possibly named after Cremona in the north of Italy, famous for its violins.
The population in 1972 was 192.

CRESSDAY   [3-2-W4]
~ former station east of Pakowki Lake.

It was named in 1922 after two wealthy ranchers, W. Cresswell and Tony Day, who had large spreads in the vicinity.

CRITCHLEY   [24-1-W5]
(See: BOWNESS)

CRIPPSDALE   [59-21-W4]
~ former post office near Thorhild.

It was named after M. J. Cripps, the first postmaster. It was opened in 1912 and closed in 1942.

CROOKED CREEK   [71-26-W5]
~ former post office near Fort McMurray.

The name is descriptive of a nearby stream.

CROSSFIELD   [28-1-W5]
~ town north of Calgary.

It was named after a railway engineer who worked for the Calgary and Edmonton Railway Company in the early days.
The population in 1972 was 618. It increased to 2,648 by 2006.

CROWELL [79-20-W5]
~ railway point near McLennan.

It was named after Frederick Crowell, a railway official in 1980.

CROWFOOT [21-20-W4]
~ hamlet east of Calgary.

It was named in honor of Crowfoot, head chief of the Blackfoot Nation, at their signing of the Treaty Number Seven at Blackfoot Crossing on the Bow River in 1877.

When Sitting Bull crossed the border into Canada after annihilating General Custer's force on the Little Big Horn, Crowfoot refused to join him in further battles. This peace-loving chief, who had survived nineteen battles himself, persuaded the Blackfoot Confederacy not to join Louis Riel in his ill-fated uprising in 1885.

CROWSNEST PASS (Municipality of)[7-4-W5]
~ a unique town.

The name is a translation of the Cree name of a nearby mountain "where nests the crow". The first mention of Crowsnest is in Captain Blakiston's report on the Palliser expedition in 1858. The altitude is 4,449 feet.

The population in 2009 was 5,749. (See: **BELLEVUE; BLAIRMORE; FRANK; HILLCREST; LUNDBRECK; PASSBURG; COLEMAN**)

CULP [78-23-W5]
~ former station northwest of Falher.

It was named after J. H. Culp, a railway official in 1915. It has since been closed.

CUMMINGS [48-7-W4]
~ hamlet near Vermilion.

It was named after John T. Cummings, the first postmaster, in 1908.

CURLEW   **[33-25-W4]**
~ former post office near Three Hills.

Possibly named because of the number of curlews found in the district. It was opened in 1906 but has since been closed.

CYGNET   **[38-28-W4]**
~ former station near Sylvan Lake.

The name of a railway station, established in 1912 near the then "Swan Lake". The young of swans are called "cygnets". Later Swan Lake's name was changed to **SYLVAN LAKE**.

CYNTHIA   **[49-10-W5]**
~ hamlet north of Drayton Valley.

It was named after the daughter of the hotel proprietor. It ranked as an Alberta town in 1958.

CZAR   **[40-6-W4]**
~ village south of Wainwright.

The Russian *Czar* means "Caesar" or "Emperor", originally so named in honor of Julius Caesar. The German form of the word, pronounced with a hard 'k', is Kaiser. This was a Ukrainian settlement.

D

(The) D - L Ranch
~ pioneer ranch near Calgary.

The D-L was the second brand registered in the District of Alberta, NWT in 1880. Cecil Denny, and John Drough Lander, after serving with the North West Mounted Police, started a pioneer ranch.

DAKIN   [67-17-W4]
~ former hamlet.

It was named after Harry Hansford Dakin, (1870-1956), Member of the Legislative Assembly from 1930 to 1935. Dakin, a former sea captain, was seriously injured in the 1917 Halifax explosion of French ammunition ship. He had been at sea for years. Later, he and 16 of his grown up children homesteaded in an isolated district of Northern Alberta. It had a post office from 1925 to 1948.

DALEHURST   [52-23-W5]
~ former station north of Drinnan.

It was named in 1919. The word "hurst" means "wooded hill", or "a grove". There is therefore a contradiction in this name. Previously the post office has been called **HINTON**.

DALMEAD   [22-27-W4]
~ hamlet south of Langdon.

It was so named in 1914: "dale" from its situation in a dale or valley, and "mead" after Dr. Ellwood Mead, an irrigation specialist.

DALMUIR   **[58-20-W4]**
~ former post office north of Lamont.

It was named in 1913 after the Scottish village, Dalmur, near Glasgow. It closed in 1956.

DALROY   **[25-27-W4]**
~ former village north of Calgary.

It was named in 1907 by the Canadian Pacific Railway after G. M. McElroy, an early settler in the district, with the prefix "dal", meaning "dale" or "valley.

DALUM   **[27-19-W4]**
~ hamlet near Drumheller.

It was named in 1915 on the suggestion of Jen Hvaar, the first settler in the area, after the district of Dalum in Denmark.

DANUBE   **[62-21-W4]**
~ former post office near Athabasca.

It was named after the large southeastern river that flows into the Black Sea. It formed part of the northern frontier of the Classical Roman Empire. It was opened in 1930 and closed in 1942.

DAPP   **[62-27-W4]**
~ hamlet north of Westlock.

It was named in 1917 for David A. Pennicuick, an account-ant of the Edmonton, Dunvegan and British Columbia Railway. Prior to then the post office was called **EUNICE**.

DARLING   **[61-19-W4]**
~ former post office.

Possibly named after the Darling River and mountain range in Australia. It opened in 1927 and closed in 1952.

DARWELL   **[54-5-W5]**
~ former village south of Lac Ste. Anne.

The railway reached here in 1915.

DAUNTLESS   [11-6-W4]
~ former station near Medicine Hat.

It was given its name by the Canadian Cement Company in 1913.

DAYSLAND   [45-16-W4]
~ former town south of Camrose.

It was named after Egerton W. Day, a prominent **EDMONTON** businessman and large land owner in the district when the railway reached here in 1905.

The population was 630 in 1972 and increased to 674 in 1989. The population increased to 818 in 2006.

DE WINTON   [21-1-W5]
~ pioneer ranch south of Calgary.

The proprietor was General Sir Francis De Winton (1835-1901). Born at Pittsford, Northhamptonshire, England, he was a career officer in the British army. He saw active service in the Crimean War. Later, he became military secretary to the Marquis of Lorne, the Governor General of Canada. Subsequently, he became the administrator general of the Congo State and the Commissioner of Swaziland. While in Canada, he organized the De Winton Ranch, which has also been know as the Brecon Ranch. He is buried at Glasbury, near Brecon, South Wales.

DEADWOOD   [89-22-W5]
~ post office north of Peace River.

It was opened in 1930. A large quantity of dead wood is carried down the Peace River during the spring run-off. It also could have been named after Deadwood, South Dakota.

DEAVER   [60-10-W4]
~ former post office near St. Paul.

It was named after G. C. Deaver, the first postmaster in 1916. The name was changed to **BOSCOMBE** in 1931.

DEBOLT   [71-1-W6]
~ *former village near Grande Prairie.*

It was named after Henry E. DeBolt, (1888-1969), a pioneer American homesteader from the State of Washington who arrived in 1919. He served as the Spirit River Member of the Legislature from 1940 to 1952. He also was the first postmaster in 1923.

DECOIGNE   [45-3-W6]
~ *former station west of Jasper.*

It was named after François Decoigne, the fair-headed fur trader stationed at Jasper House when Gabriel Franchere traveled through in the early nineteenth century. The Indians called Decoigne "Yellowhead" - the name given to the pass through the mountains.
(See: **JASPER; YELLOWHEAD**)

DECRENE   [72-2-W5]
~ *former station south of Lesser Slave Lake.*

It was named after a contractor who constructed a portion of the railway to the Peace River Country in 1914.

DEER HILL   [84-3-W6]
~ *former post office near Fairview.*

The name is descriptive. It was opened in 1936.

DEER MOUND   [52-22-W4]
~ *former community south of Edmonton.*

The black tailed deer, *odocoileus hemionus*, were once numbered in the thousands on the western prairies.

DEEP CREEK   [69-21-W4]
~ *former post office north of Athabasca.*

The name is derived from a nearby stream, which is of unusual depth. It opened in 1931.

DELACOUR [25-28-W4]
~ *former village north of Calgary.*

The railway reached here in 1913. The name is French for "of the heart".

DEL BONITA [1-21-W4]
~ *former custom post southeast of Cardston.*

According to the Geographic Board, it is the Spanish word meaning "of the pretty". This part of southern Alberta was once claimed by Spain as part of its American possession as the Milk River drains into the Gulf of Mexico via the Mississippi. The region was given to France as part of the Mississippi purchase before being claimed by Britain. According to local residents, it may have another origin: the "del" is for "dell" and "Bonita" for Saint Bonita, a tenth-century French saint, who was a goose-girl. Her feast day is October 16th. The post office was opened in 1914.

DELBURNE [37-23-W4]
~ *village south of Red Deer.*

Prior to 1911 the post office was called **GAETZ VALLEY** after Rev. Leonard Gaetz, the father of the city of **RED DEER**. Born at Musquodoboit Harbour, Nova Scotia, in 1841, he came west in 1883. He was one of the first homesteaders in the Red Deer district. In 1888, John A. Macdonald offered Gaetz a seat in the Senate, which he refused. James Lougheed, grandfather of Premier Peter Lougheed, was then appointed. Settlers decided on the name Delburne.

DELIA [31-17-W4]
~ *village north of Drumheller.*

Name given in ancient Greek mythology to Artemis, from the island of Delos, her birthplace. In Virgil's *Eclogues*, Delia is a shepherdess. The post office was opened in 1909.

The population in 1972 was 286.

DELNORTE [51-11-W4]
(See: **INNISFREE**)

DELPH   [58-18-W4]
~ former post office south of Smoky Lake.

It was named in 1913 after Delf, a city in the west Netherlands, famous in the seventeenth century for the manufacture of glazed earthenware.

DEMAY   [48-19-W4]
~ former station north of Camrose.

It was named after nearby Demay Lake which in turn was named in 1893 after a pioneer settler.

DEMMITT   [20-11-W4]
~ former station north of Brooks.

It was named after a pioneer farmer in 1914.

DEMMITT   [74-13-W6]
~ former post office near Grande Prairie.

It was named after Chelsea Demmitt, a Peace River Country pioneer, who arrived in 1919. It opened in 1929.

DENHART   [20-11-W4]
~ former station north of Brooks.

It was named after a pioneer farmer in 1914.

DENNIS   [14-8-W4]
~ former station north of Medicine Hat.

It was named in honor of John Stoughton Dennis (1820-1885), Canadian surveyor and civil servant in 1910. In 1869 he was sent by the federal government to organize a system of surveys in the North West. His handling of the difficulties confronting him was partly responsible for the Red River Rebellion. Dennis was later named Deputy Minister of the Interior.

DENISVILLE   [60-9-W4]
(See: **ST. VINCENT**)

DENWOOD   [44-6-W4]
(See: **WAINWRIGHT**)

DERWENT [54-7-W4]
~ village north of Elk Point.

It was named after the Derwent River in Cumberland, England.

The population in 1972 was 225.

DESJARLAIS [57-14-W4]
~ former post office northeast of Whitford Lake.

It was named after David Desjarlais, the first postmaster, in 1903. It closed in 1958.

DESMARAIS [80-25-W4]
~ former post office north of Lesser Slave Lake.

It was named after Rev. Alphonse Desmarais, OMI, a Catholic missionary. He was among the first to visit **WABASCA** settlement in 1891. It opened in 1927 and combined to form **WABASCA-DESMARAIS** in 1982.

(See: **WABASCA**)

DEVENISH [75-8-W4]
~ former station north of Lac La Biche.

It was named after Gwen Devenish, a friend of a railway engineer. Later she moved to Baltimore.

DEVILLE [51-20-W4]
~ former post office northwest of Tofield.

It was named after Dr. E. G. Deville (1849-1924), Director General of Surveys for the federal Department of the Interior. He was the Surveyor General from 1885 until the time of his death.

DEVON [50-26-W4]
~ town southwest of Edmonton.

This town was started as a company town after the discovery of the Leduc oil field in 1947. It is named after the geological formation in which the oil had been found.

The population was 1,446 in 1972 and increased to 6,534 by 2009.

DEVONA   [48-1-W6]
~ former station north of Jasper Lake.

The railway reached here in 1915.

DEWBERRY   [53-4-W4]
~ village north of Vermilion.

It was named in 1907 after the berry that is found in large quantities in the late summer in the district.

DEWDNEY   [20-29-W4]
(See: OKOTOKS)

DIAMOND CITY   [10-21-W4]
~ hamlet north of Lethbridge.

It was named from the fact that a coal mine was in operation in the area called "Black Diamond Mine". When a post office was opened, it was discovered the name had already been used and the alternative DIAMOND CITY was selected.

DIANA   [46-23-W4]
(See: GWYNNE)

DICKENSON STOPPING HOUSE
(See: CALGARY-EDMONTON   TRAIL   STAGING POSTS)

DICKSON   [36-3-W5]
~ former post office south of Sylvan Lake.

It was named after Dickson Creek which in turn was called after Benedickson, a pioneer homesteader who had originally come from Norway in 1906.

DIDSBURY   [31-1-W5]
~ town north of Calgary.

It was named in 1892 after the English town of Didsbury near Manchester.

The population was 1,878 in 1972 and increased to 4,599 by 2008.

DIMSDALE [71-7-W6]
~ former station west of Grande Prairie.

It was named after Henry G. Dimsdale, a railway official. The station opened in 1924 and the post office in 1927.

DINA [45-1-W4]
~ former post office north of Wainwright.

It was named after Dina Sand, the only girl living in the district when the post office was opened in 1908. It was intended to be pronounced Dina as in Norwegian. It closed in 1937.

DINANT [48-20-W4]
~ former post office north of Camrose.

It was named by François Adam, a pioneer settler, after his home in Belgium, in 1911. Previously the post office was called **PRETTY HILL**.

DINOSAUR [21-11-W4]
~ railway point near Medicine Hat.

It is located near Dinosaur Provincial Park and Museum. (See: **STEVEVILLE**)

DINTON [26-26-W4]
~ former post office south of Calgary.

It was named after one of the several Dintons found in England. When the post office was closed in 1912, the name also was given to a municipal district.

DINWOODIE [53-13-W4]
~ former post office near Innisfree.

It was named after the first postmaster in 1903. It was changed on the request of French settlers to **LAVOY** in 1913. Joseph Lavoy was the first homesteader in the district.

DIRELTON   [61-4-W4]
~ former post office east of Bonnyville.

It was named after the Scottish town of Direlton near Edinburgh. It was open from 1933 to 1960.

DISS   [48-20-W5]
~ ghost town in the Coal Branch

It was named possibly after the English town of Diss in Norfolk, in 1913. It also could be named after Dis, the Latin god of the underworld.

DIXONVILLE   [87-24-W5]
~ former post office north of Peace River.

It was named after Roy Dixon, a general merchant and the first postmaster. It was open from 1920 to 1930.

DOBSON   [29-8-W4]
~ former station southeast of Hanna.

The railway reached here in 1914.

DODDS   [49-18-W4]
~ former village south of Beaverhill Lake.

It was named after John Dodds, a pioneer settler. The post office was opened in 1911. It finally closed in 1970.

DOGPOUND   [29-3-W5]
~ former post office north of Madden.

It was named after a nearby creek, which in turn, is a translation of the Cree "wolf caught in buffalo pound". Palliser called it "Edge Creek" in his 1865 map. It opened in 1900 and has since been closed.

DONALDA   [42-18-W4]
~ village north of Stettler.

It was named possibly after Sir Donald Mann (See: **Mannville**), vice-president of the Canadian Northern Railway, in 1911. Prior to 1911, the post office was called **EIDSWOLD**.

The population was 247 in 1972 and decreased to 224 in 2006.

DONATVILLE [66-19-W4]
~ former post office east of Athabasca.

It was named after Donat Gingras, an early French home-steader in the district, in 1914.

DONGRAY [59-18-W4]
~ former post office near Redwater.

It was named after John H. Gray, the first postmaster, in 1920. It closed in 1925.

DONNELLY [78-21-W5]
~ former village west of Kimiwan.

It was named after an official of the Edmonton, Dunvegan and British Columbia Railway, in 1915. It is located 4 miles from **FALHER**.

DORAN [2-14-W4]
(See: **ALLERSTON**)

DORENLEE [43-21-W4]
~ hamlet north of Buffalo Lake.

It was named after W. O. Dore, the first postmaster, and his partner Mr. Lee in 1903. It closed in 1964.

DOROTHY [27-17-W4]
~ former post office, south of Drumheller.

It was named after Dorothy Wilson, the first and only child born in the district when the post office was opened in 1908. This Greek feminine name means "Gift from God".

DOVERCOURT [38-6-W5]
~ former post office southeast of Rocky Mountain House.

It was named after Dovercourt, Essex, England, the former home of H. Lee, the first postmaster, in 1912. It closed in 1968.

DOWLING   [32-15-W4]
~ former village near Hanna.

It was named by J. B. Tyrrell after Dr. D. B. Dowling, (1858-1925), a geological surveyor, in 1886.

DRADER   [46-3-W5]
~ former station near Lacombe.

It was named after A. E. Drader, proprietor of a large sawmill and lumberyard, in 1926.

DRAPER   [88-8-W4]
~ former station near Fort McMurray.

It was named after Thomas Draper, president of the McMurray Asphalt and Oil Company, in 1925.

DRAYTON VALLEY   [49-7-W5]
~ town southwest of Edmonton.

It was named after Drayton, Hampshire, England, the home village of W.J. Drake, the first postmaster's wife, in 1920. Previously the community was called POWER HOUSE.

The population in 1972 was 3,714. It increased to 6,893 by 2006.

DREAU   [78-22-W5]
~ station northwest of Falher.

It was named after Fr. Dreau, Oblate missionary.

DRIEDMEAT   [45-19-W4]
~ railway point near Camrose.

In ancient times, meat was hung up to dry at the site on the side of a hill. Possibly a buffalo pound was nearby. It appears on maps of Harmon in 1820.

DRIFTPILE   [73-12-W5]
~ former station south of Lesser Slave Lake.

It was named after the Cree word for the nearby river, at the mouth of which driftwood piles up.

DRINNAN [51-24-W5]
~ hamlet northeast of Entrance, Jasper National Park.

It used to rank as a village.

DRUMHELLER [28-19-W4]
~ city, former coal mining community.

It was named after Samuel Drumheller, the proprietor of several large coal mines in the district. He was born in Walla Walla, State of Washington, in 1864, and came north to Canada with a herd of cattle. Drumheller bought the town site in 1910 from Thomas P, Greentree, the original homesteader. His name was given the to post office, opened in 1911. Rail service dates from 1912. DRUMHELLER was incorporated as a village in 1913, as a town in 1916, as a city in 1930. "A veritable twentieth century Midas, everything that he undertakes brings in a rich return, and as controller of vast financial interests in the province Drumheller exercises a tremendous influence on its industrial life", (Blue).

The population in 1972 was 5,240. It increased to 7,932 by 2006.

DRYWOOD [4-29-W4]
~ station southeast of Pincher Creek.

The name is descriptive.

DUAGH [55-23-W4]
~ former post office near Edmonton.

It was named after the village of Duagh County Kerry, Ireland, in 1900 on the suggestion of John Hall, an Irishman. It closed in 1931. Translated from the Irish it means "black food".

DUCHESS [20-14-W4]
~ former village north of Brooks.

It was named after Lady Millicent Fanny, wife of the 4th Duke of Sutherland (1851-1913). She was the eldest daughter of the Earl of Rosslyn. The Duke acquired extensive land near **BROOKS** (Geographic Board of Canada: Alberta 1928).

The population in 1972 was 234. (See: **MILLICENT; ROSEMARY**)

DUET   [88-7-W4]
~ former station north of St. Paul.

The origin of this name is unknown. Duet means two.

DUFFIELD   [52-3-W5]
~ hamlet near Stony Plain.

It was named after George Duffield Hall, an American from Boston, an early pioneer, in 1911.
The population in 1972 was 57.

DUHAMEL   [45-21-W4]
~ hamlet near Camrose.

It was named after the Most Rev. Joseph Thomas Duhamel (1841-1909), Archbishop of Ottawa, in 1893. (See: **BATTLE RIVER CROSSING**)

DUNBAR   [53-23-W4]
~ railway point near Sherwood Park.

It was named after George E. Dunbar, a CNR official in 1882.

DUNBOW RANCH   [21-28-W4]
~ early ranch near High River.

The lease for 40,000 acres was granted in 1882 and its first manager was Alexander Begg (born 1840), an historian. Alexander Begg organized the ranch and was the resident manager from 1882 to 1889. He was an unsuccessful candidate for the High River constituency in the NWT Legislative Assembly in 1898. He was also the author of *History of the Northwest*.

DUNMORE   [12-5-W4]
~ former village southeast of Medicine Hat.

It was named after the 7th Earl Dunmore (1841 -1907), who served as Lord-in-waiting for Queen Victoria from 1874 to 1880. He was a large share-holder in the Canadian Agricultural Coal and Colonization Company. He visited Alberta in 1883. At one time it was called COLERIDGE.
The population in 1972 was 60.

DUNN [43-3-W4]
~ former village southeast of Wainwright.

It was named in 1914 after a railway official. Previously it was called **RIBSTONE**.

DUNPHY [29-21-W4]
~ station northwest of Drumheller.

The origin of the name is not known.

DUNSHALT [25-24-W4]
~ station northeast of Strathmore.

It was named by A. McLean, who came from Dunshalt, Fifeshire, Scotland, in 1907.

DUNSTABLE [57-2-W5]
~ former post office near Barrhead.

It was named by postal officials after Dunstable, Bedfordshire, England. It was open from 1908 to 1969.

DUNVEGAN [80-4-W6]
~ former settlement northeast of Spirit River.

It was named after the ancestral castle of the MacLeods of Skye, Scotland. Originally, there was a trading post in the Peace River Country, operated by the North West Company. According to Harmon, Northwester Archibald McLeod "used to winter here while in Athabasca". The first ascertained reference to the name is in Simon Fraser's journal in 1805.

DUNVEGAN YARDS [53-24-W4]
~ station adjoining Edmonton.

It was so named in 1911 and is the terminal of the Edmonton, Dunvegan, and British Columbia Railway, which is popularly referred to as the "Extremely Dangerous and Badly Constructed Railway"!

DURLINGVILLE   **[61-5-W4]**
~ *former post office northeast of Bonnyville.*

It was named after Mr. F. Durand and Mr. Islin, two pioneer settlers in 1908.

DURWARD   **[15-27-W4]**
~ *former station southeast of Nanton.*

It was named from the title of one of Sir Walter Scott's novels, *Quentin Durward*, in 1913.

DUSSELDORF   **[60-2-W5]**
(See: **FREEDOM**)

DUTHIL   **[25-11-W5]**
~ *former station northwest of Canmore.*

It was named after the parish of Duthil in Inverness-shire, Scotland, in 1883.

DUVERNAY   **[55-12-W4]**
~ *hamlet near Two Hills.*

It was named after Ludger Duvernay (1799-1858), the French Canadian who founded the St. Jean-Baptiste Society in 1834. Previously the community was called **SOUTH BEND**.
The population in 1972 was 71.

DUXBURY   **[15-15-W4]**
~ *former village near Stettler.*

It was named after Duxbury, Massachusetts, the original home of several pioneer settlers. (See: **FORESTBURG**)

E

E. P. RANCH   [17-3-W5]
~ ranch south of Calgary.

It was so named by His Royal Highness, Edward, Prince of Wales (1895-1972), who purchased the ranch in 1919 and owned it until the 1950's. On the death of his father, George V, in January 1936, he became King Edward VIII. But he abdicated in December of the same year to marry "the woman he loved", Mrs. Wally Simpson, an American divorcee.

EAGLE BUTTE   [7-4-W4]
~ former post office south of Medicine Hat.

It is so called because of a prominent butte or hill which was a favorite meeting place for eagles in the vicinity. There are only a few eagles found in Alberta today outside the Rocky Mountain region.

EAGLE HILL   [34-3-W5]
~ former post office near Olds.

In ancient times before the coming of the Europeans, this hill was named Eagle hill. It was opened in 1903 and closed in 1963.

EAGLESHAM   [78-26-W5]
~ village north of Birch Hills.

It was named in 1916 after the village of Eaglesham near Glasgow, Scotland. The name is derived not from "eagle", which in French is *aigle*, nor from the Gaelic *eaglais*, "church", but from a man, *Egli*, or Egil, still a Swiss surname.

The population was 242 in 1972 and decreased to 159 in 2008.

EARLIE   **[48-3-W4]**
~ *former post office west of Lloydminster.*

It was named in error for Airlie in the song "The Bonnie House of Airlie". Local residents decided to submit the name Airlie for a promised post office. The man who sent the name to the Post Office Department spelled it "Earlie". It was opened in 1909 and closed in 1947.

EARLVILLE   **[42-24-W4]**
~ *former post office south of Ponoka.*

It was named after Earl F. Heath, the first postmaster. It was opened in 1904 and closed in 1932.

EAST COULEE   **[27-18-W4]**
~ *former post office south of Drumheller.*

A coulee is a ravine or gully, usually dry, that has been worn away by heavy rains or melting snow. From the French *couler* (to flow), the word seems to have originated among French Canadian fur traders in Canada West. It's post office opened in 1929.

EAST PRAIRIE   **[79-12-W5]**
(See: **GIFT LAKE**)

EASTBURG   **[59-1-W5]**
~ *former post office southwest of Westlock.*

It was named after Mr. A. E. East, the first postmaster. The ending "burg", means "town". It opened in 1908 and closed in 1946.

EASTERVALE   **[39-8-W4]**
~ *former post office near Hardisty.*

So named because the original homesteaders arrived in the district on Easter Sunday. The post office opened in 1922 and closed in 1926.

EASTGATE   [57-22-W4]
~ former post office near Edmonton.

It was named after the first postmaster C. J. Woodward's English place of birth in Sussex, England. It was opened in 1909 and closed in 1954.

EASYFORD   [50-8-W5]
~ former post office northwest of Drayton Valley.

The name is descriptive as this post office is situated on the bank of the Pembina River where it can be forded with ease. There was a post office from 1935 to 1966.

ECHOHILL   [58-26-W4]
~ former post office near Westlock.

It was named after the first farm on the hill by pioneer settlers. It opened in 1914 and closed in 1931.

ECKVILLE   [39-3-W5]
~ town west of Red Deer.

It was named after Andrew E. Eckford, a pioneer settler. It was incorporated as a town in 1966. The railway station was at one time called **KOOTUK**.

The population was 642 in 1972 and increased to 1,002 in 2007.

EDBERG   [44-20-W4]
~ village south of Camrose.

It was named after John A. Edberg, the first postmaster who was Swedish by birth, in 1902. It became a village in 1930.

The population was 167 in 1972 and decreased to 155 in 2006.

EDENSVILLE   [43-20-W4]
~ former post office near Bashaw.

The origin of this name is unknown. Anthony Eden was a British Prime Minister in the 1950's. It opened in 1903 and changed its name to **MEETING CREEK** in 1912.

EDGERTON   [44-4-W4]
~ village south of Wainwright

It was named after H. H. Edgerton, a railway official. The post office opened in 1908.

The population was 296 in 1972 and increased to 393 in 2007.

EDISON   [60-26-W4]
~ former post office near Westlock.

The origin of the name is unknown. It was in operation from 1904 to 1913.

(See: **WESTLOCK**)

EDMONTON   [53-24-W4]
~ capital city of the Province of Alberta.

Lovell's Gazetteer of British North America, published in 1872, states that "Edmonton is a fortified village in the Northwest Territories in Lat. 53° 33´ Long. 113° 28´ west. It is built of red earth, enclosed by high pickets, and entered by a battlemented gateway. Its vicinity is rich in coal and gold and other minerals". It took its name from FORT EDMONTON, built in 1795, twenty miles farther down the North Saskatchewan River, by George Sutherland, of the Hudson's Bay Company. It was named after Edmonton, near London, England, probably as a compliment to John Prudens, Sutherland's clerk, who was born there. This fort was destroyed by the Indians in 1807. A new fort of the same name was built in 1808 on the slope of the high bank within the limits of the present city of EDMONTON. Later, the word "Fort" fell into disuse and when the first post office was opened on February 1, 1877, it was named simply, EDMONTON.

Cowper has immortalized the English town in his poem, "History of John Gilpin":

Thus all through merry Islington
These gambols did he play,
Until he came unto the Wash
Of Edmonton so gay.

The name is ultimately derived from the Anglo-Saxon Christian name Eadhelm, and Tun or ton, which means a "field" or "enclosure". The Edmonton near London was called Adelmetone in the Domesday Book (1086)

The population was 782,439 in 2009. (See also: **CLOVER BAR;**)

EDNAVILLE   **[44-4-W5]**
(See: **IOLA**)

EDOUARDVILLE   **[57-8-W4]**
~ former station southeast of St. Paul.

Edouard is the French spelling of "Edward". It was located close to the hamlet of SAINT-EDOUARD.

EDSON   **[53-17-W5]**
~ town west of Edmonton.

It was named after Edson Chamberlain, an official of the Grand Trunk Pacific Railway, which reached this point in 1910. The community was first called **HEATHERWOOD**.

The population was 4,051 in 1972 and increased to 8,365 in 2005.

EDWAND   **[59-16-W4]**
~ hamlet north of Smoky Lake.

It was named after Edward Anderson, the first postmaster. The name apparently was misspelled when sent to Ottawa. It had a post office from 1904 to 1970.

EGG LAKE   **[67-15-W4]**
~ former post office south of Lac La Biche.

It was so called in 1897 because it was located near Missawawi Lake. *Missawawi* is the Cree word for "big egg".

EGREMONT   **[58-22-W4]**
~ former post office near Thorhild.

It was named after the former English home in Cumberland of Mrs. R. C. Armstrong, the wife of the first postmaster, in 1908. It was open from 1908 to 1970.

EIDSWOLD   **[42-18-W4]**
~ former post office east of Bashaw.

The origin of the name is unknown. It was in operation in 1911, but later in the year the name was changed to **DONALDA**.

ELADESOR   **[28-19-W4]**
~ former station south of Drumheller.

The name is of uncertain etymology.

ELBRIDGE   **[60-22-W4]**
~ former post office near Westlock.

It was named after Elbridge Duval, the prospective first postmaster who died suddenly before the post office opened in 1916. It closed in 1928 but reopened in 1935. It closed for a second time in 1947.

ELCAN   **[10-17-W4]**
~ former station between Lethbridge and Medicine Hat.

The name is derived from the last part of "Tabernacle" reversed. **TABER** is the next station. Both were Mormon settlements. A post office was opened in 1910.

ELDON   **[27-15-W5]**
~ station west of Banff.

It was named after John the 3rd Earl of Eldon (1845-1926), a share holder in the Canadian Pacific Railway in 1883.

ELDORENA   **[57-20-W4]**
~ former post office near Lamont.

The origin of the name is unknown. It was open from 1914 to 1958.

ELEVENTH SIDING   **[39-27-W4]**
It was the eleventh siding of the Calgary-Edmonton Railway, built in 1891. (See: **BLACKFALDS**)

ELK ISLAND   **[55-21-W4]**
~ former station west of Lamont.

The elk or *wapita* is one of the largest members of the deer family found in Canada. Adult bulls weigh up to one thousand pounds and shed their antlers annually.

ELK POINT   **[57-7-W4]**
~ town west Lloydminster.

It is said to be named after Elk Point, South Dakota. The town was incorporated in 1962.

The population was 771 in 1972 and increased to 1,512 in 2007.

ELKTON   **[31-4-W5]**
~ former post office near Red Deer.

So named from its proximity to Red Deer River. Fur traders used the names 'deer' and 'elk' for the same animal. It was in operation from 1907 to 1970.

ELKWATER   **[8-3-W4]**
~ hamlet south of Medicine Hat.

The name of this hamlet is a translation of the Blackfoot *ponokiokeve*.

ELLAZGA   **[109-16-W5]**
~ Indian village near Fort Vermilion.

The name is the Indian word for "salt place".

ELLERSLIE   **[51-24-W4]**
~ former station south of Edmonton.

It was named after Ellerslie, one of the manors of Sir William Wallace (1272-1305), the great Scottish hero in the country's struggle against the English.

ELLSCOTT   [64-20-W4]
~ hamlet south of Athabasca.

It was named after L. Scott, a railway official, in 1916. Prior to this it was called GLENSHAW.

ELMWORTH   [70-11-W6]
~ former post office south of Beaverlodge.

It was named after, in all probability, after Elmworth in the State of Massachusetts. "Worth" is an Old English word for "enclosure" or "homestead". Thus the name means "the farm surrounded with elms".

ELNORA   [35-23-W4]
~ village north of Drumheller.

It was named after Mrs. Elinora Hogg, a pioneer settler whose husband, Alex Hogg was the first postmaster. The post office opened in 1908 and the village was incorporated in 1926.

The population was 199 in 1972 and increased to 338 in 2008. (See: **STEWARTVILLE SETTLEMENT**)

ELSPETH   [38-2-W5]
~ former station west of Sylvan Lake.

It was opened in 1914. The name is a form of the feminine Christian name, Elizabeth.

ELTHAM   [19-26-W4]
~ former station east of High River.

Probably named after Eltham near London, England.

EMBARRAS   [50-20-W5]
~ former station southwest of Edson.

It was named after the nearby River, which in turn, was probably so called because the waters are often obstructed by driftwood.

EMPRESS [23-1-W4]
~ village on the Alberta-Saskatchewan border.

This community was named after Queen Victoria (1821-1901), Empress of India. This title was given the British monarch after the crushing of the Indian uprising known as the Indian Mutiny (1856-1857).

The population was 360 in 1972 and decreased to 136 in 2006.

ENCHANT [14-18-W4]
~ hamlet north of Retlaw.

It was so named in 1915. Before this, the community was known as LOST LAKE. The name ENCHANT was suggested by W. H. Foreman, the first postmaster.

ENDIANG [36-16-W4]
~ former village near Hanna.

It was named after the Chipewyan word for "my home", according to T. Harrison. It is strange that the nearest members of the Chipewyan tribe lived hundreds of miles to the north. Homesteaders moved into the district in 1910.

ENDON [6-9-W4]
(See: **ETZIKOM**)

ENILDA [74-16-W5]
~ former post office east of High Prairie.

The feminine name, Adline, was reversed to form this name. Adline Tompkins was the wife of the first postmaster in 1913.

ENSIGN [17-25-W4]
~ hamlet northwest of Vulcan.

The district was opened up for settlement in 1910. The British ensign was the official Canadian flag until 1966, when the red maple leaf flag on a white background was adopted.

ENSLEIGH   [33-8-W4]
~ former post office near Coronation.

The origin of this name is unknown. The last portion of it: "Leigh" is found in many Devonshire, England place names. It was in operation from 1910 to 1936.

ENTICE   [29-24-W4]
~ former station west of Drumheller.

Railway officials hoped the name would encourage settlement in the district.

ENTRANCE   [51-26-W5]
~ former post office at the entrance to Jasper National Park.

The name is descriptive.
The population in 1972 was 94.

ENTWISTLE   [53-7-W5]
~ village west of Edmonton.

It was named after James G. Entwistle, a pioneer settler and railway employee. He served as the first postmaster in 1908. The village was incorporated in 1955.

The population was 329 in 1972 and increased to 534 in 2009.

EQUITY   [32-23-W4]
~ former station north of Three Hills.

It was so named in 1916. Previously it was called **GHOST PINE**.

ERIN LODGE   [80-2-W6]
~ former post office near Birch Hills.

Erin is a poetic name for Ireland. Lodge was added to distinguish it from other Erin's in Canada. The post office was opened in 1917 but has since been closed.

ERITH [51-19-W5]
~ former station southwest of Edson.

It is probably named after the English town of Erith in Kent. The Old English word *erith* means "gravelly landing-place".

ERSKINE [39-20-W4]
~ hamlet west of Stettler.

It was named after Erskine Childers (1870-1922), who served as a clerk in the British House of Commons, 1895-1910 and was one of the most popular novelist of his time. *The Riddle of the Sands* (1903), a fictional account of German preparation to invade the British Isles, was taken by the general public as fact! it resulted in the race to build battle ships. The settlement was so named by its English homesteaders.

ERVICK [47-21-W4]
~ former station west of Camrose.

It was named after Mr. Ervick, the roadmaster of the district.

ESHER [77-5-W6]
~ former station in the Peace River Country.

It was named after the English village of Esher in Surrey, former home of B. J. Prest, a railway engineer.

ESTHER [31-2-W4]
~ former post office north of Oyen.

It was named after Esther, daughter of Y. B. Olsen, the first postmaster and a pioneer Scandinavian settler in 1914. Esther was the first European child born in the district.

ETHELWYN [54-5-W4]
~ former post office near Elk Point.

It was named in commemoration of "Ethel", wife of H. Macdonald, a pioneer settler. *Wyn* is Welsh rather than Erse. But it might have been her maiden name. It was open from 1910 to 1939.

ETZIKOM   [6-9-W4]
~ hamlet east of Foremost.

This is the Blackfoot word for "valley or "coulee". It is also known in Blackfoot as *misloonsisco* or "Crows spring" coulee, as Crow Indian war parties used to water here. Before 1916 the post office was called ENDON.

EUNICE   [62-27-W4]
~ pioneer settlement, near Westlock.

How the community was given this female first name is unknown. In 1917 when the post office was established, it was changed to DAPP.

EUREKA RIVER   [86-5-W6]
~ former post office northwest of Hines Creek.

The Greek *eureka* means "I have found it". It was the cry of exultation uttered by Archimedes on the discovery of how to find the amount of alloy in Hieron's crown. It is also the motto for the State of California.

EVANSBURG   [53-7-W5]
~ village east of Chip Lake.

It was named after Harry Marshall Erskine Evans, (1876-1974) prominent Edmonton businessman and one-time Mayor of the city.

The population was 501 in 1972 and increased to 879 in 2006.

EVARTS   [38-2-W5]
~ former post office near Sylvan Lake.

It was named after Louis P. Evarts, a pioneer homesteader in 1907. It closed in 1969.

EVERGREEN   [38-4-W5]
~ former post office northeast of Caroline.

The name is descriptive. It was opened in 1910 and closed in 1969.

EWELME [6-26-W4]
~ former post office near Foremost.

It was named in 1905 after the village Ewelme in Oxfordshire. This Old English word means "source of a stream".

EWING [37-21-W4]
~ former post office near Stettler.

It was named after John Ewing, the first postmaster. The district was settled in 1898 and the post office in operation from 1903 to 1926.

EXCEL [28-5-W4]
~ hamlet northwest of Oyen.

Early pioneer settlers thought it had an "excellent" situation. The post office was opened in 1911.

EXCELSIOR [55-24-W4]
~ former station north of Edmonton.

It was opened in 1905. It is the Latin motto "higher" on the seal of the State of New York adopted in 1778.

EXSHAW [24-9-W5]
~ hamlet south of Banff.

It was named by Sir Sandford Fleming, a director of the local cement plant, in honor of his son-in-law.

EYREMORE [17-17-W4]
It was so named in 1908 by combining the name of the first postmaster, W. T. P. Eyres, with the maiden name of his wife, Moore.

F

FABYAN [45-7-W4]
~ former post office near Wainwright.

It was named after Fabyan, a holiday resort town in New Hampshire when the railway arrived in 1909. There was a post office from 1917 to 1979.

FAIRVIEW [81-3-W6]
~ town southwest of Peace River.

Many of the residents of **WATERHOLE** helped to establish this community in 1915. It was given its name because of the scenic beauty of the location.

The population was 2,093 in 1972 and increased to 3,297 in 2006.

FAIRY BANK [43-27-W4]
(See: FERRYBANK)

FAIRYDELL [58-24-W4]
~ former post office south of Westlock.

It was in operation from 1910 to 1939.

FAITH [4-9-W4]
~ former post office near Foremost.

It was named after Faith Sergeant, daughter of James Sergeant, the first postmaster, in 1911. There is also a HOPE, Alberta, But no Charity! The original CHARITY settlement changed to **CHARLES** on the request of the residents.

FALHER   **[78-21-W5]**
~ *town west of Kimiwan Lake.*

It was named in 1913 in honor of Rev. C. Falher, OMI, a Catholic missionary, who came to Canada in 1883 from Brittany, France. He attained fame for his ability to speak and interpret the Cree language, and fostered the French settlement.

The population was 971 in 1972 and decreased to 941 in 2006.

FALLIS   **[53-5-W5]**
~ *former post office near Stony Plain.*

It was named after W. S. Fallis, a Montreal manufacturer, in 1910.

FALUN   **[46-27-W4]**
~ *former post office near Wetaskiwin.*

It was named after a Swedish mining town from where many of the pioneer settlers had come. The post office was opened in 1904.

FAREHAM   **[1-23-W4]**
~ *post office near Whiskey Gap.*

It was opened in 1918 and was later closed. Probably so named after Fareham, Hampshire, England, by an early settler.
(See: **WHISKEY GAP**)

FARRANT   **[39-26-W4]**
~ *former station near Lacombe.*

It was so named in 1914.

FARROW   **[20-25-W4]**
~ *hamlet northeast of Blackie.*

The origin of this name is not known, though "farrow" means a "litter of pigs".

FAUST   [73-11-W5]
~ hamlet south of Lesser Slave Lake.

It was named in 1914 after E. T. Faust, a locomotive engineer of Edmonton, Dunvegan and British Columbia Railway. It is pronounced so that it rhymes with "lost".

FAWCETT   [64-1-W5]
~ hamlet north of Westlock.

It was known as FRENCH CREEK until 1914, when renamed FAWCETT after the resident engineer during the construction of the Edmonton, Dunvegan and British Columbia Railway.

FAWN LAKE   [58-1-W5]
~ former post office near Westlock.

It was named after a small lake of the same name, which probably commemorates some occurrence in connection with a young deer. It was opened in 1911 and closed in 1947.

FEDERAL   [36-11-W4]
~ hamlet west of Coronation.

It was so named in 1910 after the federal government, which at that time was usually referred to as the Dominion Government.

FEDORAH   [57-23-W4]
~ former post office north of Edmonton.

It was named in 1908 after the nineteenth century playwright Sardon's drama *Fedora*, in which Sarah Bernhardt played the role of the princess, Fedora. The correct spelling is Fedora; the "h" was added by postal officials.

FENN   [36-20-W4]
~ hamlet south of Stettler.

The former railway station was opened in 1911. Possibly the name refers to the fact the land in the district is rather marshy or like the Cambridgshire "fen country".

FENNER [33-10-W4]
~ former post office near Coronation.

It was named after George Fenner, the first postmaster in 1912 and closed in 1937.

FERGIE [47-19-W5]
(See: LOVETTVILLE)

FERGUSON FLATS [58-4-W4]
~ former post office east of Edmonton.

It was named after W.R. Ferguson, a Scot, who became the first postmaster in 1912. The Ferguson Clan is located in the Highlands in the Loch Fine district and many did military service with the Black Watch Regiment.

FERINTOSH [44-21-W4]
~ village south of Camrose.

The name was proposed by Dr. J. R. McLeod, MLA for the district in 1905, after the village of Ferintosh, in Ross-shire, Scotland.

The population was 150 in 1972 and increased 193 in 2008.

FERN CREEK [47-2-W5]
~ former post office near Warburg.

It was named after a nearby stream on which banks a quantity of ferns still grow. It was opened in 1913 but has since been closed.

FERRIER [39-8-W5]
~ former station west of Rocky Mountain House.

The railway reached here in 1914.

FERRYBANK   [43-27-W4]
~ former post office near Ponoka.

Postal officials changed the name of this post office in 1905 to FERRYBANK from its too romantic former name of FAIRY BANK. It was given this name because there was a peculiar shaped ravine nearby. The post office is now closed.

FERTILITY   [33-13-W4]
~ former post office near Lethbridge.

The Geographic Board of Canada, in *Place-Names of Alberta* (1928), says this name was "descriptive". It does not say of what! it was opened in 1911 but has since been closed.

FESCUE   [51-27-W4]
(See: **GOLDEN SPIKE**)

FEW RANCH   [7-2-W5]
~ large southern Alberta ranch.

The original lease in 1882 of 100,000 acres was granted to D. F. Jones, MP for South Leeds (Ontario) and F. A. Inderwick, KC, of Wichelsea, England, who was the author of many historical publications. The ranch was transferred in 1886 to A. B. Few, who died in 1896.

FIDLER   [47-23-W5]
~ former station in the Coal Branch district.

It was named in honor of Peter Fidler (1796-1822), fur trader and explorer. Born in Bolsor, Derbyshire, England, he entered the Hudson's Bay Company's service in 1788 and was sent to Cumberland House, where he studied surveying under Philip Turnor. From 1796 to 1821, Fidler was chief surveyor of the company. In 1813, he assisted in laying out the Red River Settlement that later was to become Winnipeg, and the next year he surveyed the district of Assiniboia. He served at several trading posts across Western Canada and died at Swan River. He made extensive explorations across what is now Alberta, greatly increasing the knowledge of the region.

FIELDHOLME   **[24-14-W4]**
(See: **HUTTON**)

FIFTH MERIDIAN   **[111-1-W5]**
~ isolated hamlet on the Peace River, east of Fort Vermilion.

The name is descriptive of its position Township 3, Range 67, west of the Fifth Meridian.

FINCASTLE   **[10-15-W4]**
~ former station northeast of Taber.

It was named in 1915 after Viscount Fincastle, one of the titles of the Earl of Dunmore (1841-1907). The Fincastle railway branch joins the main line at **DUNMORE** junction.

FINLAY HOUSE   **[106-16-W5]**
~ trading post in the Peace River Country.

This North West Company trading post was newly built when Alexander Mackenzie passed this way in 1792. It was named after James Finlay, a Nor'wester, who had explored the chief branch of the Peace River in 1797. It has borne his name since. It is below the Vermilion chutes.

FINNEGAN   **[25-15-W4]**
~ former post office northeast of Bassano.

It probably has an Irish derivation.

FISH CREEK   **[23-1-W5]**
(See: **MIDNAPORE**)

FISHBURN   **[5-28-W4]**
~ former post office near Lethbridge.

It was named after A. M. Fish, an early pioneer settler. The post office was opened in 1894 and since has been closed.

FISHER HOME   [47-2-W5]
~ former post office south of Warburg.

The reference in this name is to the home of Mr. Lee, a noted fisherman, who was the postmaster when the post office was opened in 1907. It was closed in 1969.

FITZALLEN   [53-14-W4]
~ former station near Vegreville.

It was named after Mr. Fitzallan, long time town official of neighboring Vegreville in 1931.

FITZGERALD   [125-10-W4]
~ hamlet northwest of Lake Athabasca.

It was named in 1915 in honor of Inspector Francis J. Fitzgerald of the N.W.M.P. who, with three companions, lost his life on the Peel River in 1911. The surname "Fitzgerald" means "son of the spear ruler". Previously the community had been called **SMITH LANDING**.

FLAGSTAFF   [43-13-W4]
~ former post office near Hardisty.

It was named after the Cree word for "flag-hanging". In ancient times, it was a gathering place for the Sarcee tribe.

FLAT LAKE   [59-8-W4]
~ former post office south of Therien.

It was opened in 1909 and closed in 1930. The nearby lake was shallow.

FLATBUSH   [66-2-W5]
~ hamlet southeast of Athabasca.

The name refers to the nature of the country. The post office was opened in 1916. In 1928 it ranked as a village.

FLEET   [37-13-W4]
~ hamlet south of Castor.

Canada was in the act of creating a navy at this time. Prior to 1912 the post office was called **HUB**.

FLOATING STONE   [61-11-W4]
~ former post office near St. Paul.

It was named after a nearby lake of the same name. In the middle of this body of water a lone 15-foot stone stands out of the water. It appears to be floating. It was opened in 1930 and closed in 1947.

FLORANN   [4-11-W4]
~ former post office south of Foremost.

The name appears to be a combination of two girls' names, Flora and Anne. It was opened in 1913 but has since been closed.

FLYINGSHOT LAKE SETTLEMENT[71-6-W6]
~ south of Grande Prairie.

The name is derived form the fact that ducks were shot during flight over the area, which lies between two feeding grounds.

FOISY   [57-11-W4]
~ former post office near St. Paul.

It was named after Aladin Foisy, a French Canadian, the first postmaster in 1919. His son, Rene P. Foisy, served as a Justice of the Alberta Court of Queen's Bench for many years.

FOOTHILLS   [47-20-W5]
~ former post office south of Sterco.

It is situated in the foothills of the Rockies. Prior to 1913, the community was called **MUDGE**. The foothills in Alberta is usually the rounding lower slopes of the east watershed of the Rockies approximately ten miles in width and reach from the United States border to some 50 miles north of **CALGARY**. In the 1880's, this was all cattle country.

(See: **COAL BRANCH**)

FORCINA   [28-14-W4]
~ former post office near Drumheller.

Prior to 1915, the post office was called **ROSE LYNN**. It was closed after 1930.

FOREMAN   [40-16-W4]
~ former post office near Stettler.

It was named after E. R. (Dick) Foreman, the first postmaster, who with his parents moved into the district in 1891. It was open from 1905 to 1946.

FOREMOST   [6-11-W4]
~ village south of Bow Island.

It was so named because in the winter of 1911 it was the "foremost" point which had been reached by the railway. The post office was opened three years later.

The population was 586 in 1972 and decreased to 524 in 2006.

FOREST LAWN   [24-29-W4]
~ former town, now a suburb of Calgary.

It was incorporated into the city of **CALGARY** in 1961. Originally it was the name of a subdivision survey, then the name of a post office, which opened in 1913.

FORESTBURG   [42-15-W4]
~ village north of Stettler

It is a descriptive name as the area was well wooded when the homesteaders moved in. The community was first called **DUXBURY**.

The population was 709 in 1972 and increased to 895 in 2006.

FORK LAKE   [63-11-W4]
~ former post office north of Whitefish Lake.

It derives its descriptive name from the nearby lake, which is shaped like the prongs of a fork. The post office opened in 1916 and closed in 1978.

FORSHEE   [41-2-W5]

It was opened in 1919. There is a community with the same name in the State of Virginia.

FORSTER   [42-21-W4]

(See: **BASHAW**)

FORT ASSINIBOINE   [62-6-W5]

~ fur trading post, village north of Westlock.

The building of a Hudson's Bay Company trading post on the Athabasca River here is referred to by John Work in his journal, September 23, 1823: "About noon arrived at a new house which Dr. McDonald, the gentleman who is superintending the building called Fort Assiniboine. It is situated on the north bank. This is the house that was to have been built at McLeod branch". The name ASSINIBOINE means "those who cook by placing hot stones in water". The post office was opened in 1913.

FORT ATHABASCA RIVER   [108-10-W4]

(See: **OLD FORT**)

FORT AUGUSTUS   [54-22-W4]

~ former fur trading post.

It is within the limits of the present town of **FORT SASKATCHEWAN** on the north bank of the river, where the Sturgeon joins the North Saskatchewan. It was an important North West Company trading post, built about 1798. FORT AUGUSTUS was abandoned in 1808, in favor of a new trading post of the same name at what is now **EDMONTON**. It was named in honor of Augustus Frederick, Prince of Wales, afterwards George IV.

FORT BERRY

~ former trading post west of Calgary.

It was named in 1872 after Dick Berry, a whiskey trader, who was killed in an ambush by a Blood Indian named Old Woman's Child. In the vicinity was LIVINGSTONE POST (named after Sam Livingstone) and KANOUSE'S POST (named after H. A. "Fred" Kanouse). All three trading posts were closed down by the North West Mounted Police.

FORT BERRY AND SHEAR
~ former trading post near High River.

Sgt. Antrobus of the North West Mounted Police reported in February 1875 that the whiskey traders "had cleared out and the fort had been burned by Indians."

FORT BOND
~ former trading post near Nanton.

It was named after William Bond, a whiskey trader. It was closed down by Captain Crozier of the North West Mounted Police in 1875.

FORT BRISEBOIS
~ former North West Mounted Police post at Calgary.

It was named by N.W.M.P. Inspector Ephraim Brisebois after himself, when he established a North West Mounted Police station on the south bank of the Bow River. Colonel Macleod changed it to FORT CALGARY. (See: **CALGARY**)

FORT CHIPEWYAN   [112-7-W4]
~ former fur trading post on the northwest shore of Lake Athabasca.

The original post of this name was built in 1788 for the North West Company by Alexander Mackenzie and his cousin Roderick Mackenzie on Lake Athabasca, about eight miles from the mouth of the Athabasca River. It was immediately prosperous and earned the name "the emporium of the North". As Mackenzie has supplied it with a library, some traders referred to it as the "little Athens of the Hyperborean region". The site was abandoned in 1804 when a new FORT CHIPEWYAN was erected on the north shore of the lake. This fort was taken over by the Hudson's Bay Company when the fur companies were united in 1821. It is still in operation. CHIPEWYAN is a Cree name meaning "pointed skins", hence the people who wear them. At one time it was called NOTTINGHAM HOUSE.

FORT CONRAD
~ an abandoned whiskey trading post near Fort Macleod.

This post, which was also called ROBBER'S ROOST and SLOUGH BOTTOM, was named in 1871 after an American free trader, Charles Conrad. It was located three miles from FORT KIPP and was burned to the ground by Indians in 1873.

FORT DE TREMBLE
~ former trading post near Fort Vermilion.

It was built by John Finlay of the North West Company in 1791.

FORT EDMONTON   [53-24-W4]
(See: EDMONTON)

FORT ETHIER
~ abandoned military fort near Wetaskiwin.

It was built on the Edmonton-Calgary trail during the North West Rebellion of 1885 by the 65th Mount Royal Rifles and named after Captain Ethier.

FORT FARWELL
~ former trading post near Cardston.

It was named after Abe Farwell, a whiskey trader. It was located on the St. Mary River and was a well-known stopping place between Fort Benton and Fort Whoop-up.

FORT FRENCH
~ former trading post near Blackfoot Crossing.

It was named after Lafayette French, a whiskey trader. It flourished in the 1870's.

FORT GEORGE [56-6-W4]
~ former trading post on the north bank of the North Saskatchewan River.

It was built for the North West Company by Angus Shaw in 1792. Nine years later the post was moved twenty miles upstream to FORT ISLAND. It was named after George III (1738-1820), who succeeded to the throne in 1760.

FORT HAMILTON [9-21-W4]
(See: FORT WHOOP-UP)

FORT ISLAND
(See: **FORT GEORGE**)

FORT KENT [61-5-W4]
~ hamlet north of Bonnyville.

So named in 1922 on the suggestion of a pioneer of the district who had come from Fort Kent in the State of Maine. The word *kent* is of Celtic origin, and means "rim" or "border".

The population in 1972 was 91.

FORT KIPP [9-22-W4]
(See: **KIPP**)

FORT KOOTENAI
~ former trading post near Waterton.

It was named after John George "Kootenai" Brown who became the first ranger in charge of **WATERTON LAKES NATIONAL PARK**. It flourished in the 1870's and may be the trading post referred to by the Mounted Police as FORT WARREN.

FORT LA JONQIUERRE
(See: **CALGARY; FORT BRISEBOISE**)

FORT LAC D'ORIGNAL
~ abandoned trading post near Bonnyville.

It was established as a North West Company trading post in 1789 by Angus Shaw on the shore of Lac d'Orignal, which is now known as Moose Lake.

FORT LEE
~ former trading post near Cardston.

It was named after W. S. Lee, a whiskey trader, and was flourishing in the 1870's. Nearby Lee Creek is not named after him but for Lee Kaiser, an early-day "bull whacker" who accidentally shot himself near the stream.

FORT MacKAY   [94-11-W4]
~ former fur trading settlement northwest of Fort McMurray.

It was named after the MacKay River which, in turn, was named after Dr. William MacKay, who worked for the Hudson's Bay Company for forty years. He died in Edmonton in 1917.

The population in 2008 was 332.

FORT MACLEOD   [9-26-W4]
~ first N.W.M.P. Post on the Western Prairie.

It was named in honor of Colonel James Farquhar Macleod (1832-1894), the commander of the first force of the North West Mounted Police to arrive in what is now Alberta. In the 1870's he brought law and order to the western prairies, and negotiated the historic Treaty Seven with the Blackfoot, Sarcee and Stony Indians. On his retirement from the force, Macleod was appointed a magistrate, and then a judge. In Blackfoot *stamix-otokan-okowy* means "bull's home", Colonel Macleod being known to the Indians as "Bull's Head" because he had a buffalo head over the door of his residence. The crest of the clan Macleod of Skye is a bull's head.

The population was 2,750 in 1972 and increased to 3,072 in 2006.

FORT McMURRAY   [89-9-W4]
~ city on the Athabasca River at the junction of the Clearwater River.

It is located at the foot of a ninety-mile stretch of rapids on the Athabasca and the beginning of a course navigable north to the Mackenzie River which has made it an important trans-shipping center. Settlement at the location began with a trading post established by the North West Company in 1788 called FORT OF THE FORKS. David Thompson descended the Athabasca River in 1799 and arrived here. The post was taken over by the Hudson's Bay Company in 1821, rebuilt in 1870 by Factor H. J. Moberly. It was renamed FORT McMURRAY in honor of William McMurray (died 1877), Chief Factor of the fur trading company who was in charge of Isle of the Cross about that time. The settlement was incorporated as a town in 1947.

The population was 6,681 in 1972 and increased to 89,950 in 2009.

FORT McPHERSON
~ former trading post near Okotoks.

It was named after whiskey trader Addison McPherson. It flourished in the early 1870's. In the vicinity was **FORT SPITZEE**.

FORT NEIL CAMPBELL
~ former whiskey trading post on Sheep Creek.

It was named after Neil Campbell, an American free trader. The Mounted Police closed it in 1875.

FORT NORMANDEAU
~ abandoned fort near Red Deer.

It was a stopping house on the Edmonton-Calgary trail used as a temporary military fortification in the North West Rebellion of 1885. Portions of the original building still stand. It is now an historic site.

FORT OF THE FORKS   [89-9-W4]
(See: FORT McMURRAY)

FORT OSTELL
~ abandoned military fort near Battle River.

It was named after Captain John B. Ostell of the 65th Mount Royal Rifles who fortified the looted Hudson's Bay Company post here during the North West Rebellion of 1885.

FORT SASKATCHEWAN   [54-22-W4]
~ city northeast of Edmonton.

It is the site of the first North West Mounted Police fort north of **CALGARY** which was built in 1875. In Cree, *simaganis wikamik* means "soldier house". The police expected the residents of **EDMONTON** to move down river; this did not happen. *Saskatchewan* is the Cree word for "swift current".

The population was 5,734 in 1972 and increased to 17,469 in 2009.

FORT SLIDE-OUT
~ an abandoned American whiskey fort near Lethbridge.

This was little more than a group of trading shacks near **STAND OFF**. When a man was killed at the post, the remaining men buried the body and decided to "slide out", thus giving the fort its name.

FORT SPITZEE
~ early American trading post near High River.

It was one of the so-called "whiskey forts" that were closed down by the North West Mounted Police n the 1870's.

FORT VERMILION{1}   [54-3-W4]
~ former trading post on the North Saskatchewan River.

Both major fur trading companies had posts on the north bank of the North Saskatchewan near the mouth of the Vermilion River from the early nineteenth century. Alex Henry wintered at the Nor'west post in 1808. Both forts were abandoned in favor of Lower **WHITEMUD HOUSE** in 1810. Indians obtained ochre to paint themselves from the iron ore deposits in the vicinity.

(See also: **HENRY HOUSE**)

FORT VERMILION{2}   [108-13-W5]
~ *on the Peace River.*

There was an early fur trading post on the Peace River in northern Alberta by this name, probably because of the ochre deposits. The first mention of FORT VERMILION is made by David Thompson who passed a Nor'west post so named when he ascended the Peace River in 1804. The third trading post in this vicinity was the "Old Establishment" mentioned by Alexander Mackenzie as being occupied in 1688.

FORT WARREN
(See: **FORT KOOTENAI**)

FORT WHOOP-UP   [9-21-W4]
~ *early American whiskey trading post.*

Old FORT WHOOP-UP was once the center of fur and whiskey trade in Southern Alberta. The naming of this trading post is traceable to a Frenchman, Charles Choquette, who freighted from Fort Benton (Montana) to what was then Fort Hamilton. He did not know much English and whenever he learned a word he had the habit of repeating "whoop up" and it became a byword. FORT WHOOP-UP became a rendezvous of badmen and evil-doing prior to the arrival of the North West Mounted Police in the 1870's. It was also called FORT HAMILTON after Alf Hamilton, an American whiskey trader.

FORTH   [38-27-W4]
~ *former station south of Red Deer.*

It was named in 1920, possibly after the rail bridge across the Firth of Forth, Scotland. When it was completed in 1890, it was one of the engineering feats of its time.

FOX   [7-1-W4]
~ *former post office near Medicine Hat.*

It was named after James H. Fox, the first postmaster in 1912. It was closed in 1964.

FOX CREEK   [62-19-W5]
~ new town south of Peace River country.

It was so named after a nearby stream in 1967. It's population was 2,278 in 2006.
(See: **IOSEGUN LAKE**)

FRAINS   [66-18-W4]
~ former post office near Lac La Biche.

Probably named after a pioneer English family whose name was "Frain". It is an English surname that means: "a person who lived near an ash-tree". There were several Frain's living in Ontario in 1900. The post office was open from 1934 to 1969.

FRANCHERE   [61-7-W4]
~ former post office west of Bonnyville.

It was possibly named after Gabriel Franchere, author of *Relation d'un voyage a Cote du Nord-Ouest de l'Amerique Septentrionale* (Montreal, 1820). This was the first published description of a journey through the Rockies by the way of the Athabasca River.

FRANK   [7-3-W5]
~ coal mine ghost town in the shadow of Turtle Mountain southeast of Blairmore.

It was named in 1901 after H. L. Frank, who opened the first coal mine in the region. At 4:10 a.m. on April 29, 1903, a ledge of limestone toppled from Turtle Mountain and buried one end of FRANK, then a busy mining community. Within 100 seconds, a ledge 4,000 feet wide and 5,000 feet thick fell from a height of 1,300 feet. It spewed ninety million tons of rock over two miles of valley. It buried thirty-two acres to a depth of 100 feet with jagged rocks as large as houses. It is believed that sixty-five persons were killed in their beds by the disaster. Miners working within the mountain at the time found their usual exit barred, but they escaped through an outlet on the other side of the mountain. . (See: **CROWSNEST PASS**)

FRANKBURG   [18-27-W4]
~ former post office near High River.

It was named after Christopher Frank, the first postmaster. It was opened in 1905 but has since closed.

FRASERTON   [27-14-W4]
~ former post office near Hanna.

It was named in 1910 after R. R. Fraser, the postmaster. The Fraser clan is located in the Beauty district near Inverness. The name is French in origin, and means "strawberry bearer", probably from an adaptation of the flower, the *fraisse,* as part of the coat-of-arms of Sir Simon Fraser in the twelfth century.

FREDA   [33-7-W4]
~ former post office near Provost.

The name was an abbreviation of the Welsh Christian name "Winifred".

FREEDOM   [60-2-W5]
~ former post office west of Westlock.

It was named in 1919 commemorating the allied victory over the central powers. Previously the post office was named DUSSELDORF. The original homesteaders were Germans. Several names of German origin were changed during the Great War.

FREEMAN RIVER   [62-6-W5]
~ former post office near Whitecourt.

It was so named after the nearby river. The river, in turn, was named to honor time-expired servants, many of them Iroquois Indians, of the Hudson's Bay Company, who settled in the district. Ex-employees of the Hudson's Bay Company were often referred to as "Freemen".

FRENCH CREEK   [64-1-W5]
(See: FAWCETT)

FRESNOY [60-6-W4]
~ former post office near Bonnyville.

It was named in commemoration of Fresnoy, near St. Quentin, France, which was captured by Canadian troops in April, 1917. It was opened in 1918 and closed in 1929.

FRIBOURG [59-9-W4]
~ former post office near St. Paul.

So named in 1911 after Fribourg in Switzerland. It was the birthplace of the first postmaster, M. Carrel.

FRIEDENSTAL [81-3-W6]
~ former post office southeast of Fairview.

It was opened in 1913 and named after the town of Friedenstal in Romania.

FROG LAKE [56-3-W4]
It was named after the nearby lake. FROG LAKE, postal district of Assinibois West, as it was then, was the site of the massacre of Hudson's Bay Company factors and Oblate missionaries by the braves of Poundmaker that started the Northwest Rebellion in 1885. On the morning of April 2, Big Bear's warriors struck. The priests were holding service when the Cree entered the village. After ransacking the Hudson's Bay Company store, they entered the church. As the people rushed from the building, they were cut down by the Indians, until nine men, including the priests (Fr. Leon Fofard, OMI, and Felix Marchand, OMI) were dead. FROG LAKE is the translation of the Cree name *Ayek*, and appears on Palliser's map in 1859. The post office was opened in 1911.

FURMAN [12-30-W4]
~ former post office south of Calgary.

It was named after an early pioneer of the district, John Furman. It was opened in 1911 but has since been closed.

G

GADSBY   [38-17-W4]
~ village east of Stettler.

It was so named after M. F. Gadsby of Ottawa in 1909.
The population was 65 in 1972 and decreased to 35 in 2006.

GAETZ VALLEY   [37-13-W4]
~ former post office near Red Deer.

It was named after Dr. Leo Gaetz, Methodist missionary
and founder of **RED DEER**. In 1911 the post office was moved to
DELBURNE, some five miles away.

GAGE   [82-4-W6]
~ former post office north of Fairview.

It was possibly named after General Thomas Gage who
commanded the British army at the Battle of Bunker Hill in 1775
during the Rebellion of the American Colonies.

GAHERN   [4-8-W4]
~ former post office south of Foremost.

It was named after H. G. Ahern, the first postmaster.

GAINFORD   [53-6-W5]
~ hamlet east of Entwistle.

It was named after the English village of Gainford, Durham,
in 1910. Previously the community was called **SEBE**. The Cree
word *si-piy* means "river".

GALAHAD [41-14-W4]
~ village near Alliance.

It was so named in 1907. The community is probably named after the famous Knight of King Arthur's Round Table. Sir Galahad was the only Knight to see the Holy Grail.
(See: **ALLIANCE**)
The population was 174 in 1972 and decreased to 134 in 2006.

GALARNEAUVILLE [25-15-W4]
It was named after G. P. Galarneau, the first postmaster in 1914. It has since been closed.

GALLOWAY [52-20-W5]
~ former station west of Edson.

It was named after David E. Galloway, an official of the Grand Trunk Railway in 1911.

GAP [24-9-W5]
~ former station east of Canmore.

It was so called because it was located at the gap in the Rockies where the Bow River issues onto the prairies.

GARDEN PLAIN [33-13-W4]
~ former hamlet northeast of Hanna.

It was so named in 1910 because of the fertility of the soil in the district.

GARDENVIEW [57-4-W5]
~ former post office northwest of Majeau Lake.

It was in operation from 1938 to 1957.

GARFIELD [30-3-W5]
~ former post office north of Cremona.

It was named after James A. Garfield (1831-1881), the 20th President of the United States. He was assassinated only four months after taking office.

GARRINGTON   [34-4-W5]
~ former post office near Olds.

It was named in 1908 after Garrington, the son of H. C. Monday, the first postmaster.

GARTH   [39-8-W5]
~ former post office near Bonnyville.

It was named after a railway official. It was in operation from 1913 to 1917.

GARTLY   [30-19-W4]
~ former station northeast of Drumheller.

It was named after the Scottish parish of Gartly in Aberdeenshire, in 1914.

GATINE   [29-21-W4]
~ former station west of Drumheller.

It was named after the cook-housekeeper of the Canadian Pacific construction crew.

GAYFORD   [26-25-W4]
~ former station north of Strathmore.

It is probably named after James Gay (1810-1891), self-styled "poet laureate of Canada". He wrote to Lord Tennyson on one occasion: "Dear Sir, now Longfellow has gone, there are only two of us left".

(The) GEDDES RANCH
~ south of Calgary.

It was named and operated by James D. Geddes, a pioneer Scottish rancher. He was the first southern Albertan to be elected to the Executive Council of the Northwest Territories, representing Calgary in 1883. He was a Scot by birth and sat in on the Council for three years.

GEIKIE   [45-2-W6]
~ former station west of Jasper.

It was named after Mount Geikie, British Columbia, which in turn, had been named in honor of Sir Archibald Geikie, the eminent British geologist.

GEM   [23-16-W4]
~ hamlet northeast of Bassano.

It obtained this descriptive name in 1914.

GENESEE   [50-3-W5]
~ former post office south of Edmonton.

It was named after Genesee, Idaho, on the suggestion of Albert White, an American in 1916.

GENEVA   [52-8-W4]
~ former post office near Birch Lake.

When it was opened in 1910 it was called LAKE GENEVA, probably after the famous Swiss lake. Later the name was shortened to just Geneva. The post office has been closed for many years.

GHENT   [9-21-W4]
~ former station near Lethbridge.

It was named after the city of Ghent in Belgium, which was one of the leading commercial and industrial centers of Europe in the fourteenth century.

GHOST LAKE   [26-6-W5]
~ hamlet near Cochrane.

It was named after Ghost River, a tributary of the Bow River. There are many Indian graves on the riverbank.

GHOST PINE   [32-23-W4]
~ former railway station near Trochu.

For more than twenty years the community had this name until in 1916 Ottawa officials changed it to **EQUITY** . No reason for the change was given at the time.

GIBBONS   [56-23-W4]
~ town north of Edmonton.

It was named after the farmer William R. Gibbons, who owned the land on which the Canadian National Railway station was built in 1917. The town was incorporated in 1977.

The population was 566 in 1972 and increased to 2,848 in 2007. (See: **BATTENBURG**)

GIFT LAKE   [79-12-W5]
~ isolated Metis community near High Prairie, Peace River.

It is named after a nearby lake. It was formerly called EAST PRAIRIE.

GILBERT   [26-10-W4]
~ former post office near Hanna.

It was named after Mrs. Alice C. Gilbert, the first postmistress. It was opened in 1913, but has since been closed.

GILBY   [40-3-W5]
~ former post office near Sylvan Lake.

It was named after O. Gilbertson, the first postmaster. It was in operation from 1906 to 1930.

GILT EDGE   [46-5-W4]
~ former post office near Wainwright.

It was called GILT EDGE on the suggestion of Edward Monaghan, an early homesteader, who on looking over the district, pronounced it "gilt edge". It was opened in 1908 but has since been closed.

GIROUXVILLE [78-22-W5]
~ village 4 miles from Falher.

It was named after a French Canadian pioneer family of the district. The post office opened and has since been closed

The population was 305 in 1972 and decreased to 282 in 2006.

GLADYS [20-27-W4]
~ former post office near High River.

It was named after Gladys Harkness, wife of the first postmaster, Charles Harkness. It was opened in 1890 but has since been closed.

GLEICHEN [22-23-W4]
~ town east of Strathmore.

It was named in honor of Count Gleichen, who traveled over the Canadian Pacific Railway lines with the company's director in 1883. His son, General Lord Edward Gleichen (1863-1937) writes: "I have never been to Gleichen, as I came up on my trip to British Columbia in 1906 from the United States, but I remember the clerk's astonishment at Calgary when I signed a telegram thence in my own name. He thought I had borrowed it from the town. I noticed it was pronounced 'Gleechen' — in those parts; it should, of course be pronounced 'Glaikhen' (KH as in Scots loch)."

Gleichen had a population in 1901 larger than it is today.

The population was 400 in 1972 and decreased to 331 in 1997.

GLEN LESLIE [72-4-W6]
~ former post office near Grande Prairie.

It was named after the first postmaster, T. Leslie. It was opened in 1914 but has since been closed.

GLENBOW [25-3-W5]
~ former station north of Calgary.

It was named in 1907 because it was situated in a "glen", or valley, near the Bow River. It is also the name of the **CALGARY** Glenbow Museum.

GLENDON   [61-8-W4]
~ *village west of Bonnyville.*

It was named in 1912 after the maiden name of the mother of the first postmaster, J. P. Spencer.

The population was 350 in 1972 and increased to 483 in 2007.

GLENEVIS   [55-4-W5]
~ *hamlet north of Lac Ste. Anne.*

It was so named in 1913 on the suggestion of John McLeod, an early homesteader, whose wife came from Glennevis, Cape Breton Island, Nova Scotia. The second "n" is omitted.

GLENFORD   [56-2-W5]
~ *former post office north of Lac Ste. Anne.*

The name is formed from the word "glen" and the last syllable of the name of the first postmaster, Thomas Rutherford. It was opened in 1909 and closed in 1960.

(The) GLENGARRY RANCH
~ *in the Porcupine Hills, west of Claresholm.*

This ranch was established by Allan B. Macdonald in 1885. Its brand was "44". He first was the manager and later the foreman. It was stocked with some 3,500 shorthorn and Hereford cattle.

In 1908, Macdonald was an unsuccessful Liberal candidate for the Macleod federal riding. Shortly after the election, he sold the ranch on his appointment as the superintendent of the Banff National Park.

By the early 1920's, the Glengarry Ranch was owned by Pat "Cattle King" Burns.

GLENHEWITT   [42-28-W4]
~ *former post office near Ponoka.*

It was named after J. J. Hewitt, the first postmaster. It was opened in 1913 and closed in 1960.

GLENISTER [58-6-W5]
~ *former post office south of Whitecourt.*

It was given this name in 1910 as a substitute for the name GLENROY, that had been suggested by residents of the district. It closed in 1964.

GLENSHAW [64-20-W4]
(See: ELLSCOTT)

GLENWOOD{1} [47-16-W4]
(See: WOODGLEN)

GLENWOOD{2} [5-27-W4]
The post office, which was opened in 1911, was called GLENWOODVILLE after Glen, the son of E. G. Wood, a large land owner in the district.

The population was 194 in 1972 and increased to 286 in 2006.

GLIDEHURST [50-26-W4]
~ *former post office south of Edmonton.*

It was opened in 1908 but has since been closed.

GODDARD [4-12-W4]
~ *former post office Foremost.*

It was named after the first postmaster,. It was opened in 1911 but has since been closed.

GOLD CREEK [57-14-W4]
~ *former post office near Vermilion.*

Small quantities of gold were panned near here in the early days. Prior to 1917 the post office was called FESCUE.

GOLDEN SPIKE [51-27-W4]
~ former post office south of Edmonton.

It was named in 1908 possibly after the golden spike driven in by Donald Smith to complete the transcontinental Canadian Pacific Railway tracks in 1885. Previously the post office was called WORLEY. It was in operation from 1907 to 1960.

GOOD HOPE [54-20-W4]
~ former post office south of Lamont.

The name is descriptive of the "good hope" of the settlers. It is likely to be confused with Good Hope Fort on the Mackenzie River. It was opened in 1907 and was closed in 1945.

GOODFARE [72-12-W6]
~ former post office north of Beaverlodge.

It was given this descriptive name in 1919. Previously it had been called KEMPTON. "Kemp" is from the Old English *cempa* meaning a "warrior" or "champion".

GOODFISH LAKE [61-13-W4]
~ former post office south of Whitefish Lake.

It was called after a nearby lake that was well stocked with fish.

GOODRIDGE [62-9-W4]
~ former post office north of Therien.

It was named after Joseph H. Good, the first postmaster.

GOODWIN [72-2-W6]
~ former post office east of Grande Prairie.

It was named in 1923 after two pioneer settlers.

GOOSE LAKE [64-11-W4]
~ former post office near Lac La Biche.

There is no lake of this name in the vicinity. The post office was in operation from 1932 to 1963.

GOPHER HEAD   **[35-19-W4]**
~ former post office near Rumsey.

It was so called from the shape of a nearby hill. It was opened in 1908 but has since been closed.

GORBALS   **[73-9-W5]**
~ former station near Lesser Slave Lake.

It was probably called after the run-down district of central Glasgow. The slums in the Gorbals are said to be some of the worst in the world.

GOURIN   **[67-17-W4]**
~ former post office west of Lac La Biche.

It was named in 1923 after the capital of the French canton from which Joseph Ulliac, the first postmaster, had come. It closed in 1967.

GRAINGER   **[29-24-W4]**
~ hamlet west of Drumheller.

It was named in 1912 after a pioneer settler, F. W. Grainger, who had come from England.

GRAMINIA   **[51-27-W4]**
~ former post office south of Edmonton.

It was named after the Latin word *gramen*, which means "grass". It was opened in 1911 and closed in 1946.

GRANADA   **[53-10-W5]**
~ former station south of Chip Lake.

It had a post office from 1927 to 1933. It is probably named after the Moorish Kingdom of southern Spain. Granada was captured by the troops of Ferdinand and Isabella in 1492 and with the fall of the city the seven hundred years of military occupation by the Moors of Spain ended.

GRANDE CACHE   [57-8-W6]
~ new town north of Edson.

The word "cache" often refers to a place where supplies have been deposited on a raised platform out of reach of wild animals. The meaning of the word in French, however, is a "hiding place", and the cache of an early fur trader was exactly that. A round piece of turf about 18" across was removed, leaving the mouth for a large bottle-shaped excavation. This excavation was lined with dry branches and the cached goods were then inserted. Finally some earth and the round piece of turf were put on top and the surplus earth all carefully removed. If the job had been done expertly, possible marauders would see no evidence that they were passing a cache. [Karamitsanis]

The population was 2,499 in 1972 and increased to 3,783 in 2006.

GRAND CENTRE   [62-2-W4]
~ town northeast of Bonnyville.

This name possibly expresses the hopes of the early settlers in 1958.

The population was 2,217 in 1972 and increased to 3,990 in 1997. (See also: **COLD LAKE**)

GRANDE PRAIRIE   [71-6-W6]
~ city in the Peace River Country.

The name is the French for "large plain", and was given in 1912 by Bishop Grouard, OMI, the Catholic missionary who described the region of gently undulating grass as "la grande prairie". This name eventually found its way into government reports.

The population was 12,054 in 1972 and increased to 50,227 in 2007.

GRANDIN [63-13-W4]
~ former post office south of Lac La Biche.

It was named in 1911 in honor or Oblate Missionary Bishop Vital-Julien Grandin (1829-1902) who became the first bishop of **ST. ALBERT**. He was born in France and joined the Oblates in 1851. He spent close to fifty years working among the Indians of the western prairies. The post office was in operation from 1911 to 1970.

GRANLEA [8-9-W4]
~ former post office south of Bow Island.

The name is a combination of "grain" and "lea", suggesting the rich agricultural products of the district near **BOW ISLAND**. It was opened in 1913 and has since closed.

GRANTA [22-19-W4]
~ station north of Bassano.

Granta is the old Saxon name of the river at Cambridge, England, now called Cam, and was suggested by two Cambridge University graduates, Van Schaik and Fairburn, who purchased tracts of land in the vicinity. The railway tracks reached here in 1913.

GRANTHAM [13-15-W4]
~ hamlet south of Lomond.

It was named after the town of Grantham, in Lincolnshire, England, in 1913.

GRANUM [10-26-W4]
~ village north of Fort Macleod.

The original name for this community was LEAVINGS. It got this name because it was the point where the Macleod-Calgary Trail left Willow Creek. The name was changed on the request of the residents in 1907. Granum, the Latin word for "grain", was suggested by Malcolm Mackenzie, MLA for Macleod.

The population was 319 in 1972 and increased to 445 in 2007.

GRASSLAND   [67-18-W4]
~ *former post office north of Athabasca.*

The name is descriptive of the abundance of grass in the district.

GRASSY LAKE   [10-13-W4]
~ *former village west of Bow Island.*

The Canadian Pacific Railway arrived here before July, 1893. The name of the small settlement was taken from a nearby lake, long since totally dried. It is a translation of the Blackfoot name, *moyi-kimi*. In 1910, some GRASSY LAKE homesteaders moved south, seeking better land, and resettled in the Foremost and Lucky Strike districts.

It became a hamlet in 1997. (See: **BOW ISLAND**)

GRATZ   [56-6-W4]
~ *former post office south of Elk Point.*

It was named in 1913 after the German birthplace of the first postmaster, J. Vogel. It closed in 1958.

GREEN COURT   [58-9-W5]
~ *hamlet south of Whitecourt.*

WHITECOURT is the next community. It is said to be called after a place of the same name in England.

GREEN GLADE   [41-1-W4]
~ *former post office near Provost.*

The name is descriptive. It was opened in 1908 and closed in 1951.

GREENLAWN   [54-5-W4]
~ *former post office near Elk Point.*

It was so named because the post office was built on a grassy slope. It was opened in 1908 and closed in 1970.

GREENSHIELDS [44-6-W4]
~ *hamlet south of Wainwright.*

It was named in 1909 after E. B. Greenshields, an important official of the Grand Trunk Railway. Previously the post office was called HOLMSTEAD.

GREENWICH HOUSE [61-5-W4]
(See: BONNYVILLE)

GRIERSON [27-21-W4]
(See: ROSEBUD[2])

GRIESBACH [54-22-W4]
~ *former station north of Edmonton.*

It was named in honor of General William Antrobus Griesbach (1878-1945), the distinguished soldier-statesman. The son of a Colonel of the North West Mounted Police, he was born in Fort Qu'Appelle. He saw action both in the Boer War and the Great War. A lawyer by profession, he was elected to Parliament for Edmonton West in 1917 and called to the Senate four years later. He sat in the Red Chamber from 1921 to 1945.

GRIESBACH [22-25-W4]
(See: CARSELAND)

GRIFFIN CREEK [81-25-W5]
~ *former post office near Peace River.*

It was named after the first white settler of the district, Thomas Griffin, who died in 1919. It was opened in 1912 but has since been closed.

GRIMSHAW [83-23-W5]
~ *town south of Peace River.*

It was named in 1922 in honor of Dr. M. E. Grimshaw, who was one of the first medical doctors to serve the people of the Peace River Country.

The population was 1,747 in 1972 and increased to 2,537 in 2006.

GRIZZLY BEAR   [78-2-W6]
~ former post office near Grande Prairie.

An Indian is said to have been killed by a grizzly bear in the vicinity. It was opened in 1916 but has since been closed.

GROSMONT   [68-24-W4]
~ former post office north of Athabasca.

The name means "big mountain" in French. There is a large hill to the north. The region was opened up for settlement in 1912. It closed in 1970.

GROTON   [3-10-W4]
~ former post office south of Foremost.

It was named in 1913 after Groton in the State of South Dakota, the former home of the first postmaster, A. J. Petersen.

GROUARD   [75-14-W5]
~ hamlet north of Lesser Slave Lake.

It was named in 1909 in honor of Father Emile Jean Baptiste Marie Grouard (1840-1931), Catholic missionary. Born in France, he came to Canada as a young man to join the Oblate Order. He spent sixty-six years ministering to the native people in the northern part of the province. He was Vicar Apostolic of Athabasca, with the title of Bishop of Ibona (1890-1929). He became a titular archbishop in 1930. He is the author of *Les eldorades de Nord-ouest* (Lyons, 1901). Previously the post office had been called **LESSER SLAVE LAKE**.

GUNN   [55-3-W5]
~ hamlet north of Alberta Beach.

It was named in 1915 after Peter Gunn, Liberal Member of the Legislature for Lac Ste. Anne from 1909 to 1917. He was born at Thurso, Scotland, and came to Canada as a young man to work for the Hudson's Bay Company.

GURNEYVILLE [59-5-W4]
~ former post office south of Bonnyville.

It was named after the maiden name of Mrs. Alex Hall, the wife of the first postmaster, in 1910.

GUY [76-21-W5]
~ former post office south of Falher.

This community is one of a group in which a considerable percentage of the inhabitants are French-speaking. They include **DONNELLY, FALHER, GIROUXVILLE, TANGENT, EAGLESHAM, CODESA** and **JEAN COTE.**

GWYNNE [46-23-W4]
~ hamlet east of Wetaskiwin.

It was named in 1906 after the maiden name of the wife of Sir Collingwood Schreiber, who was the chief engineer of the Canadian Pacific Railway during the 1880's. Lady Julia Schreiber was the daughter of a Judge of the Supreme Court of Canada. Previously the station had been called DIANA.

H

HABAY   [113-5-W6]
~ a community near Keg River.

It was one of the most northerly post offices in the province before it was closed in October, 1970.

HACKE   [1-20-W4]
(See: **TWIN RIVER**)

HACKETT   [36-18-W4]
~ hamlet south of Stettler.

This name, as a surname, is an Anglo-Norman diminutive of *hake*, a kind of fish.

HADDOCK   [56-14-W5]
~ former post office north of Peers.

It was named in 1915 after the first postmistress, Maude Haddock. It closed in 1969.

HAIGHT   [50-16-W4]
~ former post office south of Vegreville.

It was named in 1911, possibly after Captain Haight who for many years was in charge of bringing the Hudson's Bay furs down the Athabasca River. It closed in 1967.

HAIRY HILL   [55-14-W4]
~ village north of Two Hills.

The name of this community is descriptive; in the old days buffalo used to rub themselves on the thorn bushes on this hill. The post office was called **SODA LAKE** prior to 1907.

The population was 136 in 1972 and decreased to 52 in 1997.

HALACH   **[61-25-W4]**
~ former post office north of Westlock.

The name is of uncertain etymology. It opened in 1946 and closed in 1968.

HALCOURT   **[7-10-W6]**
~ former post office south of Beaverlodge.

It was named in 1913 after an early pioneer of the district, H. Halcourt Walker.

HALCRO   **[76-15-W5]**
~ Indian reserve near the Lesser Slave Lake.

It was named in 1905 after Thomas Halcro, an Indian who obtained severalty under the Treaty Number Eight.

HALFWAY LAKE   **[59-24-W4]**
~ former post office south of Westlock.

It was named in 1906 after a small body of water equidistant from Edmonton and the Athabasca River. In the old days it was the mid-point on the portage route from the North Saskatchewan River to the Athabasca. The name is a translation of the Cree name, *abitau*. It closed in 1958.

HALKIRK   **[38-16-W4]**
~ village east of Stettler.

It was named in 1909 after Halkirk in Caithness, Scotland. The word means "Holy Church". Several of the early homesteaders in this district were from Scotland.

The population was 177 in 1972 and decreased to 113 in 2006.

HALLADAY   **[28-12-W4]**
~ former station near Hanna.

It was named after Howard H. Halladay, Mayor of Hanna in 1920. He also served in the House of Commons from 1917 to 1921.

HALSBURY   [21-18-W4]
~ former station north of Brooks.

It was named in 1914 after the Earl of Halsbury (1823-1921), one-time Lord Chancellor of England.

HAMILTON LAKE   [35-9-W4]
~ former station south of Coronation.

It was named after a pioneer settler prior to the construction of the railway. Later it was changed to **THRONE** in 1912 (See: **CONSORT; CORONATION**).

HAMLET   [25-24-W4]
~ former station north of Strathmore.

It was named after William Hamlet, a railway employee of Fort William, who won the *Croix de guerre* in the Great War, in 1922.

HAMLIN   [58-13-W4]
~ former post office northeast of Two Hills.

R. H. Perley, whose mother came from Hamelin, England, suggested the name. The "e" was omitted by postal officials. It was in operation from 1913 to 1981.

HANEYVILLE
~ former station south of Fort Macleod.

It was named in 1898 after a railway official. It was abandoned in 1906 when the Crowsnest Pass line was connected with the Edmonton-Calgary Railway.

HANNA   [31-14-W4]
~ town south of Red Deer.

The community was known as **COOPERVILLE** until 1913. It was renamed in honor of David Blythe Hanna, first president of the Canadian National Railway (1918-1922). He told the story of his career in railroading in *Trains of Recollection* (1924).

The population was 2,539 in 1972 and increased to 2,847 in 2006.

HANTS [21-19-W4]
~ former station west of Bassano.

It was named after Hampshire, one of the southern counties in England. *Hants* is the abbreviation for the "Hampshire".

HAPPY HOLLOW [64-4-W4]
~ former post office north of Bonnyville.

The name expressed the hopes of the pioneer settlers. The post office has been closed for many years.

HARDIEVILLE [9-21-W4]
~ hamlet north of Lethbridge.

It was named in 1910 after W. D. L. Hardie, then superintendent of the Galt Coal Mine, who later became the Mayor of **LETHBRIDGE.**

HARDISTY [43-9-W4]
~ former town south of Edmonton.

This central Alberta community was named in 1906 after Senator Richard Hardisty (1831-1889), who was for many years chief factor of the **EDMONTON** district of the Hudson's Bay Company. Born at a trading post on Lake Nipissing, young Hardisty followed in his father's footsteps and joined the Hudson's Bay Company. In time, he was appointed inspecting chief factor for the northern department. He was called to the Canadian Senate by Prime Minister John A. Macdonald as the first Senator for the district of Alberta. He was drowned in an accident while traveling from Prince Albert to Qu'Appelle by wagon. His niece's husband was Senator Sir James Lougheed.

The population was 626 in 1972 and increased to 761 in 2005.

HARGWEN [52-22-W5]
~ former station south of Edson.

It was named in 1911 after a friend of an official of the Grand Trunk Railway. The post office opened in 1913 and closed in 1916.

HARLECH   [41-14-W5]
~ *former station northwest of Saunders.*

It was probably named after the ancient capital of Merionethshire, Wales. Harlech Castle was built by Edward I in 1285 on a precipice overlooking the sea. The castle is now in ruins. The national Cambrian war-song "The March of the Men of Harlech" is said to have originated during a siege during the Wars of the Roses.

HARMATTAN   [32-4-W5]
~ *former post office west of Olds.*

It was named by the postal department after the "harmattan", a dry, parching land wind, charged with dust that blows out of the Sahara into the Atlantic during the winter months. It had a post office from 1900 to 1966.

HARMON VALLEY   [82-19-W5]
~ *former post office south of Peace River.*

It was named after Daniel Harmon (1778-1843), a fur trader who joined the North West Company in 1800 working for many years in Athabasca and New Caledonia. What is believed to be the original text of his journal was published in *Sixteen Years in Indian Country* (Toronto, 1957). This post office was closed in 1970.

HARRISON   [39-27-W4]
(See: LABUMA)

HARRISVILLE
~ *former community south of Cardston.*

The first Catholic chapel in the extreme southern part of the province was built here in 1899. There are no records about who built it or why it was dedicated to St. Stephen. Like so many other churches in that district of higher winds, it was blown down in 1906.

HARTLEYVILLE [5-27-W4]
~ former post office northwest of Cardston.

It was named in honor of James Hartley, a Fort Macleod butcher and Social Credit MLA for Macleod from 1935 to 1967. After serving as Deputy Speaker of the Legislature, Hartley was appointed in 1955 to Premier Ernest Manning's cabinet as the Minister of Public Works.

HARWICK [25-25-W4]
(See: **ARDENODE**)

HATHERSAGE [58-8-W5]
~ former post office near Barrhead.

It was named in 1910 after the English village of Hathersage in Derbyshire. The name "Hathersage" means "Haefer's edge". "edge" in this context means "edge of a hill, "hill-side" or "an escarpment".

HAVERIGS [44-3-W5]
(See: **HOADLEY**)

HAWKSDALE [25-10-W4]
~ former post office north of Medicine Hat.

It was named in 1913 after the first postmaster, L. W. Hawkins.

HAY LAKES [49-21-W4]
~ village north of Camrose.

It was possibly so named because of the plentiful supply of grass in the region, suitable for cutting as winter fodder.

The population was 203 in 1972 and increased to 327 in 1997.

HAYNES [39-24-W4]
~ hamlet south of Alix.

It was named after Isaac Haynes, one of the first pioneers of the district, who settled here in 1891.

HAYS   [13-4-W4]
~ *hamlet north of Bow Island.*

It is probably named after Charles Melville Hays, president of the Grand Trunk Pacific Railway (now a part of the Canadian National Railway). He perished in the sinking of the *Titanic* in April, 1912.

HAYTER   [39-1-W4]
~ *hamlet east of Provost.*

It was named in 1909 after Reid Hayter, a man whose jobs ranged from Indian Commissioner at Regina, to Manager of Canadian Pacific Hotels. He later became Deputy Superintendent General of Indian Affairs.

HAZELDINE   [53-3-W4]
~ *former post office near Vermilion.*

It was named after the English village Hazeldine, Sussex, so named by a Barr colonist. It had a post office from 1927 to 1975.

HEART LAKE   [34-16-W4]
~ *former post office near Endiang.*

It was named after a nearby heart shaped lake. It was opened in 1914 but has since been closed.

HEATBURG   [39-23-W4]
~ *former station south of Alix.*

It was named in 1922 because of the high temperatures during the summer months. Previously this Canadian National Railway station had been called BULLOCKSVILLE.

HEATH   [44-5-W4]
~ *former post office south of Wainwright.*

It was named in 1908 after the one-time chief official of the Canadian National Railway water department.

HEATHERWOOD   [53-17-W5]
(See: EDSON)

HECTOR [52-7-W4]
~ former post office near Lloydminster.

It was named in 1923 after Private Hector H. Eckford, killed in action in April, 1917, at Vimy Ridge on the Western Front.

HEINSBURG [55-4-W4]
~ hamlet southeast of Elk Point.

It was named after John Heins, the first postmaster in 1913.

HEISLER [43-16-W4]
~ village northeast of Buffalo Lake.

It was named in 1915 after Martin Heisler from whom the townsite was purchased.

The population was 199 in 1972 and decreased to 153 in 2006.

HELDAR [58-7-W5]
~ former post office southeast of Whitecourt.

It was named after a hero of one of Rudyard Kipling's novels *The Light That Failed*.

HELMSDALE{1} [25-6-W4]
~ former post office southwest of Oyen.

It was named after the Scottish town of Helmsdale in Sutherland.

HELMSDALE{2} [28-1-W5]
~ former station north of Calgary.

It is named after the town in Sutherland, Scotland. This name means "valley of the helmet".

HEMARUKA   [32-8-W4]
~ hamlet south of Kirkpatrick Lake.

This name is a compound of Helen, Margaret, Ruth and Kathleen, daughters of an important official of the Canadian National Railway, A. E. Warren. Prior to 1927 the community had been called ZETLAND, after a hamlet of the same name in Huron County, Ontario.

HENRY HOUSE   [46-1-W6]
~ former station north of Jasper.

It was named in 1912 after Alexander Henry (the younger), a Nor'west fur trader. Nephew of Alexander Henry, the elder, he entered the service of the North West Company about 1792 and was a partner by 1802. He is chiefly known through his remarkable journal covering the years 1799-1814, which was edited by Elliot Coues under the title *New Light on the Early History of the Greater Northwest* (3 volumes, 1897). Henry's activities centered upon the post at FORT VERMILION[1], 1808-1811. He built a trading post at the junction of the Miette and Athabasca Rivers near here in 1811, which was referred to as having been abandoned in 1814. He was drowned off Fort George at the mouth of the Columbia River on the Pacific Coast in 1814.

HERCULES   [51-23-W4]
~ former post office southeast of Edmonton.

It was named after E. Hercules Murphy, the first postmaster in 1912.
(See: BRETONA)

HERRONTON   [19-25-W4]
~ hamlet north of Blackie.

It was named in 1912 in honor of John Heron (1852-1936), who was one of the original North West Mounted Police and helped to establish FORT CALGARY in 1874. Later Herron became a wealthy rancher in the PINCHER CREEK district who was elected to the House of Commons in 1904 for the Alberta riding. Four years later he was re-elected as the Member for MACLEOD. He sat in the House for seven years.

HESKETH [29-22-W4]
~ hamlet west of Drumheller.

It was named in 1921 after Colonel J. A. Hesketh, who graduated from the Royal Military College, Kingston, in 1883, and became an important official with the Canadian Pacific Railway. The post office was closed in 1970.

HESPERO [39-4-W5]
~ former post office south of Leslieville.

It is possibly derived from *hesperus*, the Latin word for "the evening star". The post office was called PI COX before 1916. It closed in 1960.

HIGH LEVEL [110-19-W5]
~ a new town on the Mackenzie Highway, north of Fort Vermilion.

It is the jumping off place for the oil-fields at **RAINBOW LAKE** and **ZAMA CITY** as well as being the most northerly bulk-grain shipping center in North America. It was incorporated in 1965.

The population was 2,400 in 1972 and increased to 3,887 in 2006.

HIGH PRAIRIE [74-17-W5]
~ town west of Lesser Slave Lake.

It was so named in 1910 from the nature of the surrounding country.

The population was 2,561 in 1972 and increased to 2,836 in 2007.

HIGH RIVER [19-28-W4]
~ town south of Calgary.

The name refers to the fact that the nearby Highwood River is on nearly the same level as the prairie instead of in a valley, which is much more common in Alberta. As a result, the belt of timber along the stream is much "higher" than usual and is visible for a great distance.

The population was 2,621 in 1972 and increased to 11,346 in 2009.

HIGHLAND PARK   [82-6-W6]
~ former post office north of Fairview.

It was possibly named by nostalgic Scots after their homeland.

HIGHVALE   [51-4-W5]
~ former post office south of Wabamun Lake.

It was so called on the suggestion of the first postmaster, A. C. Brook, who had come from Highgate in Ontario. The post office was in operation from 1909 to 1970.

HILDA   [17-1-W4]
~ hamlet north of Medicine Hat.

It was so named in 1910. The girl's name "Hilda" is from the Old German word meaning "battle maiden" and was the name of the chief of the Valkyries in Scandinavian mythology.

HILL END   [35-27-W4]
~ location north of Innisfail.

A range of hills terminates near this abandoned settlement. The post office was opened in 1902 and closed in 1928.

HILL SPRING   [4-27-W4]
~ village north of Cardston.

It was so named in 1911. The water from a spring on a nearby, hill is piped into the community.

HILLCREST   [7-3-W5]
~ mining community east of Blairmore.

It was named after Charles P. Hill, owner of the Hillcrest Coal and Coke Company. Post Hill in the State of Idaho is also named in his honor. One of the worst mining disasters in Canadian history occurred at No. 1 Mine of Hillcrest Collieries in June, 1914. A total of 189 persons were killed following an explosion in the mine.

The population in 1972 was 551. (See: **CROWSNEST PASS**)

HILLIARD   [54-17-W4]
~ hamlet north of Beaverhill Lake.

It was named after Hilliard McConkey, a pioneer settler in 1905.

HILLSDOWN   [38-25-W4]
~ former post office east of Red Deer.

It was named in 1902 because to the north and south of this community there are "hills" with "downs" on the east and west. "Downs" in this connection can be defined as a tract of open upland, often undulating and covered with fine turf for the grazing of sheep. It closed in 1967.

HINDVILLE   [48-5-W4]
~ former post office south of Vermilion.

It was named in 1909 after the first postmaster, Thomas Hind. It was in operation from 1909 to 1906.

HINES CREEK   [83-4-W6]
~ village north of Fairview.

It was named after a nearby stream that flows into the Peace River.

The population was 428 in 1972 and increased to 430 in 2006.

HINTON   [51-24-W5]
~ town west of Edmonton.

It was named after the Hinton Trail from **JASPER** to the Yukon, which in turn was called after W. D. Hinton, sometime General Manager of the Grand Trunk Pacific Railway. This community went through three booms in sixty years. It became a thriving center in 1910 when the Grand Trunk Pacific line reached the Rockies. In 1929, a coal mining operation here meant a population of 2,000 persons, but an explosion wrecked the mine and HINTON became a ghost town. It was reduced to a whistle stop of 180 people. The third boom came in 1955 when a multi-million dollar pulp and paper industry was established on the broad Athabasca valley.

The population was 4,690 in 1972 and increased to 9,825 in 2009.

HIRAM [34-11-W4]
~ former post office near Hanna.

The name is Jewish in origin. In the Bible, King Hiram of Tyre aided Solomon in building the temple by furnishing cedar, fir trees, and workmen. Today when used as a Christian name, it is usually associated with the Mormons. The post office was opened in 1916.

HOADLEY [44-3-W5]
~ former post office south of Pigeon Lake.

It was named in honor of George Hoadley, a United Farmers Cabinet Minister for fourteen years. Born in Cumberland, England, in 1866, Hoadley came to Canada in 1890. He settled at Sheep Creek, south of Calgary, where he became a successful rancher. He was first elected to the Legislature as a Conservative Member for Okotoks in 1909. Twelve years later he was named to Premier Greenfield's Cabinet as Minister of Agriculture and later was appointed the Minister of Health. He was descended from Dr. Hoadley, Court Physician to George II. The name *Hoadley*, which is English in origin, means "dweller on the heath". Before 1924, the community was called HAVERIGS. The post office was closed in 1969.

HOBBEMA [44-24-W4]
~ hamlet south of Wetaskiwin.

It was named in 1893 after the seventeenth century Dutch landscape painter, Meyndert Hobbema. His subjects were the woods, fields, farmhouses, streams and especially the water mills of the country around his native Amsterdam. The painting generally considered his masterpiece is "The Avenue in Middleharnis", now in the National Gallery, London

HOLBORN [51-1-W5].
~ former post office near Thorsby.

It was named in 1913 after a pioneer homesteader, Charles Holborn. It was in operation from 1913 to 1965.

HOLDEN   [49-16-W4]
~ village south of Beaverhill Lake.

It was named in 1907 after James Bismark Holden, who was elected Liberal member of the first Alberta Legislature for Vegreville where he conducted a real estate business. Holden served two terms in the provincial house, from 1905 until 1913. The previous name was VERMILION VALLEY.

The population was 503 in 1972 and decreased to 398 in 2006.

HOLLOW LAKE   [61-19-W4]
~ former post office north of Smoky Lake.

It was named after a nearby body of water which is located in a hollow. The post office was closed in 1970.

HOLMSTEAD   [44-6-W4]
(See: **GREENSHIELDS**)

HOLMSTOWN   [43-11-W4]
(See: **LOUGHEED**)

HOLT CITY   [28-16-W5]
(See: **LAKE LOUISE**)

HOLYOKE   [59-5-W4]
~ former post office south of Bonnyville.

The name originally meant a "holy oak tree". The ancient Druids worshipped the mistletoe that grows on oak. There are two towns in the United States called "Holyoke".

HOMEGLEN   [44-1-W4]
~ former post office near Wainwright.

It was named in 1909 on the suggestion of an early settler, James Burns. The name was descriptive of the location in a pleasant valley.

HOMESTEAD   [75-9-W6]
~ former post office west of Saddle Hills.

The word came into general use in Canada after the Free Land Homestead Act of 1872, under which the west was largely settled. A homestead was typically a quarter-section of 160 acres of land which the homesteader was required to occupy and improve by clearing the wood growth, or breaking the sod where the land was open prairie.

HONDO   [70-1-W5]
~ former post office south of Lesser Slave Lake.

This Spanish word is the name of the metal eye of a lariat. It is also used to describe a broad, low-lying gully in the American southwest. The post office was opened in 1914.

HOPE VALLEY   [46-4-W4]
~ former post office north of Wainwright.

The name is descriptive of the optimism of the early pioneers when the area was opened up for settlement in 1911. It had a post office that closed in 1948.

HORBURG   [40-9-W5]
~ former station north of Rocky Mountain House.

It was so named in 1914. At one time the community ranked as a village.

HORSEGUARDS   [39-5-W5]
~ near Rocky Mountain House.

It is thought that an early homesteader had been a member of the Royal Horse Guards. (See: **ALHAMBRA**)

HORSEHILLS CREEK   [54-23-W4]
~ the horse-guard or wintering ranch of the Hudson's Bay Company near Edmonton.

The livestock of the trading post was wintered here. In 1891, one hundred quarter-sections in the district were reserved by the Ottawa government for re-settlement of Germans who were abandoning their homesteads near Medicine Hat and moving north to start farming again.

HORTONBURG   [53-22-W4]
(See: **BREMNER**)

HOSELAW   [60-6-W4]
~ former post office south of Bonnyville.

It was named in 1913 after Loch Hoselaw in Roxburghshire, Scotland.

HOTCHKISS   [93-23-W5]
~ hamlet near Manning.

It is possibly named after Benjamin Hotchkiss (1826-1885), the American inventor and manufacturer of the machine gun. But more likely after C. P. Hotchkiss, a federal land surveyor. It was named in 1915.

HOWIE   [22-10-W4]
~ former post office north of Brooks.

It was named after James Howie, the first postmaster. It was opened in 1913 but has since been closed.

HUALLEN   [71-9-W6]
~ former post office south of Beaverlodge.

It was named after Hugh Allen (1889-1972) who was the Minister of Municipal Affairs and Lands and Mines in Premier Richard Reid's Cabinet. He sat in the Legislature from 1926 to 1935 as the U.F.A. member for **GRANDE PRAIRIE**.

HUB   [37-13-W4]
~ hamlet near Castor.

This community of pioneer settlers believed there was a great future for HUB - the hub of a wheel that spikes ended in what were to be only smaller cities such as **CALGARY**, **RED DEER**, **EDMONTON**, Saskatoon and Regina. A prospective and a detailed map were broadcasted across the continent and the United Kingdom. Advertisements were placed in prominent Ontario daily newspapers.

Then something happened! For some unknown reason the community name was changed to **FLEET**. Which fleet it honors is vague. Maybe it was the British Navy, or the nearer Canadian Pacific Railway North Atlantic ocean steamships.

There was a post office from 1912 to 1972. Fleet, the former Hub of the Canadian Western prairies is now a mere hamlet.

HUGGETT   [50-1-W5]
~ former post office north of Thorsby.

It was named in 1925 after the postmaster, J. Huggett. "Huggett" is a variant of the diminutive of the name Hugh, which means "inspiration sent from heaven".

HUNKA   [57-16-W4]
(See: **SNIATYN**)

HURRY   [48-14-W4]
It was so named by early settlers. Ottawa officials did not approve of this unofficial name and in 1909 changed it.
(See: **BRUCE**)

HUSSAR   [24-20-W4]
~ village south of Standard.

It was named in 1913 in honor of early German settlers in the district, many of whom had served in a regiment of the Kaiser's hussars. Originally the name "hussar" was given to soldiers belonging to a corps of light horse raised by the King of Hungary in 1458 to fight against the Turks.

The population was 167 in 1972 and increased to 187 in 2006.

HUTTON [24-14-W4]
~ former post office south of Coleman Lake.

It was named after the manager of the Northern Crown Bank, **CALGARY**, through whose influence a loan was granted to buy a townsite. The word "Hutton" means "village on the spur of a hill". Once the community was called FIELDHOLME. The post office was opened in 1911 but has since been closed.

HUXLEY [34-23-W4]
~ hamlet north of Olds.

It was named in 1907 after Thomas Huxley (1825-1895), noted British biologist whose speculations on philosophy and religion led him to a powerful advocacy of the principal of agnosticism. He was a friend of Charles Darwin, author of *The Origin of the Species*. Huxley found in Darwin's theory an intelligible hypothesis on which to base a study of evolution.

HYLO [66-15-W4]
~ hamlet south of Lac La Biche.

The post office was opened in 1914. "Hylo" is a farm term. The word is of Greek origin, meaning "wood".

HYTHE [73-11-W6]
~ village north of Beaverlodge.

It was so named in 1914 after the English town of Hythe in Kent, which is one of the Cinque Ports. The name is derived from the Old English word for "landing place".

The population was 497 in 1992 and increased to 821 in 2006.

I

IDAMAY   [33-7-W4]
~ former post office west of Grassy Island Lake.

This name appears to be formed by the combining of the two girls names, Ida and May. It operated from 1929 to 1959.

IDDESLEIGH   [20-10-W4]
~ former hamlet north of Brooks.

This community was named in 1914 in honor of Sir Stafford Henry Northcote, first Earl of Iddesleigh (1818-1887), who was the chairman of the Hudson's Bay Company during one of the most important times of the existence of the famous fur trading company. He was the son of the seventh Baronet of Pynes, in the county of Devon, and on graduating from Oxford, became the private secretary of William Gladstone, the great Liberal statesman. He was in charge of the detailed arrangements for the Great Exhibition of 1851. He was returned to the House of Commons at Westminster in 1855, and became a Cabinet Minister in Lord Derby's third government eleven years later as the president of the Board of Trade. He was elected chairman of the Hudson's Bay Company in 1869, a position he held for the next five years. He persuaded the company to accept 300,000 pounds in return for the transfer of the vast Prince Rupert's Land to the Canadian government. Alberta was created from part of this territory in 1905. Northcote was appointed Chancellor of the Exchequer in Disraeli's ministry in 1874. He became leader of the Conservatives in the House of Commons when Disraeli became a Lord.

ILLINGWORTH   [13-11-W4]
~ former station north of Bow Island.

It was named in 1914 after W. J. Illingworth, sometime director of the Canadian Pacific Railway.

IMRIE [53-8-W5]
(See: **STYAL**)

INDIAN BATTLE PARK [9-21-W4]
~ located on the Oldman River at Lethbridge.

This park marks the site of the last inter-tribal Indian battle fought on the North American continent in 1870. *The Ottawa Free Press* (April 9, 1871), states: "Latest Saskatchewan advice brings the intelligence of a fight between Cree and Blackfoot Indians in which many of the former were killed at long range by breech-loading rifles. The Crees were not aware that their enemies had been furnished with so deadly a weapon. The rifles had been furnished by American traders."

INDIAN CABINS [125-18-W5]
~ hamlet on the Mackenzie Highway east of Cameron Hills.

This isolated community is close to the boundary of the Northwest Territories.
The population in 1972 was 63.

INDUS [22-28-W4]
~ hamlet south of Langdon.

It was named in 1914, probably after the Indus, one of the sacred rivers of India.

INNISFAIL [35-28-W4]
~ town south of Red Deer River.

It was named in 1893 after the Scottish village in Argyllshire. Previously it was called POPLAR GROVE.
The population was 2,436 in 1972 and increased to 7,883 in 2009.

INNISFREE [51-11-W4]
~ village west of Mannville.

It is called after the summer residence of Sir Edmund Walker, president of the Canadian Bank of Commerce. The post office was called DELNORTE until 1909. The name in Irish, *Inis Fraoigh*, means "Heather Island".

W. B. Yeats' early poem, "The Lake Isle of Innisfree", popularized the name:

I will arise and go now, and go to Innisfree,
  nd a small cabin build there, of clay and wattles made:
Nine bean-rows will I have there, a hive for the honeybee.
  nd live alone in the bee-loud glade.

The population was 234 in 1972 and decreased to 233 in 2006.

INVERSNAY [11-10-W4]
~ former station near Bow Island

It was named in 1912 after the Inversnaid, a stream that flows into Loch Lomond, Scotland.

INVERSNAID   G. M. Hopkins

This darksome burn, horseback brown,
His rollrock highroad roaring down,
In coop and in comb the fleece of his foam
Flutes and low to the lake falls home.

A windpuff-bonnet of fawn-froth
Turns and twindles over the broth
Of a pool so pitchblack, fell-frowning,
It rounds and rounds Despair to drowning.

Degged with dew, dappled with dew
Are the groins of the braes that the brook treads through.
Wiry heathpacks, flitches of fern,
And the beadbonny ash that sits over the burn.

What would the world be, once bereft
Of wet and of wildness? Let them be left,
O let them be left, wildness and wet;
Long live the weeds and the wilderness yet.

IOLA [44-4-W5]
~ former post office near Red Deer.

There are several post offices of this name in the United States. Prior to 1909 the community was called EDNAVILLE.

IOSEGUN LAKE [62-19-W5]
~ hamlet near the Mackenzie Highway.

It was named after a nearby lake. *Iosegun* is a Cree word meaning "tail".
(See: **FOX CREEK**)

IRETON [49-25-W4]
~ former station west of Jasper.

General Henry Ireton (1611-1651) was a son-in-law of Oliver Cromwell.

IRMA [45-9-W4]
~ village west of Wainwright.

It was named in 1909 after Irma, the daughter of W. Wainwright, a vice-president of the Grand Trunk Pacific Railway.
The population was 436 in 1972 and increased to 444 in 2006.

IRON RIVER [63-6-W4]
~ former post office northwest of Bonnyville.

The name is descriptive, there being iron ore deposits on the river banks.

IRON SPRINGS [11-20-W4]
~ hamlet north of Lethbridge.

It derives its name from mineral springs in the Blackspring Ridge, which are high in iron content. The post office was opened in 1908.

IRRICANA [27-26-W4]
~ village north of Calgary.

This community is located on a Canadian Pacific irrigation canal. The name is a compound of "irrigation" and "canal". This community is on or near the site of the "slaughter camp" of Captain John Palliser (August, 1859), where the expedition killed seventeen buffalo.
The population was 126 in 1972, and increased to 1,243 in 2006.

IRVINE   [11-2-W4]
~ *town south of Medicine Hat.*

It was named in honor of Colonel A. Irvine, Commissioner of the North West Mounted Police (1880-1886).

The population was 209 in 1972 and increased to 326 in 1997.

IRWINVILLE   [53-4-W4]
~ *former post office near Lloydminster.*

It was named after J. Samuel Irwin, the first postmaster, in 1908. It was in operation from 1908 to 1927.

ISLAY   [51-4-W4]
~ *hamlet north of Vermilion.*

It was named in 1905 after Islay, in Scotland, on the suggestion of the Gilchrist family who were early settlers in the district. Professor W. J. Watson says that *islay* is old Celtic for "swollen place".

ISPAS   [56-13-W4]
~ *former post office north of Two Hills.*

It was named in 1911 after the birthplace in Bukovina of the first postmaster, N. Pawliuk. The name is Ukrainian and means "(God) the Savior".

ITASKA BEACH   [47-1-W5]
~ *summer village on the north shore of Pigeon Lake.*

It was incorporated in 1953. It's name comes from the Cree and means "edge of the woods".

The population was given as two in 1972 and increased to 35 in 2006.

J

JACKSON COULEE   [46-10-W4]
(See: JARROW)

JAMES RIVER BRIDGE   [34-5-W5]
~ former post office northwest of Olds.

It was named after the tributary of the Red Deer River, which in turn was named after the Stony Indian Chief, James Dixon, who signed Treaty Number Seven in 1877. It was opened in 1916.

JAMIESON   [9-18-W4]
~ former station near Medicine Hat.

It was named after R. R. Jamieson and J. L. Jamieson, two railway executives. On a 1916 map it was called NIEDPATH.

JANET   [24-28-W4]
~ former station east of Calgary.

An English feminine form of the Christian name "John". It was so named in 1914.

JARROW   [46-10-W4]
~ hamlet north of Hardisty.

It was named in 1919 possibly after the Monastery of Jarrow in the north of England, founded in 681 A. D., which was the home of the Venerable Bede. When the post office was opened it was called JACKSON COULEE after the first postmaster. In 1909 the name was changed to **JUNKINS** post office.

JASPER   [45-1-W6]
~ town west of Edmonton, in Jasper National Park.

It was named after Jasper House, which was a North West Company's trading post in charge of Jasper Hawes, in 1817. The post was in existence in 1814 when François Decoigne was in charge. The park was set aside in 1907 by the federal government for the perpetual use, benefit and enjoyment of the people. It contains 4,000 square miles, and is the largest of the fourteen federal reservations for park purposes. It is historic ground, many early explorers having passed this way to the Pacific, among them Alexander Mackenzie, David Thompson and Simon Fraser.
(See: **DECOIGNE**)

JASPER PLACE   [53-25-W5]
~ former town and now a suburb of Edmonton.

It was amalgamated into the city in 1960.

JAYDOT   [3-1-W4]
~ former station near Wild Horse.

It was named in 1922 after a large nearby ranch.

JEAN CÔTÉ   [79-22-W5]
~ hamlet north of Fahler.

It was named after Senator Jean Leon Côté (1867-1924), who was an active promoter of the Alberta coal industry. He sat for twelve years in the Alberta Legislature, three of them as the Provincial Secretary. He died only months after being named to the Senate.

JEFFERSON   [1-24-W4]
~ former station south of Cardston.

Thomas Jefferson (1743-1826) was the author of the Declaration of Independence and the third President of the United States. Several American cities are named in his honor.

JEFFREY **[59-24-W4]**
~ former post office southeast of Westlock.

It was named in 1922 after the first postmaster, Jeffrey Garon. It was in operation until 1961.

JENNER **[20-9-W4]**
~ hamlet north of Brooks.

It was named in 1913 after Dr. Edward Jenner (1749-1823), famous physician. Previously it was called WEBSDALE post office.

JETHSON **[26-12-W4]**
(See: **CAROLSIDE**)

JOFFRE **[39-25-W4]**
~ hamlet north of Red Deer.

It was named in 1918 after Marshal J. J. C. Joffre, Commander-in-Chief of the Allied army 1915-1917. The station previously had been called **BROOKSLEY**.

JOHN D'OR PRAIRIE **[109-7-W5]**
~ Indian Reserve east of Fort Vermilion.

It is located 550 miles northwest of Edmonton. The post office opened in 1971.

JOSEPHSBURG **[54-21-W4]**
It was named after a town in Galicia. The first settlers in the district were from this part of the Austro-Hungarian Empire. The Emperor Frans Joseph reigned from 1848-1916.

JOUSSARD **[73-13-W5]**
~ former station south of Lesser Slave Lake.

It was named in 1945 to honor an Oblate missionary, Father Celestin Joussard (1851-1932), who worked for fifty years in northern Alberta and the Northwest Territories.

JUDAH   [82-22-W5]
~ former station south of Peace River.

It was named in 1916 after Noel F. Judah, former auditor of the Edmonton, Dunvegan and British Columbia Railway Company. The post office opened in 1928.

JUDSON   [6-18-W4]
~ former station north of Raymond.

It was named in 1914 after a local businessman, Judson Bemis, of Bemis Bag Company.

JUDY CREEK   [63-10-W5]
~ hamlet near Swan Hills.

It is named after a nearby stream, which flows into the Freeman River.

JUNE   [40-26-W4]
~ former station northeast of Lacombe.

Possibly named after the sixth month of the year, when the railway siding was completed.

JUNKINS   [46-10-W4]
~ former village near Barrhead.

So named in 1910 after the vice-president of Westinghouse, Church, Kerr and Company. Previously the community was called **JARROW**.

JUNO   [10-12-W4]
~ former station east of Bow Island.

It was named in 1894 after Juno, the Roman mythological queen of the sky. Her Greek name was *Hera*. As the suspicious wife of Jupiter, she was imagined to be jealous and demanding, even willing to overthrow her husband if she could. Her faithfulness to her marriage vows and her disapproval of all who lived loosely outside of wedlock became proverbial.

K

KAHWIN   [58-16-W4]
~ former post office south of Smoky Lake.

The Canadian Geographic Board states this word is Sioux Indian for "No", expressive of the opposition to the original name proposed, OSTASIK, which is Ukrainian. However, MacGregor in *Vilni Zemli* says *kahwin* is a Slavic word denoting "peace" and "harmony". It operated from 1912 to 1969.

KALELAND   [55-13-W4]
~ former post office near Two Hills.

It was probably named by Scottish settlers. "Kale" is a type of cabbage which can stand the severe Scottish winters. "Kyle yard" is a Scottish term for "cabbage patch". It opened in 1914 and closed in 1957.

KANANASKIS   [24-8-W5]
~ park lodge, south of Calgary.

It is named after the Kananaskis River that flows north into the Bow River. Palliser says he named KANANASKIS PASS after "an Indian of whom there is a legend, giving an account of his most wonderful recovery from the blow of an axe, which had stunned but failed to kill him, and the river which flows through this gorge also bears his name".

KANOUSE'S POST
(See: FORT BERRY)

KANSAS   [30-3-W5]
(See: WESTCOTT)

KAPASIWIN   **[53-3-W5]**
~ *summer village north of Edmonton.*

This is the Cree word for "camp". It has a winter population of ten.

KATHLEEN   **[76-19-W5]**
~ *former station west of Winagami Lake.*

It was so named in 1915 after a relative of W. R. Smith, former General Manager of the Edmonton, Dunvegan and British Columbia Railway.

KATHRYN   **[26-27-W4]**
~ *hamlet north of Calgary.*

The Canadian National Railway so named it in 1913 after Kathryn McKay, daughter of Neil McKay, a large local landowner.

KAVANAGH   **[48-25-W4]**
~ *hamlet south of Edmonton.*

It was named in 1911 after Charles Edmund Kavanagh, then superintendent of Railway Mail Service in Winnipeg. It had a post office from 1925 to 1980.

KAYDEE
~ *hamlet north of Mountain Park in the Coal Branch district.*

The origin of this name is unknown.

KEEPHILLS   **[51-3-W5]**
~ *former post office south of Wabamun Lake.*

This name was suggested by George H. Collins, the postmaster in 1913, after a place in Buckinghamshire, England. The Old English *ceap* means "market-place".

KEG RIVER [101-23-W5]
~ former post office near Keg River.

It is named after a northern Alberta river that flows east into the Peace. A "keg" is a small barrel, usually less than ten gallons, that was widely used by fur traders. The word is Icelandic in origin. It is one of the most northerly settlements in the province.

KEHEEWIN [59-6-W4]
~ Cree Indian Reserve near St. Paul.

It was named in honor of Chief Keheewin, who signed Treaty Number Seven of 1877. The Chief was named after the "eagle" (*kehew* in Cree). As a young man, he distinguished himself by his bravery in many fights with the Blackfoot and became a Chief in early in life. Later, he was converted to Christianity. He died in 1887 at Onion Lake, Saskatchewan.

KEITH [25-2-W5]
~ former station north of Calgary.

It was so named in 1884 by Donald Smith, Lord Strathcona, after Keith in Banffshire, Scotland, close to where he had been born in 1820.

KELSEY [45-18-W4]
~ hamlet south of Camrose.

It was named in 1916 after Moses S. Kelsey, who came from Millbank in the State of South Dakota, and homesteaded here in 1901 on the quarter-section on which the station was later located.

(The) KEMMIS RANCH [9-26-W4]
~ on Tod Creek near Fort Macleod.

It was named after Captain John G. Kemmis, who commenced ranching in 1883. He was a pioneer rancher. Later his son, John Henry William Shore Kemmis (1867-1942), managed the family ranch. He sat in the Legislature as the spokesman for the Southern Alberta ranchers from 1911 to 1921.

KEMPTON
(See: **GOODFARE**)

KENEX
(See: **AKENSTADT**)

KENZIE   [75-18-W5]
~ former station west of Winagami Lake.

It was opened in 1915. "Kenzie" is a form of the Scottish name "Mackenzie", which in Gaelic means "son of the fair".

KEOMA   [26-27-W4]
~ hamlet north of Calgary.

It was so called in 1910 and is the Indian word for "over there" and "far away".

KERENSKY   [58-22-W4]
~ former station south of Smoky Lake.

It was named in 1920 after the Russian politician, Alexander Fedorovich Kerensky (1881-1970), the Provisional President of Russia after the fall of Czar Nicholas and before the outbreak of the Bolshevik Revolution. Son of a schoolmaster, Kerensky became a socialist as a young man and also a lawyer. He was the defense counsel for several revolutionaries in the days prior to the War. He was elected to the Duma as a labor deputy in 1912. During the early years of the war, he persistently called for democratic reforms to give the army an incentive to fight. He was only in power from July to November 1917.

KERNDALE   [83-24-W5]
~ former post office near Calgary.

It was named in 1912, possibly after the English village of Kersey in Suffolk.

KESSLER   [38-8-W4]
~ former post office northeast of Coronation.

There is a community in the State of Montana called Kessler, which is named after an honored and well-known pioneer of Helena. It was open from 1911 to 1966.

KETCHUM [82-1-W6]
(See: **LILIENDALE**)

KEVISVILLE [35-4-W5]
~ *post office southwest of Sylvan Lake.*

It was named in 1910 after the first postmaster, Charles W. Kevis. It was open until 1962.

KEW RANCH [20-3-W5]
~ *former post office northwest of Turner Valley.*

A Mr. Quirk used the letter "Q" as his brand. He was an early rancher.

KEYSTONE [48-3-W5]
~ *former post office west of Leduc.*

It was named when a post office was opened. In 1927 the name was changed to **BRETON** , after an early homesteader and Member of the Legislature.

KIKINO [63-14-W4]
~ *hamlet north of Smoky Lake.*

The origin of this name is the Cree word "home".

KILLARNEY LAKE [41-1-W4]
~ *former post office near Provost.*

It was opened in 1912, and probably named after the famous lake in Ireland.

KILLAM   [44-13-W4]
~ town northwest of Hardisty.

It was named in 1906 after Albert Clement Killam (1849-1908), Judge of the Supreme Court of Canada. Born in Yarmouth, Nova Scotia, he was educated at the University of Toronto. He practiced law first at Windsor, Ontario, and then at Winnipeg. Killam represented South Winnipeg in the Manitoba Legislature in the 1880's before he was appointed a Judge. In 1899 he became Chief Justice of Manitoba, and four years later was named to the Supreme Court. In 1905 Killam left the bench to become the first Chief Commissioner of the Board of Railway Commissioners for Canada.

The population was 878 in 1972 and increased to 1,019 in 2006.

KILSYTH   [65-2-W5]
~ former station southwest of Westlock.

It was named in 1914 after the Scottish town in Stirlingshire. Professor W. J. Watson connects this name to a Saint Syth. "Kil", Gaelic *ceall*, means "church". Thus the name could mean "Church of St. Syth".

KIMBALL   [1-24-W4]
~ hamlet south of Cardston.

It was named in 1903 after Heber C. Kimball, an early Mormon pioneer. Previously the community was called COLLES.

KINGMAN   [49-19-W4]
~ hamlet north of Camrose.

It was named in 1907 after the first postmaster, F. W. Kingsbury.

KININVIE   [16-11-W4]
~ former station south of Brooks.

It was named in 1884 after Kininvie House in Banffshire, Scotland.

KINMUNDY **[24-8-W4]**
~ former post office northeast of Brooks.

It was named in 1913 after Kinmundy in the state of Illinois, the former home of the first postmaster, Walter Flagg. There is also a Kinmundy in Aberdeen, Scotland. It is the Gaelic word for "at the head of the hill".

KINNOULL **[65-22-W4]**
(See: **COLINTON**)

KINSELLA **[46-11-W4]**
~ hamlet south of Viking.

It was named in 1910 after the private secretary of the vice-president of the Grand Trunk Railway.

KINUSO **[73-10-W5]**
~ village south of Lesser Slave Lake.

This community was originally known as SWAN RIVER, but was renamed in 1915. *Kinuso* is the Cree word for "fish".

The population was 376 in 1972 and decreased to 254 in 1997.

KIPP **[9-22-W4]**
~ hamlet northwest of Lethbridge.

It was named after FORT KIPP which had been built on the north bank of the Oldman River, above the Belly River, by an early American whiskey trader, Joseph Kipp. Born at Fort Union, an American Fur Company trading post at the mouth of the Yellowstone River, Kipp came to Canada in the 1860's to sell whiskey to the Indians in exchange for furs. Commissioner French of the North West Mounted Police found FORT KIPP in September, 1874, to consist of "three log huts without roofs".

PRAIRIE VIEW was the name of the post office until 1910.

KIPPENVILLE **[2-12-W4]**
~ former post office near Medicine Hat.

It was named in 1913 after the first postmaster, D. Kippen.

KIRKCALDY   **[16-24-W4]**
~ *hamlet north of Carmangay.*

It was named in 1911 after the Scottish town. The post office was closed in 1970.

KIRKPATRICK   **[29-21-W4]**
~ *hamlet north of Drumheller.*

It was named in 1921 after W. M. Kirkpatrick, an important official of the Canadian Pacific Railway. The name means "Church of Saint Patrick".

KIRON   **[45-19-W4]**
~ *former station south of Camrose.*

It was so named in 1916, possibly after a town in the State of Iowa.

KIRRIEMUIR   **[34-3-W4]**
~ *hamlet north of Grassy Lake.*

It was named in 1914 after the Scottish town of Kirriemuir in Angus. It is the Gaelic word for "big quarter" or "division".

KITSCOTY   **[50-3-W4]**
~ *village west of Lloydminster.*

It was named in 1905 after Coty House in Kent, England. This dolmen is the chamber of a long barrow, which has two uprights and a capstone.

The population was 342 in 1972 and increased to 808 in 2009.

KLESKUN HILL   **[72-4-W6]**
~ *former post office near Grande Prairie.*

The name is the Beaver Indian word for "white mud". The hill is visible for a long distance.

KNAPPEN [1-11-W4]
~ former post office south of Foremost.

It was named in 1913 after the Knappen family, who were early homesteaders in the district.

KNEE HILL [29-20-W4]
~ hamlet west of Elnora.

The name is descriptive of the shape of a nearby hill. It had a post office from 1894 to 1969.

KNOB HILL [46-3-W5]
~ former post office near Rocky Mountain House.

The post office was opened in 1914. The name is descriptive, there being many "knobs" and hills in the vicinity.

KNOLLTON [44-15-W4]
(See: **STROME**)

KOOTUK [39-3-W5]
(See: **ECKVILLE**)

KRAKOW [55-17-W4]
~ former post office east of Lamont.

It was named after the second largest city and ancient capital of Poland, Crakow. Though it is in an area surrounded by Ukrainian settlers, the name was chosen by a few Poles who took the lead in obtaining the post office in 1904. The first postmistress was Anna Humutka.

KRUGERVILLE [39-19-W4]
~ hamlet near Stettler.

Probably named after the great Boer leader "Oom Paul" Kruger (1825-1904). As a child he went on the Great Trek from Cape Colony to the area north of the Orange River, and later, he was the president of Transvaal Republic (1883-1900).

KSITUAN   [79-7-W6]
~ former post office north of Spirit River.

It was named after the Ksituan River, which flows into the Peace. It is an Indian word meaning "swift current".

L

LA CALMETTE **[58-26-W4]**
~ former post office near Barrhead.

It is the French word for "calm".

LA COREY **[63-6-W4]**
~ former post office north of Bonnyville.

It was opened in 1917. It appears to be the French definite article and the French surname "Corey".

LA CRÊTE **[106-15-W5]**
~ hamlet near Fort Vermilion.

This may be a descriptive name; it is the French for "crest". This is a Mennonite settlement.
The population in 1972 was 246.

LA GLACE **[74-8-W6]**
~ former post office near Beaverlodge.

The name is the French word for "ice". The post office was opened in 1917.

LABUMA **[39-27-W4]**
~ former station northwest of Red Deer.

The origin of this name is not known. It's previous name was **HARRISON**.

LAC BELLEVUE **[59-9-W4]**
~ former post office near St. Paul.

This descriptive name is the French for "the lake with the beautiful view". It was opened in 1915. It was in operation from 1915 to 1955.

LAC CANARD   [57-9-W4]
~ former post office near St. Paul.

It was opened in 1917. *Canard* is the French word for "duck". There were many wild fowls in the district when the first settlers arrived.

LAC CARDINAL   [84-25-W5]
~ former post office near Peace River.

It was opened in 1924 and named after Louis Cardinal, a pioneer settler.

LAC LA BICHE   [67-13-W4]
~ town north of Edmonton.

Its name is the French form of "Red Deer Lake", which name occurs on Turner's map of 1790. It was on the fur traders way to the far north.

The population was 1,743 in 1972, and increased to 9,123 in 2006.

LAC LA NONNE   [57-3-W5]
~ former post office east of Majeau Lake.

It appears as LAC LA NONNE in Edward Ermatigner's journal, May 18, 1827. In Cree, *mi-ka-sioo* means "eagle". As related to A. D. Henderson of **BELVEDERE**, Alberta, the lake owes its name to a duck, the white-winged scoter (*oidemia deglandi*). The species is very common on this northern Alberta lake. The birds are black with white wing bars and a white spot on the head, suggesting a black-robed nun. This explanation seems doubtful. The post office was opened in 1908.

LAC STE. ANNE [54-3-W5]
~ first mission west of St. Albert.

It is named after a nearby lake. This is the Manito Lake mentioned by David Thompson. The present name dates from 1844 when Father Jean Baptiste Thibault founded one of the first Catholic missions on the western prairies here. It is ST. ANN on Palliser's Map of 1865. Saint Ann was the mother of the Blessed Virgin Mary, whose feast date is July 26. Many Christian Indians annually go on a pilgrimage to LAC STE ANNE towards the end of July. It was a place of pilgrimage before the coming of the Europeans; the waters of this lake are believed to have healing properties.

LACOMBE [40-26-W4]
~ town north of Red Deer.

It was so named in 1893 after Father Albert Lacombe, OMI (1827-1916), who came to the western Canadian prairies in 1852 and spent the greatest part of his life there in evangelical work among the Indians and Metis. In 1874, his standard *Dictionnaire de la Langue des Cris* was published at Montreal, a work begun during his first winter (1852-53) at Edmonton. He used his influence to prevent Blackfoot Indians from joining Louis Riel in the Northwest Rebellion in 1885.

The population was 3,228 in 1972 and increased to 10,507 in 2008. (See: **CALGARY-EDMONTON TRAIL STAGING POSTS; BARNETT'S STOPPING HOUSE**)

LAFOND [57-10-W4]
~ hamlet south of St. Paul.

It was named after C. B. Lafond, the first postmaster in 1907.

LAGGAN [28-16-W5]
(See: **LAKE LOUISE**)

LAKE ELIZA [56-8-W4]
~ former post office southeast of St. Paul.

This name is a Swedish form of "Elizabeth". Swedish settlers homesteaded in this district.

LAKE ISLE   **[54-5-W5]**
~ former post office north of Isle Lake.

It got its name from the nearby lake. Prior to 1915 the post office was called SHEARWATER.

LAKE GENEVA   **[52-8-W4]**
(See: GENEVA)

LAKE LOUISE   **[28-16-W5]**
~ Banff National Park winter resort.

It got its present name from the beautiful mountain lake. Formerly the community was known as HOLT CITY(1883). Then the name was changed to LAGGAN (1883-1916), on the suggestion of Lord Strathcona after Laggan, a highland hamlet in Inverness, Scotland. It is Gaelic for "little hollow". The name was changed again to LAKE LOUISE in 1916 in honor of Princess Louise Caroline Alberta, daughter of Queen Victoria and wife of the Marquis of Lorne, Governor-General of Canada from 1878 to 1883.

LAKE MAJEAU   **[56-3-W5]**
~ former post office south of Majeau Lake.

It was named after the first French Canadian settler in the district. It was open from 1927 to 1967.

LAKE McGREGOR   **[18-22-W4]**
~ former post office near McGregor Lake.

It was named in 1909 after J. D. McGregor, who as managing director of the Southern Alberta Land Company initiated the irrigation scheme in which Lake McGregor is a reservoir. Previously it was called SNAKE VALLEY.

LAKE SASKATOON   **[72-8-W6]**
~ former post office north of Wembly.

It obtained its name because of the plentiful supply of saskatoon berries, which used to be used in manufacturing buffalo pemmican. Previous to 1912 the community was called **BEAVERLODGE**.

LAKE THOMAS   [47-12-W4]
(See: PHILLIPS)

LAKELAND   [38-8-W4]
~ former post office near Hanna.

The name is descriptive, there being a number of lakes in the vicinity.

LAKESEND COMMUNITY   [38-8-W4]
~ former post office.

The proposed railway line never was completed from Alliance to Saskatchewan's border. It had a post office for several years.

LAMERTON   [41-22-W4]
~ former station west of Buffalo Lake.

It was named in 1914 after the English village of Lamerton in the county of Devon, England by English pioneer homesteaders.

LAMONT   [55-19-W4]
~ town east of Edmonton.

It was named in 1906 in honor of Mr. Justice Lamont of the Supreme Court of Canada, by pioneer French Canadian settlers.

The population was 835 in 1972 and increased to 3,925 in 2006.

LAMORAL   [40-11-W5]
~ former station southeast of Saunders.

The railway lines reached here in 1914. The origin of the name is unknown.

LAMOUREAUX   [55-22-W4]
~ former post office north of Edmonton.

It was named in 1896 after Joseph L'Amoureaux who had migrated from Quebec to California during the gold rush of 1849. Later he prospected for gold in Montana, and finally settled in the vicinity in 1877.

LANDONVILLE   [55-6-W4]
~ former post office south of Elk Point.

It was named in 1908 after the first postmaster, J. H. Landon. The post office closed in 1970.

LANFINE   [28-5-W4]
~ hamlet west of Oyen.

It was named in 1912 on the suggestion of the first postmaster, William Davidson, after Lanfine House, in Ayrshire, Scotland. Davidson's old home was there.

LANGDON   [23-27-W4]
~ hamlet west of Strathmore.

It was named after Langdon of the railway construction firm of Langdon and Shepard. **SHEPARD** is the next station along the Canadian Pacific tracks.

LANGEVIN   [15-10-W4]
(See: **ALDERSON**)

LANGFORD PARK   [53-4-W5]
~ former post office near Wabamun Lake.

The post office opened in 1930 and was moved in 1970 to **WABAMUN**. The first postmaster was E. W. Langford.

LANUKE   [54-12-W4]
~ former post office near Vermilion.

It was opened in 1908 and named after a local farmer. It was closed in 1928.

LARKHALL   [12-4-W4]
~ former station near Medicine Hat.

It was named in 1920 after Larkhall in Lanarkshire, Scotland.

LARKSPUR **[63-25-W4]**
~ former post office north of Westlock.

The name may be descriptive of the wild flowers which row in this district.

LARMOUR **[11-1-W4]**
~ former station near Medicine Hat.

It was named in 1909 after R. E. Larmour, a general freight agent for the Canadian Pacific Railway.

LATHOM **[20-17-W4]**
~ former station south of Bassano.

It was named in 1884 after Edward George Bootle Wilbraham, Earl of Lathom (1864-1910), who was a director of the Oxley Ranch. He visited Canada in 1883.

LAVESTA **[43-3-W5]**
~ former post office near Rimbey.

It was named in 1911 after Vesta McGee, daughter of the first postmaster. It closed in 1885.

LAVOY **[52-13-W4]**
~ village east of Vegreville.

It was named in 1905 after an early settler, Joseph Lavoy. Previously the community had been called **DINWOODIE**.
The population was 118 in 1972 and decreased to 109 in 1997.

LAWSONBURG **[29-16-W4]**
~ former post office near East Coulee.

It was named in 1909 after the first postmistress, Mrs. L. L. Lawson.

LAWTON **[58-4-W5]**
~ post office southwest of Westlock.

It was opened in 1908. The origin of the name is not known.

LE GOFF   [62-2-W4]
~ former post office near Bonnyville.

It was named in 1913 after Father Le Goff, OMI, who was doing missionary work among the Indians here at the time of the Northwest Rebellion of 1885.
(See: **BEAVER RIVER**)

LEA PARK   [54-3-W4]
~ former post office near Lloydminster.

The Old English word *leah*, modern *lea*, meant originally a "wood", then a "glade" or "clearing in a wood". The more modern meaning of the word is a "piece of open land".

LEAFLAND   [40-4-W5]
~ former post office near Rocky Mountain House.

This name was suggested by Rev. Dr. C. D. McDonald and is descriptive. There are a variety of different trees in the district.

LEAHURST   [39-19-W4]
~ former station northeast of Stettler.

The railway tracks reached here in 1911. The origin of the name is unknown.

LEAMAN   [53-11-W5]
~ former post office southeast of MacKay.

It was named after a cousin of H. Phillips, secretary of the Grand Trunk Pacific Railway. Before 1914 the post office was called **CHIP LAKE**.

LEASOWE   [51-26-W4]
~ former post office near Edmonton.

It was named in 1914 after the English village of Leasowe in Chestershire. Previously the community was called MIDDLETON, a name that was retained by the school district.

LEAVINGS   [10-26-W4]
(See: **GRANUM**)

LEAVITT　　　　　　　　　[2-26-W4]
~ former post office southwest of Cardston.

It was named in 1900 after the first postmaster, William Leavitt. He belonged to a prominent Mormon pioneer family.

LECKIE　　　　　　　　　[20-17-W4]
~ former station near Brooks.

Probably named after Major R. G. Leckie of Truro, Nova Scotia, a prominent mining engineer who died in 1913.

LEDUC　　　　　　　　　[49-25-W4]
~ city south of Edmonton.

It was named in 1890 to honor Father Hippolyte Leduc, OMI. Father Leduc was a French-born Oblate missionary who labored for more than fifty years among the Indians on the western prairie. The discovery of an oil field west of the town in 1947 introduced an oil boom that is still continuing. Leduc today is part of the greater Edmonton area; there is almost no open farmland undeveloped between the two cities.

The population was 4,070 in 1972 and increased to 12,730 in 2006. (See: **CALGARY-EDMONTON TRAIL STAGING POSTS; TELFORD**)

LEEDALE　　　　　　　　[41-4-W5]
~ former post office south of Rimbey.

It was named after William H. Lee who was the postmaster for several years in the 1920's. Prior to 1917 the post office was called WITTENBURG.

LEESHORE　　　　　　　　[58-20-W4]
~ former post office north of Lamont.

It was opened in 1908. The origin of this name is unknown.

LEGAL   [57-25-W4]
~ *village north of Edmonton.*

It is a French Canadian settlement, established in 1898, and named after Emile Joseph Legal, OMI (1849-1920), first Roman Catholic Archbishop of Edmonton. Born in France, he spent many years in missionary work among the Indians on the western prairies. He is the author of *Les Indiens dans les Plaines* (1891) and *Short Sketches of the History of the Catholic Churches and Missionaries in Central Alberta* (1914).

The population was 565 in 1972 and increased to 1,192 in 2006

LEGEND   [6-12-W4]
~ *former post office west of Foremost.*

It derived its name from the fact that it was the end of the railway line. The name was originally spelled as two words: LEG END. The post office was in operation from 1914 to 1969.

LEICESTER   [78-16-W5]
~ *hamlet north of Winagami Lake.*

It was named after the English town of Leicester. This name is a hybrid of Celtic and Latin: *lei,* or *leire* is the name of a river while *castra* is the word used for a "fortified Roman camp".

LEIGHMORE   [71-11-W6]
~ *former post office near Beaverlodge.*

It was named in 1922 in error for Teigmore in the Channel Islands, former home of the first postmaster, G. J. Beadle.

LEIGHTON   [53-1-W4]
~ *former post office north of Lloydminster.*

It was named in 1911 on the suggestion of the first postmaster, J. V. Armstrong. There are five villages in England called Leighton, which means the "enclose for Leeks".

LENARTHUR [87-7-W4]
~ former station west of Gordon Lake.

It was so named in 1917. The name is a compound of the names of Dr. J.K. MacLennan and J. D. MacArthur, important officials of the Alberta and Great Waterways Railway Company.

LENZIE [9-22-W4]
~ former station near Lethbridge.

It was named in 1913 after the suburb of Lenzie, in Kirkintilloch near Glasgow, Scotland.

LEO [35-17-W4]
~ hamlet west of Stettler.

It was named in 1908 after the grandson Leo, of the first postmaster, O. Leo Longshore, who had pioneered in the district since 1906. Longshore was an American who had come from Oklahoma. One of the first grain elevators of the Alberta Wheat Pool was built here in 1924.

LESLIEVILLE [39-5-W5]
~ hamlet east of Rocky Mountain House.

It was named after the first pioneer family, Leslie, in the district. The post office was opened in 1906.

LESSARD [63-5-W4]
~ former post office north of Bonnyville.

It was named in 1921 in honor of Liberal Senator Prosper Edmond Lessard. Born in Quebec, he came west as a young man and became a successful Edmonton businessman. He sat in the Legislature for a number of years, and was briefly in Premier Stewart's cabinet as Minister Without Portfolio. He was appointed to the Senate in 1924. It operated from 1921 to 1962.

LESSER SLAVE LAKE   [75-10-W5]
~ *settlement located on the lake of the same name, east of the Peace River Country.*

Sir Alexander Mackenzie heard of this lake in 1792 from Indian hunters who told him that the Cree name was **SLAVE LAKE**, after the original Indian inhabitants; "Lesser" to distinguish it from Great Slave Lake in the Northwest Territories.

LETHBRIDGE   [9-21-W4]
~ *the third largest city in Alberta.*

It was named in honor of William Lethbridge (1824-1901), who was the first President of the North West Coal and Navigation Company. Lethbridge was a British financier who was persuaded to invest his money in the development of the coal deposits along the banks of the Oldman River by Sir Alexander Galt.   Prior to 1885, the community was called **COALBANKS**. This name in Cree is *achsaysim*, or "steep banks". The province's third University was opened here in 1967.

The population was 40,856 in 1972 and increased to 85,492 in 2009.

LEYLAND   [47-23-W5]
~ *ghost town in the Coal Branch district.*

It was named in 1913 after the English village of Leyland in Lancashire. The name means "fallow land".

(See: **COAL BRANCH**)

LILIENDALE   [82-1-W6]
~ *former post office near Grande Prairie.*

It was named in 1924 after the first postmaster, C. Lilienskold. Previously the community had been called KETCHUM.

LILLE   [7-4-W5]
~ *former coal mining community near Blairmore.*

It was named after the industrial city of Lille in northern France, the former home of one of the directors of the company that opened the mine.

LILLICO [31-16-W4]

~

This post office was named "Lillico" in 1910. Two years later it was changed.

LIMESTONE LAKE [56-17-W4]
~ former post office near Beaverhill Lake.

So called in 1917, the name is descriptive.

LINARIA [61-2-W5]

It derived its name from the fact that flax was grown in the district. Linaria is another word for "flaxseed". The post office was in operation from 1918 to 1970.

LINCOLN [65-24-W4]
~ former post office south of Athabasca.

It is most likely after Abraham Lincoln, the American president who was assassinated shortly after the end of the Civil War in 1865.

LINDALE [49-5-W5]
~ former post office northwest of Breton.

It was named in 1914 after the first postmaster, C. Lindell.

LINDBERGH [56-5-W4]
~ hamlet near Elk Point.

There were homesteaders in the area from 1906 when the post office was known as TYROL. The name was changed in 1929 in honor of Colonel Charles Lindbergh, the American pilot who successfully made a solo flight from North America to Paris.

LINDEN [30-25-W4]
~ village southwest of Three Hills.

Possibly named after the German city of Linden. There is also a city of this name in the State of New Jersey.

The population was 217 in 1972 and increased to 741 in 2008.

LINDSVILLE   [38-12-W4]
(See: BULWARK)

(The) LINEHAM RANCH   [19-3-W5]
~ *ranch south of Calgary.*

It was named and operated by John Lineham (1858-1913) who arrived from Manitoba at **CALGARY** in 1883. He was a prominent Okotoks rancher. Lineham served in the Northwest Territories Legislative Assembly from 1891 to 1902.

In 1912, he predicted that in 15 years CALGARY would have a population of 200,000. He was wrong about the date. In 1997, the City of CALGARY had a population of 780,000.

LINFIELD   [59-4-W5]
~ *former post office near Barrhead.*

It was named in 1914 after the first postmaster, C . Linfield.

LISBURN   [56-6-W5]
~ *former post office southeast of Sangudo.*

It was named in 1915, presumably after Lisburn, a town in the North of Ireland. Previously the community was called MEREBECK.

LITTLE BUFFALO   [86-14-W5]
~ *isolated hamlet east of Peace River.*

It was named after a nearby lake. The post office closed in 1957.

The population in 1972 was 103.

LITTLE CHICAGO   [20-3-W5]
~ *formerly a community.*

It was named after the American city in the State of Illinois. *Chicago* is an Indian word that means, according to Mrs. C. M. Matthews, "onion place".

LITTLE HAY LAKES   [49-22-W4]
(See: NEW SAREPTA)

LITTLE NEW YORK   [20-3-W5]
~ ghost town near Turner Valley.

So named probably by homesick Americans who had come to work in the **TURNER VALLEY** oil field in the 1920's.

LITTLE PLUME   [9-5-W4]
~ former post office south of Medicine Hat.

It was named after a Chief Little Plume (1889-1971) of the Piegan tribe. He was a veteran of World War I.

LITTLE PRAIRIE   [81-19-W5]
~ former post office near Peace River.

It was opened in 1921. The name is descriptive.

LITTLE SMOKY   [66-22-W5]
~ hamlet northwest of Iosegun.

The Smoky Rivers in northwestern Canada usually derive their names from coal beds which have become ignited and sometimes burn for years. As a result, along their banks clouds of smoke hang above the rivers.

LITTLE VOLGA   [52-5-W5]
(See: **SUNDANCE**)

LIVINGSTONE POST
(See: **FORT BERRY**)

LLOYDMINSTER   [50-1-W4]
~ city on the Alberta-Saskatchewan boundary east of Edmonton.

It was named in 1903 after Rev. George Exton Lloyd, later Anglican bishop of Saskatchewan, who came out from England as chaplain to the all-British colony which was promoted by Rev. Isaac Barr. The colony was settled near Lloydminster. BRITANNIA COLONY was the projected name of the settlement, but shortly after the settlers arrived, Lloyd became the head and the name was changed.

The Alberta portion of the population of this town was 4,308 in 1972 and increased to 17,402 in 2009. The Saskatchewan half of the community is about the same size.

LLOYDS HILL   [37-6-W4]
~ former post office southwest of Provost.

It was named in 1915 after the first postmistress, Mrs. G. L. Lloyds.

LOBLEY   [33-5-W5]
~ former post office near Red Deer.

It was named in 1909 after the first postmaster, Fred Lobley.

LOBSTICK   [53-8-W5]
~ former station west of Evansburg.

It was named after the nearby river, a tributary of the Pembina. The name first appears on Palliser's Map of 1865.

LOCHEARN   [39-7-W5]
~ former station west of Rocky Mountain House.

It was so named in 1918. Possibly it got its name from a nearby lake which is called Loch Ernie.

LOCHEND   [27-3-W5]
~ former post office northeast of Cochrane Lake.

It was opened in 1905. There are five Lochends in Scotland.

LOCHINVAR   [41-26-W4]
~ former post office near Lacombe.

It was probably named after Lochinvar, in Kirkcubbrightshire, Scotland, or Lochinvar, the hero of a ballad in Sir Walter Scott's *Marmion*:

"O, young Lochinvar is come out of the west,
Through all the wide Border his steed was the best:"

LOCKHART   [41-2-W5]
~ former post office near Red Deer.

It was named in 1906 after the first postmaster, James Lockhart.

LODGE   [39-7-W5]
~ former station east of Rocky Mountain House.

It was named in 1914 after Sir Oliver Lodge (1851-1940), the eminent British scientist. His contributions to the wireless were many and some of them were fundamental.

LOGAN   [51-19-W4]
~ post office.

The post office was opened before 1890. The origin of the name Logan is uncertain, but is believed to have been an early pioneer settler. The name was changed in 1898. (See: **TOFIELD**)

LOMOND   [16-20-W4]
~ village northwest of Lethbridge.

It was named in 1915 after the most famous of all Scottish lochs. It has been made familiar by the song:
"Oh, Ye'll take the high road, and I'll take the low road,
And I'll be in Scotland afore ye. ..."

(Few know of the story behind the song, how one of two brothers is hung by the English, but his soul is carried back to his homeland by the Wee Folk who used subterranean passages.)
The population was 201 in 1972 and decreased to 175 in 2006.

LONE PINE STOPPING HOUSE   [14-7-W4]
(See: **CALGARY-EDMONTON TRAIL STAGING POSTS; BOWDEN**)

LONE STAR   [89-23-W5]
~ hamlet south of Manning.

The communities of **RED STAR** and **NORTH STAR** are in the same vicinity.

LONEBUTTE   [27-15-W4]
~ *former post office near Medicine Hat.*

So named in 1910 because of its location on the only hill for miles around.

LONGVIEW   [18-2-W5]
~ *village west of High River.*

There is a good view of the eastern slopes of the Rockies from this community. The post office was opened in 1905.

The population was 191 in 1971 and increased to 334 in 2007.

LOOMA   [50-23-W4]
~ *former post office southeast of Edmonton.*

Originally this community was known as LOOMA VISTA.

LOON LAKE   [87-9-W5]
~ *hamlet east of Peace River.*

This isolated community is named after nearby Loon Lake which, in turn, obtained its name because it is a favorite nesting area of the *gavia imber* or loon. This Canadian bird is well known for its mournful, haunting cries in the early evenings of summer, near northern lakes.

The population in 1972 was 149.

LOST LAKE   [14-18-W4]
(See: ENCHANT)

LOTHROP   [80-1-W6]
~ *former post office near the Birch Hills.*

It was named in 1927 after an early homesteader.

LOUGHEED [43-11-W4]
~ village north of Hardisty.

It was named in 1925 in honor of Senator Sir James Alexander Lougheed (1854-1925). He practiced law in Calgary before being called to the Canadian Senate in 1889. He succeeded Sir Mackenzie Bowell as Conservative leader in the Senate in 1906 and served in the federal cabinet for many years. In 1884 Lougheed married Belle, daughter of William L. Hardisty, chief factor of the Hudson's Bay Company in Edmonton. Premier Peter Lougheed is the grandson of Sir James. Previously the community had been called HOLMSTOWN.

The population was 252 in 1972 and decreased to 240 in 2009.

LOUSANA [36-23-W4]
~ hamlet east of Delburne.

It was named in 1912 on the suggestion of W. G. Biggs, an early settler from Louisiana in the State of Missouri. The postal department curtailed the name to its present spelling.

LOVETTVILLE [47-19-W5]
~ ghost town in the Coal Branch district.

It was named in 1915 after H. A. Lovett of Montreal, president of North American Collieries. The Lovett River is also named after him. Previously it had been called after a well known mining engineer, FERGIE. The station was referred to as LOVETT when it was opened in 1913.

(See: **COAL BRANCH**)

LOYALIST [35-7-W4]
~ former post office northeast of Kirkpatrick Lake.

CONSORT, CORONATION, LOYALIST, VETERAN and **THRONE** are adjacent Canadian Pacific Railway stations named in the Coronation year of 1911 when King George V was crowned. Previously the community was called VALLEJO. There is a community near San Francisco also called by this Spanish name.

LUCKY STRIKE   [3-11-W4]
~ *former post office south of Foremost.*

When this post office was opened in 1910, those who obtained land in the vicinity were considered to be fortunate.

LUNDBRECK   [7-2-W5]
~ *hamlet northwest of Pincher Creek.*

It was so named in 1904. The name is a compound of Lund and Breckenridge (Breckenridge and Lund Coal Company). These two men commenced operating collieries and sawmills here at the turn of the century. (See: **CROWSNEST PASS**)

LUNDEMO   [48-20-W4]
~ *former post office northwest of Camrose.*

It was named in 1908 on the suggestion of the first postmaster, John Waldun, after his old home in Norway.

LUNNFORD   [59-3-W5]
~ *former post office southwest of Westlock.*

It was named in 1910 after the first postmaster, E. L. Lunn.

LURE   [37-11-W4]
~ *former post office northwest of Coronation.*

The name may be indicative of the hopes of the early settlers.

LUSCAR   [47-24-W5]
~ *ghost town in the Coal Branch district.*

It was named in 1922 after the Luscar Colliery, which in turn, was named after Luscar in Fifeshire, Scotland.
(See: **COAL BRANCH**)

LUZAN   [55-16-W4]
~ *former post office north of Beaverhill Lake.*

The name was suggested in 1913 by Simon Iconiuk, postmaster, after Luzan, in the Ukraine.

LYALTA   [26-25-W4]
~ former post office north of Calgary.

The name is a compound of Lyall and Alberta. It was suggested by A. Harry Parsons of Lyall Trading Company. Before 1914 the post office was called LYALL.

LYMBURN   [73-12-W6]
~ former post office north of Beaverlodge.

It was named in honor of John Farquhar Lymburn, K.C., a prominent Edmonton lawyer. Born in Scotland in 1881, he was educated at Glasgow University and came to Canada in 1911. Lymburn was first elected to the legislature as one of the members for Edmonton in 1926. He served as the Attorney General of Alberta for nine years. He died in 1969. The post office was opened in 1932 and has since closed.

LYNDON   [12-29-W4]
~ former post office west of Claresholm.

It was named in 1881 after Charles A. Lyndon, a pioneer settler of the district.

M

MACBETH   **[18-14-W4]**
~ station south of Brooks.

It was named in 1912 after Hugh Macbeth of the North West Coal and Navigation Company. He was the purser aboard the *Alberta*, the company's riverboat that plied between Lethbridge and Medicine Hat during the 1880's. Macbeth died in 1923. The station was in operation from 1912 to 1924.

MacDONALD CROSSING   [58-3-W5]
(See: BELVEDERE; PEMBINA CROSSING)

MacKAY{1}   [54-11-W5]
~ hamlet west of Chip Lake.

The former station was opened in 1911. The community is named after J. C. MacKay, a railway contractor. The post office closed in 1981.

MacKAY{2}
~ fur trading post on the Athabasca River.

It was named after Dr. William MacKay, chief trader for the Hudson's Bay Company in the district for forty years.

MACSON   [12-5-W4]
~ former station near Medicine Hat.

The name is derived by compounding parts of McArthur and Jamieson, who were two superintendents of the Canadian Pacific Railway.

MADDEN [28-2-W5]
~ hamlet northwest of Calgary.

The origin of this name is not known.

MAGNOLIA [53-6-W5]
~ former post office near Entwistle.

It was named after the magnolia tree, which in turn, was named after the seventeenth century French botanist Pierre Magnol. There are some thirty-five communities in the United States called Magnolia. It was in operation from 1908 to 1970.

MAGRATH [5-22-W4]
~ town south of Lethbridge.

It was named in 1900 in honor of Charles A. Magrath (1860-1949). Born in Upper Canada, he came west to practice as a land surveyor. In 1885, he joined the Galt interest in various enterprises. He was the first mayor of Lethbridge. He represented the city as a member of the Northwest legislature from 1891 to 1902, serving as Minister without Portfolio in the Haultain administration. Entering federal politics as a Conservative, he represented Medicine Hat in the House of Commons from 1908 to 1911, when he was defeated by Liberal W. A. Buchanan. His second wife was a daughter of Sir Alexander Galt.

The population was 1,233 in 1972, it increased to 2,254 in 2008.

MAHASKA [57-13-W5]
~ former post office near Peers.

It was named after a county in the State of Iowa which in turn was called after an Indian chief. The post office was opened in 1913 and closed a few years later.

MAJESTIC [21-6-W4]
~ former station southwest of Empress.

This descriptive name was given in 1914.

MAJORVILLE   [19-20-W4]
~ *former post office near Bassano.*

Before 1915 the post office was called merely MAJOR. It was closed in 1970, the mail being sent to Milo.

MAKEPEACE   [23-19-W4]
~ *former station north of Bassano.*

It was named in 1913 after William Makepeace Thackeray, the nineteenth century British novelist who wrote *Vanity Fair*. It closed in 1951.

MALEB   [8-10-W4]
~ *former post office north of Foremost.*

It was so called in 1911 by combining the initials of the names of the children of Mr. And Mrs. Bowen: Morley, Amy, Lorne, Elizabeth, and the initial of their surname. The Bowens settled in this district in 1910.

MALLAIG   [60-10-W4]
~ *hamlet south of Therien.*

It was named after the Scottish west coast fishing village of Mallaig in Inverness-shire.

MALMO   [44-23-W4]
~ *former post office near Wetaskiwin.*

It was named in 1911 by American settlers from Malmo in the State of Nebraska. There is also a community called Malmo in Sweden. It was closed in 1933.

MALOY   [62-8-W4]
~ *former post office north of Glendon.*

It was opened in 1915. There is a place with the same name in Iowa. It was closed in 1966.

MA-ME-O BEACH   [46-28-W4]
~ *summer village on the south shore of Pigeon Lake, near Wetaskiwin.*

The population was 109 in 1972, it increased to 155 in 2006.

MANCE   [47-14-W4]
~ *former post office near Camrose.*

Possibly it is named after the English village of Mancea in Cambridgeshire. *Mancea* means "a place that was communally owned". The post office was opened in 1913.

MANIR   [78-4-W6]
~ *former station southeast of Rycroft.*

It was so named in 1916 after Madame Manir Polet, a Belgian painter, who for fifteen years was a resident of Alberta.

MANNING   [91-23-W5]
~ *Peace River town north of Grimshaw.*

It was named in 1947 in honor of the then Premier of Alberta, Ernest C. Manning. Born in 1908 and raised on a farm near Carnduff, Saskatchewan, Manning was William Aberhart's first student at the Calgary Prophetic Bible Institute. He was closely associated with Aberhart as a radio preacher of fundamentalist Christianity. He was an ordained Baptist minister.

In 1935, Manning was elected as a Social Credit member of the legislature for Calgary. He entered the first Aberhart cabinet as Provincial Secretary and Minister of Trade and Industry. On Aberhart's death seven years later, he succeeded to the premiership, which he held for the next twenty-five years. He assumed the additional portfolios of Provincial Treasurer (1944-1954), and Mines and Minerals (1952 -1968). His government was returned with large majorities in seven provincial general elections. With no resort to unconventional financial expedients, his government carried on an extensive program of social legislation, particularly in public health. On December 12, 1968, he resigned as premier and at the end of the year, he resigned his seat in the legislature. In 1970 he was appointed by Prime Minister Trudeau to the Senate.

The townsite was originally called AURORA, but postal officials changed the name. The hotel is still called Aurora Hotel.

The population was 1,322 in 1972, it increased in 1,493 in 2006.

MANNVILLE [50-9-W4]
~ village west of Vermilion.

It was named after Sir Donald D. Mann (1853-1934), one of the builders and chief executive of the Canadian Northern Railway. Sir Donald and Sir William McKenzie owned and operated the railway until it was taken over by the government in 1918. He was created K.B. in 1911.

MANOLA [59-2-W5]
~ hamlet west of Westlock.

It was named in 1907 after the daughter of James Albert McFee, an early settler in the district.

MANY ISLAND [14-1-W4]
~ former post office near Medicine Hat.

It received its name from a nearby lake in 1919. Previously this post office had been called TARVES.

MANYBERRIES [5-6-W4]
~ former post office south of Foremost.

This name is descriptive. The nomadic Indians of the prairies have for generations gathered here in the autumn to pick the wild berries and saskatoons for use in the making of pemmican. The word is a translation of the Blackfoot *akoniskway*. The post office was opened in 1911.

MAPOVA [61-22-W4]
~ hamlet near Westlock.

The first three settlers were Ukrainians. The name was a combination of letters of their names. "M" for Murlak, "A" for Alho and "P" for Papowich.

(The) MARCELLUS RANCH
~ at/near Pincher Creek.

It was named and operated by John Plummer Marcellus (1846 -1932) who came with his sons in 1888. He was a pioneer cattle and horse rancher. He served in the Alberta Legislature from 1905 to 1909.

MARGIE   **[74-9-W4]**
        ~ *former station north of Lac La Biche.*

It was opened in 1916. Mrs. Margie Judge was the wife of a railway official. Margie is a shortened form of Margaret and is a popular girl's name in Scotland. Saint Margaret of Scotland (1050-1093) married King Malcolm Canmore in 1070, and promoted justice, even having a special thought for the poor.

MARIE-REINE   **[82-21-W5]**
        ~ *hamlet south of Peace River.*

This is French for "Queen Mary", and may refer to the Blessed Virgin Mary.

MARKERVILLE   **[36-2-W5]**
        ~ *hamlet south of Sylvan Lake.*

It was named in 1902 after C. P. Marker, one-time dairy commissioner for the NWT it is an Icelandic settlement.

MARLBORO   **[53-19-W5]**
        ~ *hamlet south of Edson.*

It was named from marl deposits in the vicinity, used in the making of cement. A cement plant was erected here in 1912, the same year as the post office was opened.

MARWAYNE   **[52-3-W4]**
        ~ *village north of Lloydminster.*

It was named in 1906 on the suggestion of the first postmaster S. C. Marfleet, who had come from the English town of Wainfleet (old spelling Waynflete). He named his farm Marwayne.
        The population was 351 in 1972, it increased to 569 in 2007.

MARY LAKE   **[53-7-W4]**
        ~ *former post office near Vermilion.*

It was named after a lake in the vicinity, which in turn, had been named by Charles Hogoban, the first postmaster, after his wife Mary. It was in operation from 1912 to 1932.

MASINASIN   [2-13-W4]
~ *former post office south of Foremost.*

Masinasin is the Cree name meaning "writing on stone", referring to figures and writing cut in the sandstone cliffs along the banks of the Milk River. (See: **WRITING-ON-STONE PARK**)

MASSIVE   [26-13-W5]
~ *former station north of Banff.*

The name is taken from nearby 7,990 foot Mount Massive, which describes its appearance.

MATZHIWIN   [21-15-W4]
~ *former station northeast of Bassano.*

The origin of this name is not known.

MAUGHAN   [52-7-W4]
~ *former post office north of Vermilion.*

It was named in 1907 after the first postmaster, A. Maughan. It closed in 1958.

MAUNSELL   [7-29-W4]
~ *former hamlet near Pincher Creek.*

It was named after Edward Maunsell (1854-1923), who after serving with the Northwest Mounted Police, became the proprietor of the IVY ranch in 1877. He was an unsuccessful candidate in the 1910 Macleod provincial by-election. His grandson, also a rancher, was a member of the Legislature in the 1960's.

MAYBUTT   [6-19-W4]
~ *former post office east of Raymond.*

It was named in 1912 after May Butt, wife of Mr. Fisher, the original owner of the townsite.

MAYCROFT   [10-2-W5]
~ former post office north of Blairmore.

It was named in 1910 after Mrs. A. C. Raper, wife of the postmaster. Her Christian name was "May". The post office closed in 1964.

MAYERTHORPE   [57-8-W5]
~ town northeast of Chip Lake.

It was named in 1905 after the first postmaster, R. I. Mayer. "Thorpe" is the Old English word for village. The population was 1,042 in 1972 and increased to 1,574 in 2006.

MAYTON   [33-27-W4]
~ former post office near Olds.

The first settlers in this district came from May City in the State of Iowa. It was in operation from 1902 to 1932.

MAZEPPA   [19-27-W4]
~ hamlet east of High River.

It was named in 1912 after the Cossack hero of Lord Byron's poem "Mazeppa", published in 1819. Byron found the chief incidents for his story in Voltaire's *Historie de Charles XII*, from which he quotes three excerpts to serve as preface to his poem. His Mazeppa is essentially Ivan Stepanovitch Mazeppa, 1644-1709, a Cossack. Letman (leader) became a symbol of Ukrainian struggle for independence.

McDONALDVILLE   [47-3-W4]
~ former post office near Wainwright.

It was opened and named after an early settler Adam McDonald in 1908.

(The) McINTYRE RANCH
~ south of Lethbridge.

It is located on the wind swept Milk River Ridge and is one hundred square miles in size. Originally part of the Senator Cochrane Ranch, it was founded by William H. McIntyre who purchased the land from the Alberta Railway and Irrigation Company in 1894. He stocked it with shorthorn cattle from the State of Utah. His brand was IHL. The McIntyre family owned this ranch until they sold it to the former foreman Ralph Trall, in 1945.

McLAUGHLIN [46-2-W4]
~ hamlet northeast of Wainwright.

It was named in 1908 after a settler of that name, John M. McLaughlin.

McLENNAN [77-19-W5]
~ town in the Peace River district.

It was named after Dr. J. K. McLennan, secretary of the Edmonton, Dunvegan and British Columbia Railway when it reached the site in 1915. It was incorporated as a town in 1948. Many of the settlers were French Canadian.

The population was 1,157 in 1972, it increased to 824 in 2006.

McLEOD RIVER [52-18-W5]
~ former station southwest of Edson.

The railway reached here in 1912. It is named after the McLeod River which flows into the Athabasca River. Archibald N. McLeod, was fur trading in the district in 1799.

McMURRAY [89-9-W4]
(See: **FORT McMURRAY**)

McNAB [5-18-W4]
~ former station south of Raymond.

It was named in 1912 after Donald McNabb of Lethbridge. For a few months in 1909 McNabb was the MLA for Lethbridge. He was returned unopposed in the January 8 by-election caused by the resignation of W. C. Simmons. In the general election, held on March 22, McNabb, who was a Labor candidate, was defeated by the young Liberal publisher of *The Lethbridge Herald*, W. A. Buchanan. One "B" in the name was dropped.

McRAE [62-12-W4]
~ former post office east of Whitefish Lake.

It was named after W. M. McRae, the first postmaster in 1924.

MEADOW CREEK [11-29-W4]
~ former post office near Blairmore.

The name is descriptive, there being good hay land in the vicinity. The post office was opened in 1895 and closed some years later.

MEADOWBROOK [63-25-W4]
~ former post office near Athabasca.

The name was descriptive. It was open from 1915 to 1951.

MEANDER RIVER [115-22-W5]
~ hamlet north of Hay River.

This is one of the most northerly post offices in the province. The stream for which the post office is named is first called this in H. Footner's *New Rivers of the North*. The name is descriptive.

MEANOOK [64-22-W4]
~ hamlet seventy miles north of Edmonton.

This small community is the "Center of Alberta", being half way from the American border to the south and the boundary of the Northwest Territories in the north. *Meanook* is the Cree word meaning "good camping ground".

MEARNS   [56-26-W4]
~ hamlet northwest of Edmonton.

It was named in 1912 after Mearns near Glasgow, Scotland. This Gaelic word means "plains of Eire".

MEDICINE HAT   [12-5-W4]
~ city in southeastern Alberta.

The site of the present city is so called in the report of the North West Mounted Police for 1882 and about this year the first house was erected. Medicine Hat is a translation of the Blackfoot name *saamis*, meaning "head-dress of a medicine man".

One of the many explanations connected with the name was a fight between the Cree and Blackfoot tribes, when the Cree medicine man who was running away lost his war bonnet in the river. Another connects the origin of the name with the slaughter of a party of white settlers in the early days and the appropriation by an Indian medicine man of a woman's fancy hat worn by one of the victims. Yet another story states that the name was applied originally to a hill east of the city, from its resemblance in shape to the head-gear of an Indian medicine man. This hill is styled Medicine Hat on a map of the Department of the Interior dated 1883. In addition, there is an Indian legend that a young brave rescued a squaw from drowning in the turbulent waters of the South Saskatchewan, and for the courageous deed, received the hat of a famous medicine man as a token of admiration.

But of all the stories connected with this unusual name, the one we like best says that Medicine Hat was the name given to the locality because an Indian chief once saw in a vision an Indian rising out of the swift flowing river, wearing the plumed head-gear of a medicine man.

The population was 25,713 in 1972 and increased to 61,097 in 2009.

MEDLEY   [62-2-W4]
~ former post office north of Bonnyville.

It was named after C. Medley of Calgary.

MEETING CREEK   **[43-19-W4]**
~ hamlet north of Buffalo Lake.

Before 1905 the community was called **EDENSVILLE**. The Crees of the northern woodlands and the Blackfoot of the southern plains, in their buffalo hunts, frequently met here.

MEKASTOE   **[9-26-W4]**
~ former station west of Fort Macleod.

It was named in 1915 after Mekastoe or Red Crow, head chief of the Southern Bloods, who signed the Indian Treaty Number Seven, September 22, 1877 at Blackfoot Crossing. Mekastoe was loyal throughout the Northwest Rebellion of 1885. He was next in rank in the Blackfoot Confederacy to the famous chief Crowfoot.

MELLOWDALE   **[60-3-W5]**
~ former post office northwest of Westlock.

It was opened in 1909. **MELROSE** was the name requested by the homesteaders in the district, but postal officials in Ottawa modified the suggested name to the present form.

MENAIK   **[43-25-W4]**
~ former post office northeast of Ponoka.

This is a variation of the Cree word for "tamarack". It was open from 1928 to 1980.

MERCOAL   **[48-22-W5]**
~ ghost town in the Coal Branch district.

It is in the coal mining district in the foothills, forty-four miles southwest of **EDSON**. Served by a rail line, the name given in 1913 is a compound of portions of the McLeod River Hard Coal Company.
    (See: **COAL BRANCH**)

MEREBECK   **[56-6-W5]**
    (See: **LISBURN**)

MESEKUM   **[17-12-W4]**
~ former station near Brooks.

It was named in 1912 after the Indian word for "the land is rich". It is descriptive of the fertile soil in this district.

METISKOW   **[40-5-W4]**
~ hamlet north of Provost.

It was so named in 1909 and is the Cree word for "many trees".

MEWASSIN   **[51-2-W5]**
~ former post office near Wabamun.

This name is the Cree word for "good". It was opened in 1903, and closed after 1930.

MICHICHI   **[30-18-W4]**
~ hamlet northeast of Drumheller.

It is named after the Cree word for "little hand". The Hand Hills are in the vicinity.

MICHIGAN CENTRE   **[48-26-W4]**
~ former hamlet east of Leduc.

It is possibly named after the State of Michigan. The state's name is derived from an Indian word meaning "vast body of water" or "monstrous lake".

MIDDLE CREEK   **[56-4-W4]**
~ former station south of Elk Point.

It is named after a nearby stream that is a tributary of the North Saskatchewan River. It first appeared on Arrowsmith's Map in 1859.

MIDDLETON   **[51-26-W4]**
(See: **LEASOWE**)

MIDLANDVALE [29-20-W4]
~ hamlet north of Drumheller.

The first name of this community was MIDLANDVILLE, named after the nearby Midland Coal Mine. The post office was opened in 1917.

MIDNAPORE [23-1-W5]
~ suburb of Calgary.

Originally named FISH CREEK, it is the first community south of Calgary on the Macleod Trail. There is a story that it obtained its present name when John Glen, a squatter who was acting as the postmaster, even though he could neither read nor write, claimed a letter addressed to "The Postmaster, Midnapore, India". The post office opened in 1883.

MIETTE [49-27-W5]
~ former station northeast of Jasper Lake.

It was named in 1915 after nearby Roche Miette, which in turn, was named after a trapper who climbed it in the early nineteenth century. This incident is mentioned by Franchere in *Relation d'un Voyage a la côte du Nord-ouest de l'amerique Septentrionale* (1820). Previously the community was called BEDSON.

MILK RIVER [2-16-W4]
~ town south of Lethbridge on the Coutts Highway.

It was named after the nearby river that rises in the State of Montana and flows north into Canada before turning south to join the Missouri-Mississippi, and finally flows into the Gulf of Mexico.

The river is so named because of the milky-white color of its water. This is due to the amount of sediment that is carried by this swift flowing river. It is so called on an 1817 map. In Blackfoot, it is called *Kinuhsisuht*, "the little river".

This part of Alberta has been, at one time, part of the American possessions of Spain, France and Britain, and was also claimed in the nineteenth century by the United States of America.

The population was 861 in 1972 and decreased to 846 in 2007.

MILLARVILLE   [21-3-W5]
~ former post office southwest of Calgary.

It was named in 1885 after an early settler in the district, Malcolm Millar.

MILLERFIELD   [27-18-W4]
~ former post office near East Coulee.

It was named in 1913 after the first postmaster, John M. Miller. It was closed after 1930.

MILLET   [47-24-W4]
~ town southeast of Leduc.

It was named in 1893 after Jean Francois Millet (1814-1875), the famous French painter. His best known paintings are "The Angelus" and "The Man with a Hoe", works in which he imparted a largesse and a pathetic dignity to his figures of men and women who labor in the fields.

The population in 1972 was 480 and increased to 2,125 in 2005.

MILLICENT   [20-13-W4]
~ hamlet north of Brooks.

It was named after Lady Millicent Fanny, the fourth Duchess of Sutherland. Her husband, the Duke (1851-1933), held a large amount of property in southern Alberta.

DUCHESS is also named in her honor and **ROSEMARY** is named after her daughter, Lady Rosemary Millicent.

MILO   [18-21-W4]
~ village north of Vulcan.

It was named in 1908 after Milo Munroe, the first postmaster.

MINARET   [32-1-W5]
~ former station north of Didsbury.

It was named in 1912 from the fact that it is the highest point between Calgary and Edmonton. Previously it was called ROSEBUD[1].

MINBURN   [50-10-W4]
~ village west of Mannville.

It was named in 1905 after Miss Mina Burns of Ottawa who described the Canadian West in magazine articles.

MINEHEAD   [49-21-W5]
(See: ROBB; COAL BRANCH)

MINISTIK LAKE   [51-21-W4]
~ former post office near Edmonton.

Ministik is the Cree word for "island". It was opened in 1908 and closed in 1928.

MINTLAW   [37-28-W4]
~ former station southwest of Red Deer.

It was named in 1914 after Mintlaw in Scotland. The Scandinavian word *law* means "hill". This name means "the hill on which grows mint".

MIRROR   [40-22-W4]
~ village north of Alix.

It was named in 1911 after the famous London newspaper *The Daily Mirror*.

MISSION BEACH   [47-1-W5]
~ hamlet on the north shore of Pigeon Lake.

The name is descriptive, there being once a Catholic mission located here.

MITFORD   [26-5-W5]
~ former station north of Cochrane.

T. B. H. Cochrane, son of Admiral Sir Thomas Cochrane, held ranching leases in the vicinity and the name was suggested by his wife, Lady Adela Cochrane, after Mrs. Percy Mitford, sister of the Earl of Egerton, who was a friend of hers. The post office was opened in 1889.

MITSUE   [72-4-W5]
~ former station southeast of Lesser Slave Lake.

Mitsue is the Cree word for "eating". There was an abundance of game in the district at one time.

MIZPAH   [25-14-W4]
~ former post office near Hanna.

This name, which appears in the Bible, means "Watchtower". It was opened in 1913 and closed after 1930.

MOLE LAKE   [56-17-W4]
(See: WOSTOK)

MOLSTAD   [45-17-W4]
It was named after a pioneer homesteader. The name was changed by Ottawa officials in honor of a Winnipeg wheat baron. (See: BAWLF)

MONARCH   [10-23-W4]
~ hamlet northwest of Lethbridge.

The post office was opened in 1908. Before it was called the DUTCH SETTLEMENT.

MONITOR   [35-4-W4]
~ hamlet north of Grassy Island Lake.

Before 1913, the post office was called SOUNDING LAKE.

MONKMAN [54-7-W4]
~ former post office near St. Paul.

It was named in 1920 after the first postmaster, P. J. Monkman, who was one of the original settlers in the district. Previously the community was called PEGUIS, after Peguis in Manitoba where Monkman had come from.

MONTGOMERY [24-2-W5]
~ hamlet west of Calgary.

Possibly named after Hugh John Montgomery, who was elected Liberal member of the legislature in 1914 for Wetaskiwin. He held the seat until 1921 when he lost out to the U.F.A.. He was re-elected to represent this constituency from 1930 to 1935.

MONVEL [41-19-W4]
~ former post office near Buffalo Lake.

When it was opened in 1906, the name was spelt MONVAL. It was closed after 1930.

MOON LAKE [51-7-W5]
~ former post office near Wabamun.

The name is the translation of a Cree name applied to an adjacent lake. It was in operation from 1926 to 1971.

MOOSE PORTAGE [72-26-W4]
~ former post office west of Calling Lake.

The moose is the largest member of the deer family and roams throughout the coniferous forest regions of Alberta. Some adult bulls weigh up to 1,800 pounds. Compared to the graceful deer, this animal is a grotesque creature, with humped shoulders, ungainly legs and broad, drooping nose. The moose is rapidly disappearing from being over-hunted.

MOOSE RIDGE [35-3-W5]
~ former post office near Red Deer.

The name is descriptive, numerous moose being found in the vicinity. Before 1925, the post office was called MOUNTAIN HOUSE.

MOOSWA   [56-5-W4]
~ former post office near Lloydminster.

Mooswa is the Cree word for "moose". Before 1912, the post office was called TYROL.

MORINVILLE   [56-25-W4]
~ town northwest of Edmonton.

This community was founded in the spring of 1891 by Abbé Morin. He was born at St. Paul-de-Joliette in Quebec, and studied at Montreal, where he was ordained in 1884. He published a pamphlet *Le nord-ouest Canadian et ses Resources Agricole* (1894). It is predominantly French-speaking, as a community, a large number of the original settlers having come from the French-speaking part of Belgium.

The population was 1,251 in 1972 and increased to 7,636 by 2009.

MORLEY   [25-7-W5]
~ post office west of Calgary.

It was named after Rev. George McDougall's ranch, which in turn was named in honor of Rev. Morley Punshon, prominent Methodist preacher. In the summer of 1872, McDougall met Punshon at a missionary conference at Winnipeg and secured the latter's endorsement of a plan for the establishing of a new mission at the foot of the Rockies. In a letter (Edmonton, May 28, 1873). McDougall says, "In the evenings we camped on the bank of the Bow River, close to the mountains. The prospect was one of the grandest I had ever witnessed and Morleyville will yet become a favorite resort of tourists".

MORNINGSIDE   [41-26-W4]
~ hamlet southwest of Ponoka.

It was named in 1892 after Morningside, a suburb of Edinburgh, capital of Scotland. It had a post office from 1901 to 1982.

MORRIN [31-20-W4]
~ village north of Drumheller.

Prior to 1911, the post office was called BLOOMING PRAIRIE.

The population was 272 in 1972 and decreased to 253 in 2006.

MOSSIDE [58-4-W5]
~ post office southwest of Westlock.

It was named in 1908 after Mosside, which is a suburb of Manchester, England.

MOUND [33-4-W5]
~ former post office west of Olds.

The name originally referred to the cabin of H. A. Muntz, and early settler, who built it in 1896. The name was suggested by a hillock. The post office was opened in 1905.

MOUNTAIN HOUSE [35-3-W5]
(See: **MOOSE RIDGE**)

MOUNTAIN MILL
~ former lumbering community west of Fort Macleod.

Located 60 miles west of the Fort at the junction of Mill Creek and Castle River. It was so named in 1882. The settlement boomed during the construction days of the Crowsnest Pass railway in the late 1890's due to the demand for ties and bridging timber.

MOUNTAIN PARK
(See: **COAL BRANCH**)

MOUNTAIN VIEW [2-27-W4]
~ hamlet west of Cardston.

The name is descriptive of the wonderful view obtained of the Rockies. The post office was opened in 1895.

MUDGE   **[47-20-W5]**
(See: FOOTHILLS)

MUIRHEAD   **[16-1-W5]**
~ *former post office near High River.*

It was named in 1912 after Peter Muirhead, pioneer homesteader.

MULGA   **[49-8-W4]**
~ *former post office near Wainwright.*

It was named in 1911 after the Australian mulga tree. The suggestion came from Percy Fielding, the first postmaster, who resided for a time in Australia.

MULHURST   **[47-28-W4]**
~ *post office east of Pigeon Lake.*

It was named after G. Mulligan, the first postmaster, in 1912.

MUNDARE   **[53-16-W4]**
~ *town east of Edmonton.*

(NB: The author of this work has spent more time in attempting to find the origin of this name than any other in the book.)

In 1903 the spelling of the name was MUNDAIRE.

The Encyclopedia Canadiana (1963) states the community "was named after a French missionary, Father Mundare." The Ukrainians, who now form a large portion of the population, say it is a free deformation of the Ukrainian word for "monastery". The station agent in 1906 was William Mundare.

The population was 590 in 1972, and increased to 823 in 2009.

MUNSON   **[30-20-W4]**
~ *hamlet north of Drumheller.*

It was named after J. A. Munson, K.C., a Winnipeg lawyer, in 1911.

MURRAY VALLEY   [33-2-W5]
~ former post office near Alsask, Saskatchewan.

It was named in 1905 after one of the first settlers in the district, James Murray. The Murrays who came from Northumberland, England, started here in 1892.

MUSAKO FORT   [50---6-W5]
~ trading post on the North Saskatchewan River.

This North West Company trading post was often called QUAGMIRE HOUSE and was visited by David Thompson in 1808.

MUSKEG RIVER   [57-5-W6]
~ former station east of Grande Cache.

It was named after the nearby river. The word is derived from the Chipewyan *muskig*, meaning "grassy bog".

MYRNAM   [54-9-W4]
~ village east of Two Hills.

These apt words, *myr nam*, are Ukrainian for "peace to us". Most of the early settlers had come from the Ukraine. The post office was opened in 1908.

MYSTERY LAKE   [60-7-W5]
~ former post office near Whitecourt.

There is no lake of this name in the vicinity. It is a "mystery" how it obtained its name. It was closed by postal officials in August, 1970.

N

NACMINE   [29-20-W4]
~ hamlet west of Drumheller.

The name was formed by the combination of the initial letters of "North American Collieries", a mine near here, and the word "mine". The post office was opened in 1919.

NACO   [31-6-W4]
~ hamlet northwest of Oyen.

The post office was opened in 1926 and was named after a community called Naco in the State of Arizona. It closed in 1968.

NAKAMUN   [52-2-W5]
~ former post office northeast of Lac St. Anne.

The name is the Cree word for "song of praise". It operated from 1911 to 1960.

NAMAKA   [23-24-W4]
~ hamlet southeast of Strathmore.

It is named from the Blackfoot words nama, "bow", and nietakhtai, "river", pronounced by the Indians namokhtai, but corrupted by those who did not know the language to NAMAKA. Archdean J. W. Timms says, "I think the late General Strange was responsible for the name and probably the spelling of it. I remember him telling me that the Canadian Pacific Railway had suggested that the station be called "Strange", but he asked the company to call it NAMAKA, as that was the name he had chosen for his ranch on the Bow River, and his friends would know where to leave the train." The railway tracks reached here in 1884.

NAMAO [54-24-W4]
~ hamlet north of Edmonton.

Namao is the Cree word for "sturgeon". The community is situated on the banks of the Sturgeon River. The post office opened in 1892.

NAMPA [81-20-W5]
~ village south of Peace River.

It is named after the town of Nampa in the State of Idaho.

The population was 317 in 1972 and increased to 373 in 2007.

NANTON [16-28-W4]
~ town on the Fort Macleod-Calgary Trail.

It was named in 1893 after Sir Augustus Meredith Nanton (1860 -1925), the Canadian financier. At the age of thirteen he entered the service of the brokerage firm of Pellat and Osler of Toronto, and in 1884 he was sent west to represent his firm in Winnipeg. Nanton became one of the outstanding figures in the financial life of the country, and was knighted for his service in connection with financial management of Canada's part in the Great War. For many years he was a director of the Canadian Pacific Railway. The firm of Pellat and Osler dealt in townsite properties in Southern Alberta.

The population was 940 in 1972 and increased to 2,124 in 2009.

NAPLES [60-2-W5]
~ former post office north of Westlock.

The post office was in operation from 1924 to 1970. There were a large number of Italians among the first settlers in the district. The name "Naples" or "neapolis" means "new city". It was an Italian settlement.

NATEBY   [23-13-W4]
~ former post office near Brooks.

It was named in 1910 after Nateby Triumph, a famous stallion that had been imported from Nateby, England, by J. W. Forster, a famous horse rancher in the district.

NAUGHTON GLEN   [53-10-W4]
~ former post office near Vermilion.

It was opened in 1909 but has since been closed.

NAVARRE   [45-24-W4]
~ former station south of Wetaskiwin.

It was so named in 1912 after the northeast province of Spain, which in medieval times was an independent Kingdom. Henry of Navarre became King Henry IV of France in 1589.

NEEDMORE   [6-6-W4]
(See: ORION)

NEEDERLANDIA (NEERLANDIA) [61-3-W5]
~ former post office north of Westlock.

The first settlers and homesteaders who came into the district in 1913 were from the Netherlands. The name itself in Dutch means "lowlands".

NEEPEE CHIEF   [80-3-W6]
~ former Beaver Indian Reserve in the Peace River country.

The name was given in 1907, and is the Cree *nipi (neepee)* for "water".

NELSPUR   [46-4-W5]
~ former station near Wainwright.

In 1926 it served the Nelson's mill, and the name is a contraction of Nelson Spur.

NEMISKAM [6-10-W4]
~ hamlet east of Foremost.

The name is the Blackfoot word for "two coulees". Before 1916, the post office was called **BINGEN**. The post office was closed in 1970.

NESTOW [60-24-W4]
~ hamlet west of Westlock.

Nestow is the Cree word for "brother-in-law". The post office was opened in 1908.

NEUTRAL HILLS [37-7-W4]
~ former post office north of Coronation.

It was named in 1913 after the nearby hills which lie west of Sounding Lake. In the early days, the locality was frequented by various tribes of Indians and buffalo hunters in summer, and the necessities of that period of the year suggested the cessation of the usual hostilities for the time being. These hills are so called on the Palliser Map of 1860.

NEVIS [39-22-W4]
~ hamlet south of Alix.

The Ben Nevis Coal Mine was once in operation in the vicinity. The original *Ben Nevis* is the highest mountain in the British Isles near Fort William in Inverness-shire. Collin Livingstone suggested that the name is derived from the Gaelic *ben*, "mountain", and *ni-nhaise*, appropriate to this ungainly mountain.

NEW BRIGDEN [31-4-W4]
~ hamlet south of Grassy Island Lake.

It was so called in 1912 on the suggestion of settlers who had come from Brigden in Ontario.

NEW DAYTON [5-18-W4]
~ hamlet south of Lethbridge.

The post office was opened in 1908, and named by settlers who had come from Dayton in the State of Ohio,

NEW KIEW [53-13-W4]
~ former post office east of Mundare.

It was named by Ukrainian settlers after the capital of the Ukraine. A solid block of some 2,000 square miles of land east of Edmonton was colonized by Ukrainians during the first decade of the century.

NEW LINDSAY [47-1-W4]
~ former post office near Lloydminster.

It was named in 1911 after the first postmaster, John Lindsay. The "new" was added to distinguish it from Lindsay in Ontario.

NEW LUNNON [55-23-W4]
~ former post office north of Edmonton.

It was named after London, the capital of England. But it has an unusual spelling.

NEW NORWAY [45-21-W4]
~ village south of Camrose.

The post office was opened in 1903. Many of the early settlers were Norwegians.

The population was 228 in 1972 and increased to 323 in 2006.

NEW SAREPTA [49-22-W4]
~ village south of Edmonton.

It was named in 1905 after the city of Sion, mentioned in Chapter Four of Luke's Gospel. Previously the community was called LITTLE HAY LAKES.

The population was 202 in 1972 and increased to 530 in 2009.

NEWBROOK [62-20-W4]
~ hamlet west of Smoky Lake.

The first post office in 1917 was located in a building beside a creek. The creek was discovered when a trail was cut to the settlement in 1914.

NEWCASTLE MINE [29-20-W4]
~ hamlet west of Drumheller.

This former village was named after the nearby Newcastle coal mine.

NESTOR [48-14-W4]
(See: TORLEA)

NIEDPATH [9-18-W4]
(See: JAMIESON)

NIGHTINGALE [25-24-W4]
~ hamlet northeast of Calgary.

It was named in 1911 after Florence Nightingale, the English nurse, celebrated for her devotion to the wounded during the Crimean War, 1854-1856. The post office was in operation from 1911 to 1957.

NILREM [41-9-W4]
~ former post office near Hardisty.

The name is "Merlin" spelt backwards. Merlin was the half-legendary bard of the sixth century, who was King Arthur's wisest councilor.

"NINE RANCH"
~ near Carseland, south of Calgary.

It was a horse ranch from 1908 to 1930. The proprietor was John James Bowlen (1876-1959). Later he sat as a Legislative member and then served as Lieutenant Governor from 1950-1959. He had seen active service in Teddy's Rough Riders in Cuba while in the American army during the Spanish American War, 1899-1900.

In later life, Bowlen used to boast that he went to Harvard for four years. As a young man he was a Boston bus driver who drove his bus up to the front door of the university on his route.

NIOBE [36-28-W4]
~ former station east of Innisfail.

It was named after the Canadian Cruiser, "Niobe".

NISBET [34-28-W4]
~ former post office near Olds.

It was named in 1912 after the first pioneer H. M. Nisbet. It closed in 1943.

NISKU [50-25-W4]
~ hamlet south of Edmonton.

The International Edmonton Airport is located near it. According to the Geographic Board of Canada, the name is the Cree word for "goose". The post office was opened in 1908. Many of the original settlers were Ukrainians, and the name may be the Ukrainian word *nisku*, meaning "flat marsh land".

NITON [54-12-W5]
~ hamlet west of Edmonton.

It was so named in 1911. The name is "not in", reversed. The post office was in operation from 1908 to 1970.

NOBLEFORD [11-23-W4]
~ village north of Lethbridge.

It was named in 1913 after Charles Noble, farmer and founder of the community. He made a fortune in inventing farm machinery.

The population was 401 in 1972 and increased to 877 in 2009.

NOJACK [53-11-W5]
~ hamlet near Niton.

"No Jack" means "no way!" This means no credit.

NOLAN [9-26-W4]
~ former station north of Fort Macleod.

It was so named in 1911 after Patrick James Nolan (1864-1913), the well-known Calgary lawyer. Born in Ireland, he was educated in Dublin University before coming to Canada in 1889. Nolan was one of the most famous trial lawyers of his day.

NORAL [65-16-W4]
~ hamlet south of Lac La Biche.

The railway reached here in 1914. It could be a contraction of "Northern Alberta". It had a post office from 1921 to 1969.

NORBUCK [46-4-W5]
~ former post office south of Breton, situated on the trail to the north end of Buck Lake.

The name is coined by combining the first letters of North with the name of nearby Buck Lake. The post office was in operation from 1926 to 1970.

NORDEGG [45-15-W5]
~ ghost coal mining town west of Red Deer.

It was named after Martin Nordegg, manager of Brazeau Collieries.

NORFOLK [24-27-W4]
~ former station east of Calgary.

It was named in 1914, after the English county of Norfolk. The word means the "north" folk (people) as compared to Suffolk "south"(people).

NORMA [54-14-W4]
~ hamlet north of Vegreville.

In 1918 a prize was offered for the best name of not more than five letters; the name NORMA was selected, after Mrs. Norma V. Richardson, a resident of the district.
(See: **PREVO**)

NORMANDEAU [64-12-W4]
~ *former post office south of Lac La Biche.*

It was named in 1915 after Abbé Joseph-Aldric Normandeau, OMI, a Catholic missionary.

NORTH FORK [9-1-W5]
~ *former post office west of Pincher Creek.*

The name is descriptive, it being located near a north fork of the Oldman River. Before 1912, the post office was called OLIN CREEK.

NORTH STAR [90-23-W5]
~ *former post office south of Manning.*

The "North Star" is the bright star at the tip of the tail of Ursa Minor. It is also referred to as Polaris, the polestar, and Cynosure.

The population in 1972 was 90.

NORTH VERMILION [108-13-W5]
~ *former post office in northeast Alberta.*

It was so named in 1911, probably after beds of red ochre on the Vermilion River. Previously the post office was called FORT VERMILION[2].

NORTHBANK [58-18-W4]
~ *former post office near Smoky Lake.*

The name is descriptive of the post office's location. It was opened in 1907 but has since been closed.

NORTHLEIGH [50-6-W5]
~ *formerly a post office near Smoky Lake.*

It was named in 1915 after Northleigh in the County Down, England. The name was suggested by H.G. Foye, the first postmaster.

NORTON [10-4-W4]
~ former post office near Medicine Hat.

It was named in 1923 after the first postmaster, H. A. Norton. It has since been closed.

NORWAY VALLEY [55-3-W4]
~ former post office near Frog Lake.

It was named in 1923 after the school district. It was a nostalgic transplanted toponym, by Norwegian homesteaders.

(The) NOSE HILL RANCH
~ west of Calgary, now part of the city.

The proprietor was Thomas Riley (1842-1913) who came west with his seven sons in 1888. He was a pioneer rancher. Two of his sons, Ezra H. Riley and Harold W. H. Riley served in the Legislature, and his grandson. Justice Harold W. Riley served for many years as an Alberta Supreme Court Trail Division Judge.

NOTIKEWIN [92-23-W5]
~ former post office north of Manning.

This word is the Indian for "battle". Prior to 1924, the community was called **BATTLE RIVER PRAIRIE**.

NOTTINGHAM HOUSE [112-7-W4]
(See: **FORT CHIPEWYAN**)

NOVA VUKKOURNYA [60-8-W4]
It was named by pioneer Romanian homesteaders. Later it was anglicized to BEACON CORNER.

NOYES CROSSING [55-1-W5]
~ former post office near Alberta Beach.

It was named after Daniel E. Noyes. It was closed in 1956.

NUGENT   [44-3-W5]
~ former station west of Gull Lake.

It was named in 1911 after the maiden name of the wife of the first postmaster. The post office was in operation from 1911 to 1928.

O

OBED   [53-22-W5]
~ former post office west of Edson.

It was named in 1915 after Colonel Obed Smith, some-time Canadian Commissioner of Immigration in London, England.

OBERLIN   [38-21-W4]
~ former station south of Stettler.

It was named in 1914, probably after Oberlin in the State of Ohio.

OGDEN   [23-1-W5]
~ hamlet south of Calgary.

It is possibly named in honor of Peter Skene Ogden (1794-1854), one of the most important figures during the golden days of the fur trade in Western Canada. He was a partner in the North West Company by 1820, but he was so prominent in the violence used against the Hudson's Bay Company officers that he was dropped when the two fur companies were united in 1821. Re-engaged two years later, Ogden was sent beyond the Rocky Mountains, and his aggressiveness was useful in exploiting the fur resources of the Snake River country where American traders had penetrated. In 1835, he was one of the company's chief factors, taking charge of the New Caledonia district, with his headquarters at Fort St. James. Ross Cox described him thus in 1817: "... the humorous, honest, eccentric, law-defying Peter Ogden, an important official of the Canadian Pacific Railway, one-time vice-president in charge of Finance."

It was the location of large railway maintenance work shops.

OHATON   [46-19-W4]
~ hamlet south of Camrose.

It was named in 1906, this community obtains its name by the combination of the names Osler, Hammond and Nanton, a prominent Winnipeg financial firm which recently changed its name to Midland Securities.

OIL CITY   [1-29-W4]
~ a ghost settlement on Cameron Creek near Waterton townsite.

It is the site of the first petroleum discovery made in Alberta in 1902.

There was a tendency in mining-camp days to add "City" to the name of the community. Perhaps it gave a certain status to a conglomeration of tents or log and mud huts; perhaps it indicated a dream for the future of the camp, though it was rough and primitive when the name was chosen.

OKE   [49-21-W5]
~ ghost rail town in the Coal Branch

It was opened in 1912 and was later closed.

OKOTOKS   [20-29-W4]
~ town on the Fort Macleod-Calgary trail.

It was so named in 1897. The name is the Blackfoot word *okatoksituktai* meaning "lots of stones". It refers to the stony ford of Sheep Creek on the Calgary-Fort Macleod Trail. Previously the community was called DEWDNEY. Edgar Dewdney (1835-1916), was a civil engineer and administrator. He was first elected to the British Columbia legislature in 1869 and three years later elected to the House of Commons. Dewdney was a supporter of Sir John A. MacDonald during the period of the "Pacific Scandal" and during the Mackenzie regime. In 1880 he was appointed Indian Commissioner and two years later, Lieutenant-Governor of the Northwest Territories. It was while he held this position that the North West Rebellion breakout of 1885 took place, and his careful handling of the situation was partly responsible for the pacific behavior of the Indians. He was later Minister of the Interior (1888-1892), and Lieutenant-Governor of British Columbia (1892-1897).

The population was 1,175 in 1972 and increased to 21,690 in 2009.

OLD FORT [108-10-W4]
~ abandoned trading post.

Former Northwest Company trading post north of **FORT MCMURRAY**. It was also known as FORT ATHABASCA RIVER. It was originally built by Peter Pond in 1778.

OLD FORT POINT [45-1-W6]
~ south of Jasper.

It is the site of an old trading post built by William Henry in 1812 as a cache for supplies and furs.

OLD RED RIVER FORT [94-11-W4]
~ trading post on the Athabasca River.

It was situated three miles below where the MacKay River joins the Athabasca. Formerly the MacKay River was called the Red River.

OLDS [32-1-W5]
~ town north of Calgary.

The Canadian Pacific Railway track reached this point on the Calgary-Edmonton trail in 1893. The community is named after George Olds, sometime traffic manager of the railway.

The population was 3,408 in 1971 and increased to 7,248 in 2006.

OLD WOMEN'S BUFFALO JUMP [17-29-W4]
~ *archaeological site near Cayley.*

This important archaeological site was used continuously by inhabitants of this region over a period of about 1,500 years until the sixteenth century. Excavations by Dr. Forbis reveal that herds of bison were forced over the cliff and killed at its base. The stratified OLD WOMEN'S BUFFALO JUMP has yielded the best evidence in Alberta for the sequence of cultural changes during the last two millennia of our history. Kill sites, such as this, present the archaeologist with hundreds of artifacts, almost entirely the stone tools used to slaughter, skin and butcher bison.

OLIN CREEK   [9-1-W5]
(See: NORTH FORK)

OLIVER   [54-23-W4]
~ *former station northeast of Edmonton.*

It was named in 1905 after Frank Oliver (1853-1933), the publisher of the *Edmonton Bulletin* from 1880 to 1923. Born in Ontario, he was one of the most influential Liberals on the prairies for many years. He was elected to the Northwest Territories legislature in 1888 and after serving eight years in that assembly, was elected to the House of Commons. In 1905 Oliver could have, if he had wanted, become the first premier of Alberta. However, he preferred to be Minister of the Interior in Laurier's cabinet. He did much to encourage immigration to the prairies.

ONEFOUR   [2-4-W4]
~ *former post office southeast of Pakowki Lake*
on the United States border.

It was so called in 1904 from its situation in township one, range four, west of the Fourth Meridian. There was an error in measurement!

ONOWAY [54-2-W5]
~ *village northwest of Stony Plain.*

It was so named in 1904. It is said that this small community on the pilgrim's route from **ST. ALBERT** to **LAC STE ANNE** obtained its name when Indians would cry out as they passed, "We are ON-OUR-WAY". On the other hand, the Geographical Board states that the name is an error for Onaway, after the character in Longfellow's poem *Hiawatha*.

The population was 473 in 1972 and increased to 875 in 2006.

OPAL [58-22-W4]
~ *hamlet northeast of Edmonton.*

It is a selected name. It was so named in 1912, and since has been closed.

ORBINDALE [47-8-W4]
~ *former post office near Wainwright.*

It was named in 1907 after Orbin and Dale, the first two white babies born in the district. It closed in 1938.

ORION [6-6-W4]
~ *hamlet south of Foremost.*

It was named after the brilliant constellation, south of the zodiac, figured as a hunter with belt and sword. Prior to 1916 it was known as **NEEDMORE**. This name expresses the plight of the early homesteaders.

ORTON [9-2-W4]
~ *hamlet near Foremost.*

It was named after Josiah Orr, the postmaster. A large number of persons in this Mormon community had ORR as their surname and were all related to each other. The post office was in operation from 1907 to 1926.

ORVILTON   **[57-8-W4]**
~ former post office near St. Paul.

It was named in 1913 after the son of the first postmaster, Orville Wilson.

OSTASIK   **[58-16-W4]**
(See: **KAHWIN**)

OTLEY   **[54-13-W5]**
~ former station near Whitecourt.

It was named in 1911 after the English village of Otley in Yorkshire.

OTWAY   **[39-7-W5]**
~ a ghost village near Rocky Mountain House.

It was named after the Restoration dramatist Thomas Otway (1652-1685), whose best known play is *Venice Preserved*.

OULLETTEVILLE   **[23-21-W4]**
~ former community east of Gleichen.

In 1908 Father O. Oullette, O.M.I. founded a settlement of French Canadians on township 23, range 21, west of the fourth meridian. It seemed ill-fated from the outset. The colonists did not know prairie farming, and many returned to Quebec after a couple of years.

OUR LADY OF PEACE MISSION   **[24-1-W5]**
~ near Calgary.

A Catholic mission was established on the banks of the Bow River in 1873 and named after the Blessed Virgin Mary. It predates the building of Fort Calgary in 1875.

OWL RIVER   **[68-13-W4]**
~ hamlet north of Lac La Biche.

It is located where Owl River enters Lac La Biche and is near Sir Winston Churchill Provincial Park.

OWLSEYE LAKE [58-10-W4]
~ hamlet southwest of Therien.

It was so named in 1913, and is said to commemorate a hunter so nicknamed who was killed by Indians in the vicinity. The post office closed in 1971.

OXVILLE [46-2-W4]
~ former settlement northeast of Wainwright.

The settlers were still using oxen in the neighborhood in 1907 when the district was opened up for homesteaders. It had a post office from 1907 to 1931.

OYEN [27-4-W4]
~ town east of Drumheller.

It was named in 1912 after a pioneer Norwegian settler, Andrew Oyen.

The population was 954 in 1972 and increased to 1,190 in 2009.

OZADA [25-8-W5]
~ former community near Morley.

It was near the junction of the Bow and the Kananaskis rivers. The Stony word *Oozed* means fork. During World War Two, there was a German Prisoner of War camp located here.

P

PADDLE PRAIRIE   [103-21-W5]
~ hamlet south of High Level.

This northern settlement is situated where Highway 35 to the Territories crosses the Boyer River. A post office was established in 1945.

PADDLE RIVER   [59-2-W5]
~ former post office north of Hawk Hills.

It was named in 1913 after the nearby river, which is mentioned by this name in E. Ermatinger's *York Factor Express Journal* in 1827. The name is derived from the fact that a canoe could be propelled on it upstream by use of the paddle alone, while on the nearby swifter Pembina River the pole and track line had to be used.

PADSTOW   [58-8-W5]
~ former post office near Mayerthorpe.

It was named after the Cornish village of Padstow. The Old English word "stow" had the meaning of "place", "place of assembly", or "Holy Place", This English village is named after St. Petroc, indicating the existence there of a church dedicated to that particular saint. It was opened in 1911 and was closed in 1951.

PAKAN   [58-17-W4]
~ former post office east of Edmonton.

It was named in 1887 after an important Cree Chief whose English name was James Seenum. The Cree word *pakan* means "nut". This former community, which was established by Rev. George McDougall as a Methodist Mission in 1862, was first called **VICTORIA** after the Queen. The name was changed to avoid confusion with other "Victoria"s across Canada.

PAKOWKI [6-8-W4]
~ *former station east of Foremost.*

It was named after the nearby Pakowki Lake. This descriptive word is the Blackfoot for "bad water". It appears on Palliser's Map of 1865 as PEEKOPEE.

PAMAGA [15-10-W4]
~ *former station west of Claresholm.*

It was a composite name designating members of the family of Sir George Bury.

PANCRAS [21-4-W4]
~ *former station near Medicine Hat.*

It was probably named after St. Pancras, one of the metropolitan boroughs of London and also an important railway station for the north. It reminds one of the old saying (that Scots abhor): "St. George for England and St. Pancras for Scotland".
(See: **CAVENDISH**)

PARADISE VALLEY [47-2-W5]
~ *village southwest of Lloydminster.*

It was named in 1910 by the California Land Company, which advertised and promoted land in this district. The name is intended to be descriptive.

The population was 174 in 1972 and increased to 183 in 2006.

PARK COURT [54-7-W5]
~ *former post office near Entwistle.*

The appearance of the countryside, it is said, reminded an old lady of an English park. The post office was opened in 1910 and closed in 1955.

PARKLAND [15-27-W4]
~ *hamlet west of Claresholm.*

It was named in 1907 after a pioneer resident of the district, Park Hill.

PARTRIDGE   **[9-22-W4]**
~ *former station near Lethbridge.*

There used to be a large number of wild fowls in the district.

PASHLEY   **[12-3-W4]**
~ *former station southeast of Medicine Hat.*

It was named in 1910 after the maiden name of the wife of David McNicoll (1852-1916), an executive of the Canadian Pacific Railway.

PASSBURG   **[7-3-W5]**
~ *former village near Blairmore.*

It was named by combining the word "Pass" from **CROWSNEST PASS** and the word "burg" in the sense of town. The community died in 1936.

PATIENCE   **[47-26-W5]**
~ *former post office near Pigeon Lake.*

When this region was first settled in 1902, it required "patience" to travel over the roads in the vicinity.

PATRICIA   **[20-13-W4]**
~ *hamlet north of Brooks.*

It was named in honor of Princess Patricia, daughter of His Royal Highness, Duke of Connaught, Governor-General of Canada, 1911-1916. The first Canadian Contingent, Great War, 1914-1918, was named the Princess Pat's Light Infantry. She presented the corps with regimental colors made by herself. At the close of the War the Princess married Captain Ramsay of the British Navy. She died in 1972.
(See: **PRINCESS**)

PAUL'S CORNERS   **[82-24-W5]**
~ *former post office near Peace River.*

It was named after H. Paul, the first postmaster

PAXSON [66-20-W4]
~ former post office south of Athabasca.

It was named in 1913 after a former employee of the postmaster, G. Schaffer. It closed in 1969.

PEACE POINT
~ locality on the north shore of the Peace River.

In the account of his voyage to the Pacific in 1792-1793, Alexander Mackenzie narrates that he entered the Peace River on October 12, and continues: "On the 13th noon we came to Peace Point, from which, according to the report of my interpreter, the river derives its name; it was the spot where the Knistenaux (Crees) and Beaver Indians settled their dispute; the real name of the river and point being that of the land which was the object of contention. When this country was formerly invaded by the Knistenaux, they found the Beaver Indians inhabiting the lands, and the adjoining tribes were those they called Slaver. They drove both these tribes before them; the latter proceeded down the river from Lake of the Hills (Lake Athabasca) in consequence of which that part of it obtained the name of Slave River. The former proceeded up the river; and when the Knistenaux made peace with them, this place was settled to be the boundary".

PEACE RIVER [83-21-W5]
~ town in Peace River Country.

The Peace River Country extends across a large section of Northern Alberta between the fifty-fourth and fifty-ninth parallel. The soil of this region is similar to that parkland along the banks of the North Saskatchewan River with an annual rainfall of about fifteen inches. Despite its northern latitude, the area is blessed with an average temperature range that assures normal harvests. This rich region is populated by a breed of Albertans that Lord Tweedsmuir describes as "one of the few aristocrats left in the world. I think he is one of the most steadfast human beings now alive." The town of PEACE RIVER is located at the junction of the Peace and Little Smoky Rivers. Before 1919 the community was called PEACE RIVER CROSSING ST. MARY'S HOUSE, the first Hudson's Bay Company trading post to be built in the Peace River Country in 1818, was located near here.

The population was 5,384 in 1972 and increased to 6,315 in 2006.

PEACOCK [13-23-W4]
~ former station southeast of Carmangay.

It was named after William Peacock on whose land the station was built in 1928.

PEARCE [10-25-W4]
~ former post office west of Lethbridge.

It was named in 1910 after William Pearce (1848-1930), Canadian civil engineer and land surveyor. He played an important part in the development of the prairies in regard to settlement, mining, irrigation and railways. He left behind him, in manuscript, a valuable account of his service in the west, which has not yet been published.

PEAT [55-7-W4]
~ former post office near Elk Point.

It was named in 1915 in error for Peet after the first postmaster, John Peet. It had a post office from 1915 to 1955.

PEAVINE [59-7-W5]
~ former post office near Whitecourt.

It was opened in 1908. Pea vines grow abundantly in the vicinity.

PEERLESS [19-8-W4]
~ former post office near Brooks.

It was named in 1911 because of the bumper grain crops that were being grown in the district at this time.

PEERS [54-14-W4]
~ hamlet west of Chip Lake.

It was named in 1911 after the family name of the mother of Sir Charles Peers Davidson (1841-1929), of Montreal, Chief Justice of Quebec from 1912 to 1915. He was the author of *Statutes Relating to Banks and Banking* (1876).

PEGUIS [54-7-W4]
(See: MONKMAN)

PEIGAN POST
(See: BOW FORT)

PEIGAN [8-27-W4]
~ former station northeast of Pincher Creek.

Possibly a misspelling of the word "Piegan". The Piegans, an Algonkian-speaking Indian tribe of the western prairies, once occupied the region around the present city of **LETHBRIDGE**. They were part of the Blackfoot Confederacy.

PEKISKO [17-2-W5]
~ former post office southwest of High River.

It is the Blackfoot word for "foothills" or "rolling hills". This name was suggested by Fred Stimson in 1896.

PELICAN PORTAGE [78-17-W4]
~ former post office near Pelican Lake.

The white pelican, *Pelicanus erythronhynchos*, is locally common about lakes of the prairies, where it makes its nest on bare islands. There were a large number of these birds in the district. The post office was closed in 1969.

PEMBINA CROSSING [58-3-W5]
It was named by early settlers moving north across the north flowing river. Later its name was changed to MacDONALD CROSSING after its first permanent ferry boat operator. This name first appeared on David Thompson's map of 1814. (See: **BELVEDERE**).

PEMBRIDGE [57-5-W5]
~ former post office near Sangudo.

The name is formed by combining part of the name "Pembina River" with a "bridge" over it. It was closed in 1970.

PEMBURTON HILL   [50-2-W5]
~ former post office near Thorsby.

It was named after the first postmaster, C. Burton. The "Pem" part was added to distinguish it from **BURTONSVILLE**. There was a post office there from 1913 to 1937.

PEMUKAN   [35-4-W4]
~ hamlet north of Grassy Island Lake.

The Cree word *pemukan* means "across the water". The railway reached here in 1914.

PENDANT D'OREILLE{1}   [3-7-W4]
~ former post office south of Foremost.

It was opened in 1910. The name is French and means "earring" and is also the name of a tribe of native people.

PENDANT D'OREILLE{2}   [3-7-W4]
~ former custom post near Wild Horse.

It was opened in 1904 and closed in 1917 to permit the police to enlist in the Canadian Army and go overseas. It was never re-opened.

PENDRYL   [46-5-W5]
~ former post office east of Buck Lake.

It was named in 1916 after an English family of Pendryl that had come from Boscobel, in Shropshire, England. The name itself is Welsh.

PENHOLD   [36-28-W4]
~ town southwest of Red Deer.

The railway tracks reached here in 1893. During the Second World War Penhold had a large air-training station, one of the many located across the Canadian prairies.

The population was 430 in 1972 and increased to 2,114 in 2008.

PEORIA [73-3-W6]
~ former post office south of Birch Hills.

There is a city of this name in the State of Illinois. The pioneer settlers and homesteaders had come from the United States.

PERBECK [34-32-W4]
~ former post office near Trochu.

It was named in 1908 after the Isle of Purbeck in the County of Dorset, England. The spelling was changed by the Post Office Department of Ottawa. It closed in 1944.

PERRYVALE [63-23-W4]
~ hamlet west of Athabasca.

It was named after Mr. Perry, the first postmaster, with the word 'vale' added to the end.

PHIDIAS [22-22-W4]
~ former station near Gleichen.

It was named in 1912 after Phidias, the ancient Greek sculptor and architect, who designed the Parthenon.

PHILLIPS [47-12-W4]
~ former station east of Viking.

It was named in 1909 after Henry Phillips, an official of the Grand Trunk Railway. Previously the community was called LAKE THOMAS.

PHILOMENA [71-11-W4]
~ hamlet northeast of Lac La Biche.

It was opened in 1916. It derives its name from the Greek word for "nightingale". In Greek mythology, Philomela or Philomena is a princess of Athens who was raped by her brother-in-law, Tereus, who then tore out her tongue. When, in revenge, she and her sister Procne killed Tereus' son, the gods changed the fleeing sisters - one into a swallow and the other into a nightingale.

PHOENIX   [39-10-W5]
~ hamlet near Rocky Mountain House.

The phoenix is, according to legend, a bird of great beauty which, after living 500 years in the Arabian wilderness, builds for itself a funeral pyre, lights the pyre with the fanning of its wings, and is burnt. It rises from its ashes new and young. The post office was opened in 1923 and closed some years later.

PIBROCH   [61-26-W4]
~ hamlet west of Westlock.

A pibroch is a martial air played on the bagpipes. This former village was so named in 1910 because it was a Scottish settlement. It had been previously called DEBNEY after Philip Debney, railway engineer.

PICKARDVILLE   [58-27-W4]
~ hamlet south of Westlock.

It was named in 1909 after the first postmaster, William Pickard. The post office closed in 1966.

PICTURE BUTTE   [11-21-W4]
~ town north of Lethbridge.

The name is descriptive, being a translation of the Blackfoot "the beautiful hill".

The population was 1,062 in 1972 and increased to 1,592 in 2006.

PIEGAN   [8-27-W4]
~ former station near Cardston.

It was named before 1901 after the Piegan tribe of the Blackfoot Confederacy, whose reserve is nearby. The name is a corruption of *pikuni*, referring to this Algonkian-speaking tribe having badly dressed robes. The Piegan once occupied the region around the present city of LETHBRIDGE.

PIERRE-AU-CALUMET [97-11-W4]
~ former North West Company trading post on the Athabasca River.

The name referred to a pipestone cliff nearby. The post was abandoned in 1820 for want of provisions.

PINCHER CREEK [6-30-W4]
~ town west of Fort Macleod.

The name derives from the finding on the site, in 1874, of a pair of pinchers lost by prospectors in 1868. The first white settlement dates from 1878, when it became a North West Mounted Police wintering horse ranch.

The population was 3,337 in 1972 and increased to 3,712 in 2008.

PINCHER STATION [7-30-W4]
~ former station north of Pincher Creek.

PINCHER CREEK is the only large community in Southern Alberta not on a railway line. The station is three miles from the town.

PINE LAKE [36-25-W4]
~ former post office southeast of Red Deer.

The nearby lake is called Ghost Pine Lake. Indians believed the vicinity to be haunted by a headless horseman since a battle was fought here before the coming of European settlers. Many traces of this battle have been found. The post office was opened in 1895.

PINE POINT
~ community on the Mackenzie Highway.

The railway reached here in 1965.

PINGLE   **[80-6-W4]**
~ former station near Fort McMurray.

It was named in 1925 after Captain Charles Stewart Pingle, Speaker of the Alberta legislature. Born in Morris, Manitoba, in 1880, Pingle was a **MEDICINE HAT** druggist when first elected to the legislature in 1913 as the Liberal member for Redcliff. He was named the Speaker on the death of Fisher in 1920. He lost his seat in the 1921 general election. Pingle sat again in the legislature as the Liberal member for Medicine Hat in 1925, and died while still a member three years later.

PINHORN   **[1-8-W4]**
~ former post office and a custom post near Pakowki Lake, east of Coutts.

It was named after Dr. G. C. Pinhorn, first Veterinary Inspector appointed to represent the federal Department of Agriculture. Earlier a quarantine station was located near here. The post office opened in 1914 but has since been closed. The custom post was moved to **ADEN** in 1924.

PIONEER   **[55-15-W5]**
~ former post office northeast of Edson.

The name is another word used to describe the first settlers.

PIPESTONE CREEK   **[70-8-W6]**
~ former post office southwest of Wembley.

It was named from the occurrence on the nearby stream of fragments of soft, fine-grained, gray-blue argillite, which the Indians have used for the manufacture of pipes.

PIRMEZ CREEK   **[24-3-W5]**
~ former post office west of Calgary.

It was named in 1910 after Count Raoul Pirmez, owner of the Belgian Horse Ranch.

PITLOCHRIE   **[69-12-W4]**
~ former station northeast of Lac La Biche.

It was named in 1916 after Pitlochry, in Perthshire, Scotland. It is the Gaelic word for "hamlet of the assembly".

PIVOT   [17-1-W4]
~ former station northeast of Medicine Hat.

The name is a reference to the fact that this is a turning point of the railway. The railway reached here in 1924.

PIYAMI   [10-21-W4]
~ former station north of Lethbridge.

It is named after a nearby coulee. It is the Blackfoot word for "far out."

PLAIN LAKE   [53-12-W4]
~ former post office south of Two Hills.

The name is derived from the fact that the nearby lake is situated between two plains. The post office was opened in 1910.

PLAMONDON   [68-16-W4]
~ village west of Lac La Biche.

It was named in 1909 after American settler Joseph Plamondon, from the State of Michigan, who had first settled in the **MORINVILLE** district before moving on.

The population was 220 in 1972 and increased to 253 in 1997.

PLEASANT VIEW   [68-20-W4]
~ former post office north of Athabasca.

The name is descriptive. Before 1915 the post office had been called WINDY RIDGE, which apparently had discouraged settlement in the district.

POCAHONTAS   [49-27-W5]
~ former post office near Jasper Lake.

The name was first used as that of a coal mining community near here, that has since been abandoned. The post office was so named in 1911 after Pocahontas, a coal mining town in the State of Virginia. The historical Pocahontas was the Indian princess who saved the life of Captain John Smith after his capture by her father in 1608. The veracity of this is still a subject of dispute.

POE   **[49-16-W4]**
~ *hamlet southeast of Beaverhill Lake.*

It was named in 1909 after Edgar Allan Poe (1809-1848), American poet and author of horror stories. His best known poem is "The Raven". It closed in 1964.

POINT BRÛLÉ   **[50-27-W5]**
(See: BRÛLÉ)

POINT PROVIDENCE   **[115-11-W4]**
(See: CARLSON LANDING)

POLLOCK   **[40-12-W5]**
(See: ANCONA)

POLLOCKVILLE   **[25-12-W4]**
~ *hamlet southeast of Coleman.*

It was named in 1910 after the first postmaster, R. Pollock. James Henry (Jack) Horner, colorful member of Parliament from 1958 to 1979, operates a ranch near here.

POND HOUSE   **[25-12-W4]**
~ *North West Company trading post, now abandoned, on the bank of the Athabasca River above the confluence of the Embarras and Athabasca Rivers.*

This trading post was built in 1778 by Peter Pond (1740-1807), the fur trader and explorer. The maps he drew of his explorations in the North West were among the first which exercised an influence over future events. He died in poverty.

PONOKA   **[43-25-W4]**
~ *town north of Lacombe.*

The Blackfoot word *ponoka* means "deer" or "elk". The railway reached here in 1893.

The population was 4,554 in 1972 and increased to 6,576 in 2006. (See: **BARKER'S STOPPING HOUSE; CALGARY-EDMONTON TRAIL STAGING POSTS**)

POPLAR GROVE [35-28-W4]
(See: INNISFAIL)

POPLAR RIDGE [80-7-W6]
~ former post office northwest of Spirit River.

The name is descriptive, there being a large number of poplars in the vicinity.

POWER HOUSE [49-7-W5]
(See: DRAYTON VALLEY)

PRAIRIE VIEW [9-22-W4]
(See: KIPP)

PRENTISS [39-26-W4]
~ former station north of Red Deer.

It was opened in 1914. There is another Prentiss in the State of Mississippi, near Jackson.

PRESTVILLE [78-4-W6]
~ hamlet southeast of Rycroft.

It was named in 1916 after B. J. Prest, a railway engineer. It used to rank as a village.

PRETTY HILL [47-20-W4]
Postal officials gave this name to a site of a proposed post office, but local homesteaders objected. Soon the name was changed to **DINANT**, after the town the Belgian settlers had come from.

PREVO [39-1-W5]
~ former station north of Sylvan Lake.

This place was at one time called **NORMA**. Prevo may be an incorrect spelling for Prevot, the French for "provost" or "mayor".

PRIDDIS   [22-3-W5]
~ former post office south of Calgary.

It was named in 1894 after the first postmaster, Charles Priddis. It is now part of **CALGARY.**

PRIMROSE   [57-4-W4]
~ former post office near Elk Point.

Possibly so named in 1930 after Philip Carteret Hill Primrose (1865 -1937), who after serving for 30 years with the North West Mounted Police, rose to the rank of superintendent, and then served for twenty years as an Edmonton Police Magistrate. In 1935, Primrose was appointed the Lieutenant Governor of Alberta. He died 18 months later. The post office operated from 1930 to 1970.

PRIMULA   [56-5-W4]
~ former post office near Elk Point.

It probably was named after the primula or the primrose which is found in large numbers in springtime on the prairies. It was opened in 1913, and closed in 1970.

PRINCESS   [20-12-W4]
~ hamlet north of Brooks.

It was named in 1918 in honor of Her Royal Highness Princess Patricia, daughter of the Duke of Connaught, then Governor-General of Canada. The adjoining community is called **PATRICIA.** She died in 1972.

PROSPECT VALLEY   [45-2-W4]
~ former post office near Wainwright.

It was opened in 1910, and closed twenty years later. It has a good view of Buffalo Lake.

PROSPERITY   [67-19-W4]
~ former post office northeast of Athabasca.

The name expresses the hopes of the early homesteaders.

PROVOST [39-2-W4]
~ *town southeast of Wainwright.*

"Provost" is the title applied to the Chief Magistrate of a Scottish town and is the equivalent to the English "Mayor". The post office was opened in 1908. Many of the original homesteaders came from Scotland.

The population was 1,502 in 1972 and increased to 2,078 in 2005.

PUFFER [39-10-W4]
~ *former post office near Alliance.*

It was named in 1908 after William Franklin Puffer, Liberal member of the legislature for **LACOMBE** from 1905 to 1917. Born in Ontario of United Empire Loyalist descent, Puffer came to Alberta as a young man to homestead in the LACOMBE district. He became a successful lumber merchant prior to entering politics.

PURPLE SPRINGS [10-14-W4]
~ *hamlet west of Bow Island.*

It is so named after a spring in a coulee where purple flowers grow. The Canadian Pacific Railway tracks reached here in July, 1893. Nellie McClung used the name, *Purple Springs*, as the title of a novel she wrote in 1921 in which the campaign for women's rights is relived by the author's ability to portray real characters and the life of rural Canada vividly as she knew it.

Q

QUAGMIRE HOUSE   [50---6-W5]
(See: MUSAKO FORT)

QUARREL   [46-16-W4]
~ *former post office near Daysland.*

It was so called after a lake, now dry, known in Cree as *kekatomokichewonepekah sakigan*, or "quarrel spring lake". General Sam Steele says in *Forty Years in Canada* that it was an old Indian camping place where there were many quarrels between hunting parties. From 1905 to 1928, there was a post office.

QUEENSTOWN   [19-22-W4]
~ *hamlet south of Gleichen.*

The name was first given to the district in 1881 by Captain Dawson, manager of the Canadian Pacific Colonization Company. The Queen referred to is Victoria, Queen of Great Britain and Ireland and Empress of India, who reigned from 1837 to 1901. She was the daughter of Edward, Duke of Kent, fourth son of George III, and Princess Mary Louise Victoria of Saxe-Cobourg. In the 1920's this community ranked as a village, but it has been on the decline since. The post office was closed in 1970.

QUIGLEY   [82-6-W4]
~ *former station south of Gordon Lake.*

It was so named in 1917 after James N. Quigley, a railway contractor. Quigley is an Irish surname and means 'escort' or 'companion'.

QUORN RANCH [20-2-W5]
~ south of Calgary.

It was part of the original land leased to Fred Stimson in 1882. It was later transferred to Charles Martin and Associates of Quorn, England. There is a town of this name near Adelaide, Australia. The QUORN RANCH has also been called the SHEEP CREEK RANCH.

R

RABBIT HILL
~ hamlet near Edmonton.

There were a number of Ukrainian settlers in the district. Father Albert Kulawy, who had come from Winnipeg, built a church here in 1903.

RADNOR   [26-5-W5]
~ former station west of Cochrane.

It was named in 1884 after Lady Wilma, daughter of the fifth Earl of Radnor, and wife of the second Earl Lathom. She was awarded the C.B.E. in 1920.

RADWAY   [58-20-W4]
~ village south of Smoky Lake.

It was named after Orland S. Radway, first postmaster. His father had settled in the district in 1897, and was one of the first homesteaders. The word is the Old English for "road suitable for riding".

The population was 158 in 1972 and increased to 173 in 1997.

RAHAB   [78-1-W6]
~ former station on the Edmonton, Dunvegan and British Columbia Railway line in the Peace River district.

It was named in 1916 after the biblical character, Rahab, who was the woman who took Joshua's two spies into her house in Jericho and hid them from the king. Rewarding her for her assistance, the Israelites spared her and her household when they captured Jericho. (See: Joshua 2:1 - 18)

RAINBOW LAKE   [109-9-W6]
~ oil town in northern Alberta near Hay Lake.

Probably named after the rainbow trout which are found in large numbers in northern lakes.

The population was 565 in 1972 and increased to 1,082 in 2007.

RAINIER   [16-16-W4]
~ hamlet north of Vauxhall.

It was named in 1911 after Mount Rainier in the State of Washington.

RALEY   [4-24-W4]
~ former station south of Magrath.

It was named after C. Raley of **LETHBRIDGE** in 1902.

RALSTON   [15-9-W5]
~ former post office north of Medicine Hat.

It was named after Colonel James L. Ralston, Minister of National Defense during World War II, who expanded the nearby Suffield Army Firing Range.

RANFURLY   [51-12-W4]
~ hamlet north of Viking.

It was named in 1905 after the fifth Earl of Ranfurly who was Governor of New Zealand from 1897 to 1899.

RAT LAKE   **[63-4-W4]**
~ former post office north of Bonnyville.

The name is a misnomer because, since 1950, the province has prided itself on being almost free of rats. Its prevention program has been the subject of inquiries from many of the rat-infested areas of the world. The crux of the program is a series of poison-bait stations, using the pesticide warfarin, situated on about 3,500 premises from the border to twelve miles into the province. Joe Gurba, head of the government Pest Control Branch, states that an estimated 33,900 rats were killed coming into Alberta during 1970. The rat referred to in this name may, of course, be a muskrat.

RAVEN   **[36-4-W5]**
~ former post office south of Sylvan Lake.

The north and south branches of the Raven River traverse the municipal district of RAVEN and join at the post office. It was opened in 1905 and closed in 1970.

RAVINE   **[54-9-W5]**
~ former post office near Mayerthorpe.

Located in a ravine, it was in operation from 1911 with a break until 1952.

RAWDONVILLE   **[30-24-W4]**
(See: SWALWELL)

RAYMOND   **[6-20-W4]**
~ town south of Lethbridge.

It was named in 1902 to honor Raymond Knight, the eldest son of Jesse W. Knight, a prominent Mormon southern Alberta rancher. Knight, Sr. was the proprietor of the large K-2 (Bar K Two) ranch, near **CARDSTON**. In 1901, he contracted with the irrigation and railway company for 26,000 acres for growing sugar beets and building a sugar factory. A townsite was selected on the open prairie and named RAYMOND. The project attracted 1,500 people within two years, mostly young Mormon settlers from the State of Utah.

The population was 2,063 in 1972 and increased to 3,674 in 2009.

READY MADE
~ hamlet east of Lethbridge.

It derived its name when the railway company built sod huts on each quarter-section prior to the arrival of settlers.

REARVILLE
~ former post office near Medicine Hat.

The post office was opened in 1914 but has since been closed.

RECO   **[49-19-W5]**
~ ghost town in the Coal Branch district.

The name is a compound of Reliance Coal Company, which once had a mine near here. The post office, which was opened in 1926, has been closed for many years.

(See: **COAL BRANCH**)

RED DEER   [38-27-W4]
~ *city halfway between Calgary and Edmonton.*

It was named after the Red Deer River which flows east across central Alberta. The name is a translation of the Cree Indian *was-ka-sioo*. Three miles west of the present city is a ford where the trail from the south to Edmonton crossed the river. Traffic north over the prairie greatly increased after the Canadian Pacific Railway reached Calgary in 1883, and in the autumn of that year, a stopping place and trading post were erected at the RED DEER CROSSING. As time passed, the word "crossing" dropped out of use. In 1884, a post office was opened. In 1891, the railway line reached the Red Deer River from the south and the present townsite was laid out near the original settlement, and after debate, it was agreed to retain the name RED DEER for the new community.

The population was 27,431 in 1972 and increased to 89,891 in 2009. It is the fourth largest city in the province.

RED EARTH (RED EARTH CREEK) [27-22-W4]
(See: REDLAND)

RED LODGE   [34-2-W5]
~ *former post office near Olds.*

It was opened in 1896. Originally Red Lodge was the name of the ranch of the first postmaster, Colin Thomson. It has since been closed.

RED STAR   [81-2-W6]
~ *former post office near Fairview.*

It was opened in 1927, and got its name from the school district. It has been now closed for several years.

RED WILLOW   [40-18-W4]
~ *hamlet northeast of Stettler.*

The post office was opened in 1903. On some of the early maps, the nearby stream is either called Red Willow Creek or Old Wives Creek.

The population in 1972 was 63.

REDCLIFF   [13-6-W4]
~ town northwest of Medicine Hat.

The name refers to the red cliffs along the banks of the South Saskatchewan River.

The population was 2,242 in 1972 and increased to 5,096 in 2006.

REDLAND   [27-22-W4]
~ hamlet southwest of Drumheller.

The name is descriptive. The former station was opened in 1914 and was named by the Canadian National Railway. In the 1920's it ranked as a village, but it has since declined. On some maps it is referred to as RED EARTH, or RED EARTH CREEK.

REDLOW   [72-10-W6]
(See: **BEAVERLODGE**)

REDWATER   [57-21-W4]
~ town northeast of Edmonton.

It got its name from the nearby Redwater River, a tributary of the North Saskatchewan. This river appears as "Vermilion River" on David Thompson's :map of 1814. The change was made to avoid duplication.

The population was 1,303 in 1972 and increased to 2,192 in 2006.

REID HILL   [17-22-W4]
~ former post office near High River.

It was named after Orick A, Reid, the first postmaster. It was opened in 1906 but has since been closed.

REIST   [31-10-W4]
~ former post office near Hanna.

It was named in 1911 after the first postmaster, E. B. Reist.

RELIANCE   [10-16-W4]
~ former station near Taber.

It is called after a former coal mine in the district, which was operated by the Reliance Coal Company.

RENO   [81-20-W5]
~ hamlet northwest of Kimiwan Lake.

It was named in 1915, presumably after the famous Reno in the State of Nevada.

The population in 1972 was 62.

RETLAW   [13-17-W4]
~ hamlet northwest of Taber.

This is a coined word - Walter spelled backwards. It was named after Walter R. Baker, private secretary to the Earl of Dufferin while he was Governor-General of Canada in the 1870's. Baker afterwards became the assistant to the General Manager of the Canadian Pacific Railway. Prior to 1913 the post office was called **BARNEY**.

RIBSTONE   [43-2-W4]
~ hamlet southeast of Wainwright.

It was named in 1907 after nearby Ribstone Lake. The name first appears on Palliser's Map of 1865, and may refer to a large stone that bears marks resembling a man's ribs. The name was once used for a provincial constituency.

The population in 1972 was 53. (See: **DUNN**)

RICH LAKE   [64-11-W4]
~ former post office south of Rich Lake.

The name is descriptive because of the abundance of fish in the nearby lake.

RICHDALE   [30-12-W4]
~ hamlet east of Hanna.

The post office was opened in 1910. The community once ranked as a village. The name is descriptive.

RICHMOND PARK [68-21-W4]
~ former post office northwest of Athabasca.

Probably named after Richmond, near London, England.

RICINUS [36-7-W5]
~ former post office west of Caroline.

Ricinus is the Latin word for the castor-oil plant. The post office was opened in 1913.

RIDGECLOUGH [46-1-W4]
~ former post office near Wainwright.

It was named in 1912 after the Ontario farm of W. B. Gordon, the first postmaster.

RIFE [60-7-W4]
~ former post office southeast of Therien.

The name was selected by the postal officials in Ottawa in 1910.

RIMBEY [42-2-W5]
~ town west of Ponoka.

It was named in 1903 after the first three settlers in the district, the Rimbey brothers, who came from the State of Illinois.

The population was 1,465 in 1972 and increased to 2,496 in 2008.

RINARD [1-22-W4]
It was named in 1924 after Rinard in the State of Illinois, the former home of the first postmaster, R. J. Miller.

RIO GRANDE [70-12-W6]
~ former post office southwest of Beaverlodge.

"Grande" because it is the **GRANDE PRAIRIE** country and "rio" because the Red Willow River is half a mile distant. It was opened in 1919.

RIVERBEND   **[54-23-W4]**
~ former station northeast of Edmonton.

The name is descriptive.

RIVERBOW   **[16-15-W4]**
~ former post office near Retlaw.

It was opened in 1909. The name is descriptive.

RIVERCOURSE   **[46-1-W4]**
~ hamlet south of Lloydminster on the Alberta-Saskatchewan border.

The post office was opened in 1907.

RIVERTON   **[54-3-W4]**
~ former post office near Lloydminster.

It was opened in 1914.

RIVIERE CASTOR   **[63-4-W4]**
~ former post office near Lloydminster.

The name is the French for "river of beavers". The post office was opened in 1914 but has since been closed.

RIVIÈRE-QUI-BARRE   **[55-26-W4]**
~ former post office northwest of Edmonton.

It is named after the nearby river that flows southeast into the Sturgeon. It received its name before 1880 by lumbermen who could not use the river for driving their logs. The post office was opened in 1895.

ROBB [49-21-W5]
~ ghost town in the Coal Branch district.

It still has a post office. It was first called MINEHEAD, then until 1923, BALKAN. Robb is probably named after James A. Robb (1850-1929), Canadian industrialist and politician. He was considered for the leaderships of the Liberal party following the death of Sir Wilfred Laurier. He joined Mackenzie King's first cabinet as Minister of Trade and Commerce. He later was named Minister of Immigration and Colonization and was the Finance Minister at the time of his death.
(See: **COAL BRANCH**)

ROBBER'S ROOST
(See: **FORT CONRAD**)

ROBERTSON [25-2-W5]
~ former station northwest of Calgary.

It was named in 1917 after Private James Robertson, V.C., a Canadian infantry locomotive engineer, who was killed in action during the Great War in November, 1917, when his platoon was held up by a machine gun and uncut barbwire. Private Robertson reached the machine gun post, shot four of the crew and turned the gun on the remainder, thus saving the lives of several of his comrades.

ROBINSON [9-3-W4]
~ former post office southeast of Medicine Hat.

It was named after Dr. John Lyle Robinson (1890-1953), Social Credit member of the legislature for **MEDICINE HAT** for eighteen years. Born at Belfast, Ireland, he was educated in Dublin as a chiropractor before coming to Canada in 1913. He was first elected to the legislature in 1935 and was appointed by Premier Manning Minister of Industries and Labor in 1948. He died while still a sitting member.

ROCHESTER   [62-24-W4]
~ hamlet northeast of Westlock.

It was named in 1912 after Herbert Rochester, secretary to M. H. Macleod, who was General Manager, western lines of the Canadian National Railway from 1909 to 1915.

ROCHFORT BRIDGE   [57-7-W5]
~ hamlet southeast of Mayerthorpe.

It was so named in 1920. Originally the community had been called ROCHFORT and then its name was changed to WANEKVILLE. There is a Rochfort in France; it is a naval station on the Bay of Biscay, where Napoleon surrendered to Captain Maitland, a British naval officer, on July 15, 1815, thus ending the Napoleonic Wars!

The population in 1972 was 77.

ROCHON SANDS   [40-20-W4]
~ summer village northeast of Stettler.

It is situated in a 158 acre provincial park of the same name on the shore of Buffalo Lake.

ROCKY MOUNTAIN HOUSE   [39-7-W5]
~ town fifty-three miles west of Red Deer on the North Saskatchewan River.

It was the site of a North West Company trading post as early as 1799 and remained the most westerly Hudson's Bay post on the river until 1875, in spite of being twice burned by the Blackfoot Indians. The area was surveyed for homesteads in 1906 and received rail service in 1912. Nearby was another trading post known as **ACTON HOUSE.**

The earliest reference to the Rocky Mountains is that of John Knight, governor of York Factory who, in his diary for 1716, states that Indians had told him that very far to the west there were prodigious mountains. In 1730, Beauharnois, the French Governor, transmitted to France a sketch drawn for La Vérendrye by the Indian Ochagach on which is indicated the "Montagnes de Pierres Brilliantes" or "Mountains of Bright Stones". First mention of their present name is to be found in Legardeur St. Pierre's journal for 1752, which refers to the "montagnes de Roche".

Rocky Mountains is a translation of the Cree Indian name for them, *as-sin-wati*. Seen from the east across the prairies, they appear as a great rocky mass. Towering to altitudes of 12,000 feet, they form over half of the western boundary of Alberta. From the United States border, their ranges sprawl northwestward for approximately 450 miles, and leave Alberta near the headwaters of the Smoky River.

The population of the town was 3,153 in 1972 and increased to 7,231 in 2007.

ROCKY RAPIDS   [50-7-W5]
~ former post office north of Drayton Valley.

It was named in 1915 after the rapids that occur in the nearby swift-flowing North Saskatchewan River.

The population in 1972 was 69.

ROCKYFORD   [26-23-W4]
~ village southwest of Drumheller.

It was so named in 1914 after a ford over a nearby stream.

The population was 285 in 1972 and increased to 349 in 2006.

RODEF   [57-17-W4]
~ former post office northeast of Lamont.

The origin of this name is not known.

RODINO   [48-10-W4]
~ former post office near Wainwright.

It was so named in 1911 by the Postal officials in Ottawa. It has been closed for many years.

ROLLING HILLS   [15-13-W4]
~ hamlet southeast of Brooks.

The name is descriptive and is in contrast to the coulee country to the south.

The population in 1972 was 132.

ROLLINSON   **[32-7-W4]**
~ *former post office near Hardisty.*

It was so named in 1914 after the first postmaster, Frank Rollinson.

ROLLY POINT   **[17-3-W4]**
~ *former post office near Medicine Hat.*

It was so named in 1924 after the school district.

ROLLY VIEW   **[49-23-W4]**
~ *former post office south of Edmonton.*

The name is descriptive.

ROMA   **[83-22-W5]**
~ *former post office southwest of Peace River.*

It was named after Stanley Roma Lamb, a former resident engineer of the railway company in 1922.

RONALANE   **[13-12-W4]**
~ *former station northwest of Bow Island.*

It was named in 1914 after General Ronald Lane, who had a distinguished military career, seeing active service in the Zulu War (1879), Boer War (1881) and Egyptian War (1882).

RONAN   **[56-9-W5]**
~ *former post office southwest of Mayerthorpe.*

It was named in 1905 after Ronan in the State of Montana. The American community had been named for Major Peter Ronan who wrote the history of the Flathead Indians.

ROROS   **[45-2-W4]**
~ *former post office near Wainwright.*

It was named in 1914 after the Roros copper mines in Norway. Many of the original settlers in this district were Norwegians.

ROSALIND [44-17-W4]
~ village southeast of Camrose.

It was so named in 1905.

The population was 174 in 1972 and increased to 214 in 2009.

ROSE LYNN [28-12-W4]
~ hamlet southeast of Hanna.

It was so named in 1910 because the ridge on which this community is situated is covered with rose bushes. The floral emblem of Alberta is the wild rose.

(See: **FORCINA**)

ROSEBERG [10-6-W4]
~ former post office near Medicine Hat.

It was so named in 1911.

ROSEBUD[1] [32-1-W5]
(See: **MINARET**)

ROSEBUD[2] [27-21-W4]
~ hamlet southwest of Drumheller.

It was so named in 1896. It derives its name from the Blackfoot name of the river which was *akokiniskway*, meaning "many rose buds". This is the Edge Coal Creek where Peter Fidler noticed coal in 1792, and was referred to as Edge Creek by Dr. James Hector in 1859. Previously the community had been called GRIERSON.

ROSEDALE [28-19-W4]
~ hamlet southeast of Drumheller.

It was named after the Rosedale Colliery, a nearby coal mine. The post office was at one time called ROSEDALE STATION.

The population in 1972 was 499.

ROSEDEER [28-19-W4]
(See: **WAYNE**)

ROSEGLEN   [15-3-W4]
~ former post office near Red Deer Lake.

It was named in 1913 due to the fact that there are a large number of wild roses in the neighborhood.

ROSEMARY   [21-16-W4]
~ village northwest of Brooks.

It was named in 1914 in honor of Lady Rosemary Millicent, daughter of the fourth Duke of Sutherland, who acquired an extensive farm in the district. In 1919, Lady Rosemary (1893-1930) married the Earl of Dudley. She died tragically as a result of an airplane accident.

The population was 211 in 1972 and increased to 388 is 2006. (See also: **DUCHESS; MILLICENT**)

ROSENHEIM   [37-2-W4]
~ former post office near Provost.

It was so called in 1909 after a town in Bavaria, from where many of the first homesteaders had come.

ROSENROLL   [46-22-W4]
~ hamlet near Wetaskiwin.

It was named after Anthony Sigwart de Rosenroll, Liberal MLA for Wetaskiwin in 1905. Born at Castellamore, Italy, in 1857, he came to Canada as a young man. He became a successful lumber merchant before entering politics in 1898 when he was elected by acclamation to the territorial legislature. Rosenroll ranked as a village in 1906.

(See: **BITTERN LAKE**)

ROSEVEAR   [54-15-W5]
~ former post office northeast of Edson.

It was named in 1911 after J. M. Rosevear, an official of the Grand Trunk Pacific.

ROSSINGTON [60-1-W5]
~ former post office west of Westlock.

It was named in 1910 after a village in Yorkshire which means "the enclosure of the people on the moor."

ROSYTH [42-9-W4]
~ hamlet southeast of Hardisty.

It was named in 1909 after Rosyth, the famous Scottish naval base. The name means "headland with a landing place" from the Gaelic *ros*, "headland", and Old English *hithe*, "landing place".

ROUND HILL [48-18-W4]
~ hamlet northeast of Camrose.

It was named in 1904 from a round hill situated two miles west of the community.

ROUND VALLEY [50-7-W4]
~ post office north of Drayton Valley.

The name is descriptive.

ROWLEY [32-20-W4]
~ hamlet west of Drumheller.

It was named after C. W. Rowley, one-time assistant general manager of the Canadian Bank of Commerce, Toronto. While he was in **CALGARY**, he assisted the community to obtain a large bank loan.

ROXANA [78-20-W5]
~ station west of Kimiwan Lake.

It was so named in 1915.

ROYAL CITY
~ former community southeast of Calgary.

It was named after Joseph Royal (1837-1902), journalist and politician. Born in Lower Canada, he was educated in Montreal and called to the Quebec Bar in 1864. After moving to Winnipeg in 1870, he founded *Le Metis*(renamed in 1882 *Le Manitoba*) and entered politics as a Conservative. He sat in the Manitoba Legislature for nine years, holding a number of cabinet posts before being elected to the House of Commons in 1879. In 1883 Sir John A. Macdonald named him the Lieutenant-Governor of the Northwest Territories to replace Dewney. Royal held this position for five years.

ROYDALE   [58-7-W5]
~ former post office northwest of Sangudo.

It was opened in 1908 but has since been closed.

RUMSEY   [33-21-W4]
It was named in 1911 after R. A. Rumsey, one-time assistant general manager of the Canadian Bank of Commerce in Toronto.
The population was 113 in 1972 and decreased to 60 in 1997.

RUSKA SVOBODA   [56-17-W4]
(See: WOSTOK)

RUSYLVIA   [53-6-W4]
~ former post office north of Vermilion.

The name is a combination of two Latin words, *rus sylvia,* meaning "wooded country". It was opened in 1912.

RYCROFT   [78-5-W6]
~ village southeast of Spirit River.

It was named in 1920 after R. H. Rycroft, a local Justice of the Peace. He was a pioneer resident of the district. Previously the community was called **SPIRIT RIVER**.
The population was 528 in 1972 and increased to 638 in 2006.

RYLEY   [50-17-W4]
~ village southwest of Vegreville.

It was named in 1909 after railroader G. U. Ryley. He was the land commissioner when the railroad arrived in 1908.

The population was 469 in 1972 and decreased to 458 in 2006. (See: **YELGER**)

S

SABINE   [37-19-W4]
~ former station south of Stettler.

It is probably named after the ancient people of Central Italy, who lived chiefly in the mountains north of Rome. The Sabines were defeated by the Romans in 290 B.C. and subsequently formed an important ethnic element in the composition of the Romans. The so-called rape of the Sabine women is a notable incident in the legendary history of Rome.

SACRED HEART   [57-13-W4]
~ former post office near St. Paul.

There were a large number of Roman Catholics among the early settlers in this district. The post office was opened in 1903 but has since been closed.

SAGE CREEK   [1-2-W4]
(See: **WILD HORSE**[1])

ST. ALBERT   [54-25-W4]
~ incorporated city now surrounded by Edmonton.

It was named by Bishop Taché of St. Boniface, Manitoba, in 1861, after the patron saint of Father Albert Lacombe. It was at St. Albert, where the Sturgeon River winds its way through a valley of poplar and pine trees, that Father Lacombe built the first bridge of any size west of the Great Lakes in 1863. It is the location of Alberta's fourth degree-granting institution of higher learning, the University of Athabasca.

The population was 11,249 in 1972 and increased to 58,501 in 2008.

ST. BRIDES   [58-11-W4]
~ former post office west of St. Paul.

The patron saint of the Douglas family was St. Brides. *Brides* is the Scottish word for "Bridget".

ST. EDOUARD   [58-8-W4]
~ former post office near St. Paul.

The first two settlers in this district were Edouard Coté and Edouard Labrie. *St. Edouard* was the church's name before the first post office was opened in 1909.

ST. FRANCIS   [50-3-W5]
~ former post office north of Warburg.

Since there were a number of French Canadians among the early settlers, the saint referred to is most likely St. Francis de Sales (1567-1622), author of *Introduction to the Devout Life*.

ST. ISIDORE   [83-20-W5]
~ former post office near Peace River.

It was named after Rev. Isadore Clut. It was opened in 1964.

ST. JOSEPH
~ former community near Foremost.

This settlement was established by Germans in 1910 when the district was opened for homesteading. It was named after the Catholic church. After the drought years, which began in 1916, many farmers moved on.

ST. KILDA   [1-12-W4]
~ former post office near Foremost.

Opened in 1911, it was probably named after St. Kilda, a lonely group of four islets off the west coast of Scotland. In August, 1930, the entire population of the islands (35 in number), interesting for their isolation and primitive ways, were removed to the mainland. The Gaelic name of the main island is *hirta*: "St. Kild" (there is no such saint), is probably a sailor's corruption of that, by way of the island dialect which, it is said, replaced the "r" sound by "e".

ST. LINA   [61-10-W4]
~ *former post office northwest of Therien.*

Said to have been named in 1912 after a relative of L. Mageau, the first postmaster.

The population in 1972 was 59.

ST. LOUIS DE MOOSE LAC   [61-5-W4]
~ *pioneer French Canadian settlement.*

It was named after St. Louis, King of France. (See: BONNYVILLE)

ST. MICHAEL   [56-18-W4]
~ *former hamlet northeast of Lamont.*

It was so named in 1923 after a local Catholic church. Michael is one of the three angels liturgically venerated by the Catholic church. His feast is September 29, probably the anniversary of the dedication of a church of St. Michael and All the Angels at Rome in the sixth century.

The population in 1972 was 97.

ST. NAZAIRE
~ *Indian missionary settlement near Lac La Biche.*

In 1905 Fr. W. Lomire built a church of hewn logs, possibly naming it after the patron saint of Rev. Nazaire Dozois, the official visitor of the missionaries of the Oblate of Mary Immaculate.

ST. PAUL   [58-9-W4]
~ *town northeast of Edmonton.*

This community was founded by Father Lacombe, missionary, who in 1894 obtained four townships for a metis settlement. He called it ST. PAUL DES METIS. After twelve years the project was abandoned and settlement was opened to other settlers. The village of ST. PAUL DES METIS was incorporated in 1912 and the railway service reached it in 1920.

The population was 4,241 in 1972 and increased to 5,441 in 2007.

SAINT-PIERRE [54-26-W4]
~ hamlet west of St. Albert.

It was named by pioneer French settlers in the 1880's, after the leader of Christ's Apostles and the first Bishop of Rome. It was changed in 1900. (See: **VILLENEUVE**)

ST. VINCENT [60-9-W4]
~ former post office south of Therien.

Probably named after St. Vincent de Paul (1576 -1660), a French priest who founded several hospitals in Paris and was noted for his charitable works. Prior to 1918 the post office was called DENISVILLE. St. Denis is the patron saint of France. Early trappers called this settlement *La Croupe au Chien* or Dog's Rump.

SALT PRAIRIE [77-14-W5]
~ former post office north of Lesser Slave Lake.

The name is descriptive, there being several salt flats in the vicinity.

SAMPSONTON [28-3-W5]
~ former post office near Didsbury.

It was named after Arthur Sampson, the first postmaster in 1906. It has since been closed.

SAMSON RESERVE [44-24-W4]
~ located west of Red Deer Lake.

It was so called after a Cree chief who was the leader of the band that was established here.

SANDERVILLE [36-11-W4]
~ former station near Red Deer.

The name of the railway station. It was changed to **CONSORT** at the time of the Coronation of King George and his consort Queen Mary in 1910. Adjacent railway stations also were changed including **CORONATION, DUCHESS, LOYALIST, PATRICIA, THRONE** and **VETERAN**.

SANDHOLM BEACH   **[47-1-W5]**
~ hamlet on the north shore of Pigeon Lake.

There is a pleasant sandy beach near the community.

SANDSTONE   **[21-1-W5]**
~ former station north of Calgary.

It was named in 1907 after sandstone quarries in the
vicinity.

SANDY BEACH   **[55-1-W5]**
~ summer village west of Morinville.

The name is derived from Sandy Lake on which it is
located. The lake is so called on Palliser's map of 1865.

SANDY LAKE   **[79-22-W4]**
~ isolated northern community north of Athabasca.

It is named after a nearby lake.
The population was 78 in 1972.

SANDY RAPIDS   **[63-8-W4]**
~ former post office northeast of Therien.

This descriptive name is derived from a nearby river.

SANGUDO   **[56-7-W5]**
~ village northwest of Lac Ste. Anne.

The name could be a contraction of Santa Gudo, and was
submitted by residents in 1912, or it may have received its name
from two American towns, Santa and Gudo.
The population was 360 in 1972 and increased to 405 in
1997.

SARCEE RESERVE   **[23-29-W4]**
~ west of Calgary.

It was established in 1882 and named after the Sarcee or
Sarsi, a tribe of the Athabascan families who were allies of the
Blackfoot Confederacy. The name is of Blackfoot origin, meaning
"not good", or "the bad ones".

SARRAIL **[66-18-W4]**

~ former post office northeast of Athabasca.

It was named in 1916 after General Maurice Paul Emmanuel Sarrail, the French commander of the allied forces at Salonika during the Great War.

SAULTEAUX **[72-3-W5]**

~ former station southeast of Lesser Slave Lake.

the Saulteaux or Ojibway are an Algonkian-speaking Cree tribe who formerly occupied both shores of Lakes Superior and Huron. The name is derived from their practice of gathering annually at the rapids (sault) of Sault Ste. Marie. They moved west and traveled up the North Saskatchewan to trade with other Indian tribes. Many Saulteaux Indians worked for the Hudson's Bay Company.

SAUNDERS **[40-13-W5]**

~ former station west of Rocky Mountain House.

It was named after B. J. Saunders, who surveyed the 11th base line in 1908. This surname is ultimately derived from Alexander.

SAWBACK **[25-13-W5]**

~ former station west of Banff.

It was named after a nearby mountain range that in turn was given this name by Dr. James Hector of the Palliser Expedition. The range consists of vertical beds of gray limestone that form a number of separate peaks.

SAWDY **[68-23-W4]**

~ former post office northwest of Athabasca.

It was named in 1913 after the first postmaster, W. E. Saudy.

SCANDIA **[15-15-W4]**

~ hamlet northeast of Vauxhall.

Many of the pioneers who homesteaded in this district had come from Scandinavia, several by way of the northern United States. The post office was opened in 1924.

SCAPA   [33-14-W4]
~ hamlet northwest of Hanna.

It was named after Scapa Flow in the Orkney Islands, north of Scotland. This is one of the most important British naval bases in the United Kingdom, Admiral Jellicoe, who commanded the Grand Fleet at the Battle of Jutland, took Scapa as his title when he was created a peer.

SCARLET'S STOPPING HOUSE
(See: CALGARY-EDMONTON   TRAIL   STAGING POSTS)

SCHULER   [16-1-W4]
~ hamlet northwest of Medicine Hat.

It was named in 1910 after the first postmaster, N. B. Schuler.

The population in 1972 was 116.

SCOLLARD   [34-20-W4]
~ hamlet north of Drumheller.

The post office was in operation from 1911 to 1969. Probably named after Clinton Scollard (1860-1932), the American author and poet.

SCOPE   [13-14-W4]
~ former station northwest of Bow Island.

The district was opened up for settlement in 1913.

SCOTFIELD   [30-10-W4]
~ hamlet southeast of Hanna.

It was named in 1914, possibly because there were a number of Scots among the early settlers. The post office was closed in 1970.

SCOTFORD [55-21-W4]
~ former station northeast of Edmonton.

It was named in honor of the first premiers of Saskatchewan and Alberta: Walter Scott and Alexander Cameron Rutherford. Scott (1867-1938), was the publisher of *The Regina Leader* for many years. He was a Liberal Member of Parliament for the Northwest Territories from 1900 until he resigned to become Saskatchewan's first premier. He retired undefeated because of ill health in 1915. Rutherford (1858-1941), was a lawyer in **STRATHCONA** when he was elected to the Northwest Territories legislature in 1902. Three years later Prime Minister Laurier called on him to form the first Alberta government. He resigned the premiership in 1910 as a result of a railway scandal.

SEBA BEACH [53-5-W5]
~ summer village west of Wabamun Lake.

Prior to 1907 the post office was called SEBA. The name may be a misspelling of the Cree word *si-pi*, meaning "river".

The population was 163 permanent residents in 1972 and increased to 203 in 2006.

(See: **GAINFORD**)

SEEBE [24-8-W5]
~ former post office east of Canmore.

The name is derived from the Indian word for "river". It is located near the Bow River.

SEDALIA [31-5-W4]
~ hamlet northwest of Oyen.

It was named in 1911 after Sedalia in the State of Missouri where many of the early settlers had come from.

SEDGEWICK [44-12-W4]
~ town northwest of Hardisty.

It was named in 1906 after Robert Sedgewick (1848-1906), a Scottish born lawyer who became the Deputy Minister of Justice in 1888 before he was named to the Supreme Court of Canada. It was also the name of a provincial constituency.

The population was 758 in 1972 and increased to 891 in 2006.

SENTINEL   [8-5-W5]
~ former station west of Coleman.

It was named in 1905, possibly because of its isolated position.

SEVEN PERSONS   [11-7-W4]
~ hamlet southwest of Medicine Hat.

According to Dawson, the name is a deformation of the Blackfoot name of the nearby river, *Ki-truki-a-topi.*

SEXSMITH   [73-6-W6]
~ town north of Grande Prairie.

It was named in 1913 after David Sexsmith, a longtime Peace River district resident. Previously the community was called **BENVILLE**.

The population was 491 in 1972 and increased to 2,255 in 2007.

SHAFTESBURY SETTLEMENT   [83-22-W5]
~ settlement southeast of Peace River, above the junction with the Smoky River.

Hereabout was the site of the trading post where Alexander Mackenzie wintered in 1792-93 prior to crossing the Rockies and reaching the Pacific Ocean at Bella Coola. In 1896, Rev. J. Gough Brick, an Anglican minister of the community, sent some grain he had grown to the Chicago International Exposition, where it won a prize.

SHALKA   [56-14-W4]
~ former post office near Two Hills.

It was named after the first postmaster, Matt Shalka. It was in operation from 1911 to 1969.

SHAMROCK VALLEY
~ former community near St. Paul.

This name has an Irish sound to it.

SHANDRO [57-15-W4]
~ former post office near Lamont.

It was named in 1905 after the first postmaster, Andrew W. Shandro, who was the first Ukrainian-Canadian to be elected to the Alberta legislature. He was the Liberal member for **WHITFORD** from 1913 to 1922.

SHARPLES [29-22-W4]
~ former station west of Drumheller.

It was named in 1922 after John Sharples, a Saskatoon railway fireman who won the D.C.M. during the Great War.

SHARROW [22-2-W4]
~ former station southwest of Empress.

The name is from the title of a story by Baroness Von Hutton. The station was opened in 1914.

SHAUGHNESSY [10-21-W4]
~ former post office north of Lethbridge.

It was named in honor of Baron Thomas George Shaughnessy (1853-1923), the American-born president of the Canadian Pacific Railway from 1898 to 1918. In 1916 he was created Baron Shaughnessy, in the peerage of the United Kingdom.

The population in 1972 was 287.

SHAW [48-22-W5]
~ ghost town in the Coal Branch District.

It was named after R. L. Shaw, member of the Alberta legislature for **STETTLER**. (See: **COAL BRANCH**)

SHEARWATER [54-5-W5]
(See: **LAKE ISLE**)

SHEERNESS   [29-12-W4]
~ hamlet southeast of Hanna.

It was named in 1910, probably after the English coastal town in Kent. The post office was closed in 1969.
The population was 73 in 1972.

SHEEP CREEK RANCH   [20-2-W5]
(See: QUORN RANCH)

SHEPARD   [23-28-W4]
~ hamlet southeast of Calgary.

It was named in 1884 after Shepard of Langdon and Shepard, who were two railway contractors. The next station along the line is called **LANGDON**.
The population was 50 in 1972.

SHEPENGE   [56-12-W4]
~ former post office near Two Hills.

The name goes back to Ukrainian *Shypynci*, a town in Bukovina. It was opened in 1910 but has since been closed.

SHERWOOD PARK   [53-23-W4]
~ former post office east of Edmonton, now part of the city.

It was developed in the 1950's as a dormitory town for Edmonton. The school is called "Robin Hood".
The   population   in   1972   was   14,282, it increased to 61,660 in 2009. (See: **CAMPBELLTOWN**)

SHINING BANK   [57-14-W5]
~ former post office east of Edson.

The name refers to the yellow clay bank from which dirt and stones keep falling; they shine like gold in the sun and are visible for miles.

SHOAL CREEK   [61-2-W5]
~ former post office near Westlock.

It was in operation from 1915 to 1970.

SHONTS [50-18-W4]
~ former station south of Beaverhill Lake.

It was named in 1909 after Theodore Perry Shonts (1856-1919), an American lawyer and railway executive, who was responsible for the construction of the Panama Canal.

SHOULDICE [20-22-W4]
~ hamlet southeast of Gleichen.

It was named in 1925 after James Shouldice, the original owner of the townsite. The post office was closed in 1970.

SIBBALD [28-2-W4]
~ hamlet northeast of Oyen.

It was named in 1912 after Frank Sibbald, nearby rancher, the son of Andrew Sibbald, who settled near Morley in 1875. The population in 1972 was 73.

SIDCUP [46-3-W4]
~ former post office near Wainwright.

It was opened in 1913 and probably named after the English village of Sidcup in Kent. It is now closed.

"SILVER CITY"
~ ghost town on the higher reaches of the Bow River.

Around 1883, when the Canadian Pacific Railway's line was pushing through the Rockies, a syndicate of crooked mining promoters, with rich samples of silver ore from Montana, began showing them around Calgary, saying these were samples from their claims near Castle (Eisenhower) Mountain. They succeeded in starting a rush and a small mining town named SILVER CITY came into existence where before there had been only a railway construction camp.

SILVER HEIGHTS [39-9-W4]
~ former post office northeast of Coronation.

It was named in 1923 after the residence of Donald Smith, Lord Strathcona, near the city of Winnipeg.

SILVERWOOD   [77-5-W6]
~ former post office south of Spirit River.

It was named in 1926 after the school district. A large number of silver birch are growing in the neighborhood.

SIMMONS   [54-22-W4]
~ former station northeast of Edmonton.

It was named after Chief Justice of the Alberta Supreme Court -Trial Division and long-time chancellor of the University of Alberta, William Charles Simmons. A Lethbridge lawyer, he was returned to the First Alberta Legislature in 1905. Two years later, he vacated his seat to unsuccessfully attempt to enter the House of Commons. Later he was appointed a judge. He died in 1952.

SIMONS VALLEY   [26-2-W5]
~ former post office near Calgary.

It was named in 1907 after the first postmaster, W. E. Simons. It has since been closed.

SION   [56-2-W5]
~ former post office south of Lac La Nonne.

It was opened in 1904. This is a Biblical name, meaning Jerusalem land from the Hebrew *tsiyon*, "hill". The first church built here by F. Simonin is called "Our Lady of Sion".

SKARO   [57-19-W4]
~ former post office north of Lamont.

It was named after the first postmaster, K. H. Skaro, who had originally come from Norway. It opened in 1904 and closed in 1964.

SKIFF   [6-14-W4]
~ hamlet south of Lethbridge.

The streets in this small community are named after parts of a small boat or skiff. Thus we have Bow Avenue, Stern Avenue, Rudder Street and Tiller Street.

SLAVE LAKE [72-5-W5]
~ town south of Lesser Slave Lake.

The community gets its name from the nearby lake, which in turn, gets its name from the Slave or Slavey Indians, an Athabasca-speaking tribe of northern Alberta. The name is the one by which they were known to the Cree; it was a derogatory appellation, used because of their peaceful habits and inefficiency in war.

The population was 2,059 in 1972 and increased to 7,031 in 2007.

SLAVEY CREEK [118-21-W5]
~ near Meander River

It was named after the Slavey tribe chief who signed Indian Treaty Number Eight on behalf of his people in 1898.

SLAWA [54-8-W4]
~ former post office south of St. Paul

Religious minded Ukrainian pioneers bestowed this name on the district, which can be translated as "Glory (to God)". The post office named SLAWA was opened in 1912. It was closed in 1950.

SLEEPER [41-5-W5]
~ near Rocky Mountain House.

It was named after an early pioneer homesteader, Carlos Sleeper. In 1914 the name was changed to Carlos. (See: CARLOS)

SLEEPY HOLLOW [33-1-W4]

(See: **COMPEER**)

SLIDE OUT
~ whiskey fort located on the Belly River.

The whiskey traders "slid out" when the Mounted police came into the district in 1874.

SLOUGH BOTTOM
(See: FORT CONRAD)

SMITH   [71-1-W5]
~ *landing settlement, hamlet north of Athabasca,*

This former trading post was established in 1874 on the 60th Parallel. Its name was changed to FITZGERALD SETTLEMENT in 1915.

SMITH LANDING   [125-10-W4]
(See: FITZGERALD)

SMITHMILL   [86-24-W5]
~ *former hamlet north of Grimshaw.*

It was named after Harry Smith, proprietor of a sawmill and lumberyard in the district.

SMOKY   [77-24-W5]
(See: WATINO)

SMOKY HEIGHTS   [74-3-W6]
~ *former post office north of Grande Prairie.*

It was named after the nearby Smoky River, which in turn, derived its name from the fact that smoldering coal beds along the river banks resulted in a perpetual haze. The post office at one time was called SMOKY RIVER.

SMOKY LAKE   [59-17-W4]
~ *town northeast of Edmonton.*

It was named in 1920 after the nearby lake. A body of smoke appears to hang over the lake at certain times of the year from forest fires in the neighborhood.

The population was 1,075 in 1972 and decreased to 1,010 in 2006. (See: WARSPITE)

SNAKE VALLEY   [18-22-W4]
(See: LAKE McGREGOR)

SNARING   [47-1-W6]
~ former station west of Jasper Lake.

It was named after the nearby Snaring River which was first so-called on Palliser's Map of 1865. Dr. Hector of the Palliser Expedition states the river is named after the Snare Indians that once lived here, dwelling in holes dug in the ground, and subsisting on animals which they captured with snares of green hide, in which manner they used to kill the big horn, small deer and even moose.

SNIATYN   [57-16-W4]
It was named in 1907 after a town in Galicia from which many of the pioneer Ukrainian settlers came. The community had been called HUNKA from 1960 to 1936.

SOCIAL PLAINS   [20-2-W4]
~ former post office near Empress.

Originally it was the name of the school district. The name was chosen to express the sociable character of the pioneer settlers. It was opened in 1915 but has since been closed.

SODA LAKE   [55-14-W4]
~ former station north of Vegreville.

It was named in 1903 after the nearby shallow lake, so called because of the high soda content in its shallow waters. It had a post office between 1907 and 1939.
(See: **HAIRY HILL**)

SOUNDING LAKE   [36-4-W4]
~ former post office near Provost.

When the deep lake, for which it was named, freezes in winter, the ice often cracks, causing strange moaning sounds. (See: **MONITOR**)

SOUTH BEND   [55-12-W4]
~ *former hamlet on the Vermilion River, north of Two Hills.*

It was a descriptive name of a community for several years. Later it was changed to **DUVERNAY**, after the founder of the St. Jean-Baptiste Society. There was a post office in the community from 1908 to 1970.

SOUTH FERRIBY   [54-2-W4]
~ *former post office near Lloydminster.*

It was named in 1913 after the English village of Ferriby in Lincolnshire, the former home of the postmaster's wife. It closed in 1939.

SOUTHESK   [19-16-W4]
~ *former station southeast of Bassano.*

It was named in 1884 in honor of Sir James Carnegie, Earl of Southesk. He was the author of *Saskatchewan and the Rocky Mountains* (1875), a travel diary of an expedition that he made in 1859-60 through the Canadian Northwest.

SPARLING   [47-20-W4]
It was named thus by early settlers. It was officially changed due to confusion with **STERLING**, Alberta, and Sperling, Manitoba, to **CAMROSE**.

SPEDDEN   [59-12-W4]
~ *hamlet west of Ashmont.*

It was named after R. Spedden, a pioneer homesteader. Prior to 1923 the post office was called CACHE LAKE.

SPENNYMOOR   [24-4-W4]
~ *former post office near Oyen.*

The name, given in 1914, was suggested by English settlers who had come from the parish of Spennymoor in the county of Durham.

SPITEFIRE LAKE   [74-7-W6]
(See: **BUFFALO LAKE**)

SPIRIT RIVER [78-6-W6]
~ town in the Peace River country.

The name, a translation of the Indian, applied to a small stream two miles away from the present community. The original settlement, on the banks of the stream, grew about two trading posts; Hudson's Bay Company and Revillon.

The population was 1,130 in 1972 and decreased to 1,148 in 2006.

SPONDIN [33-12-W4]
~ former post office northeast of Hanna.

The etymology of this name is uncertain. It was opened in 1933 and closed in 1969.

SPRING COULEE [4-23-W4]
~ hamlet south of Lethbridge.

The name is descriptive, there being a number of springs in this coulee. It was so named in 1902.

SPRING CREEK [54-14-W4]
~ former post office near Mundare.

It was named in 1926 after a nearby stream which flows only in the months of April, May and June, in the spring months.

SPRING LAKE [44-16-W4]
~ former post office near Daysland.

The name was derived from a small lake formerly known as "Never-go-dry Lake". The post office was opened in 1904, but has since been closed.

SPRINGBURN [80-19-W5]
~ former station north of Kimiwan Lake.

It was so called in 1915 and since has been closed.

SPRINGDALE [44-2-W5]
~ former post office near Camrose.

It was named in 1906 after a spring in the vicinity.

SPRINGPARK   [57-6-W4]
~ former post office near Elk Point.

A spring used to run through the community. It was so called in 1913. It closed in 1970.

SPRUCE GROVE   [53-27-W4]
~ city west of Edmonton.

The post office was opened in 1894. There were a large number of big spruce trees in this area when the early settlers arrived.

The population was 2,706 in 1972 and increased to 23,326 in 2009.

SPRUCE VALLEY   [68-19-W4]
~ former post office northeast of Athabasca.

The name is descriptive, there being a large number of spruce trees in the vicinity. The name was officially rescinded in 1970.

SPRUCE VIEW   [36-3-W5]
~ hamlet west of Innisfail.

There are large stands of spruce in the vicinity. It was named by an early homesteader Knud Knudson, a Norwegian settler.

SPRUCEFIELD   [60-19-W4]
~ former post office northwest of Smoky Lake.

It was so called because of the number of spruce trees in the vicinity. It was in operation from 1913 to 1969.

SPURFIELD   [72-2-W5]
~ former station southeast of Lesser Slave Lake.

So named in 1926.

SPUTINOW   [57-2-W4]
~ hamlet east of Frog Lake.

It was named from the Cree word for high hill.

STAIR RANCH   [13-7-W4]
~ near Medicine Hat.

It was named after the 11th Earl of Stair (1848-1914) who had a controlling interest in the Stair Ranching Company, established in 1884.

STANDARD   [25-22-W4]
~ village southwest of Drumheller.

It was named after the English former home of A. J. Butler, the first postmaster in 1911. The population was 263 in 1972 and increased to 380 in 2006.

STAND OFF   [6-25-W4]
~ native community in the middle of the Blackfoot Reserve.

A. Stavely Hill says that it "has its name from the fact that [here] in the early days Wachter and two or three of his comrades had 'stood off' the United States police, who had come up to serve some process, under the impression that it was south of the boundary line". The words imply the resistance which had been offered.

STANGER   [55-6-W5]
~ former post office south of Sangudo.

It was named in 1911 after the postmaster's former home in England. There is a Stanger Head in the Orkney islands, Scotland.

STANMORE   [30-11-W4]
~ hamlet south of Hanna.

The post office was opened in 1913. It is probably called after Stanmore in Middlesex, England.

STANSLEIGH   [40-2-W4]
~ former post office near Hardisty.

It was named in 1907 after the first postmaster, Hugh Stainsleigh.

STAPLEHURST   [50-1-W4]
~ former station northwest of Lloydminster.

It was named in 1910 after the former English home of the postmaster, H. C. Rawle, in Kent.

STAR   [56-19-W4]
~ hamlet north of Lamont.

The first postmaster was Mr. Knowlton. The post office was in operation by 1900. Many of the pioneer Ukrainian homesteaders received their mail from here. There are four communities in the United States called Star, including one in the State of Texas.

STAUFFER   [37-5-W5]
~ post office north of Caroline.

It was named in 1907 after C. H. Stauffer, an American settler from Idaho, who opened a store on the post office site.
(**NOTE:** Not named after Captain J. Emmett Stauffer (1874 -1917) who was a homestead inspector and former teacher. He was a Member of the Legislature from 1905 to 1917 and served as a deputy speaker. He was killed in action at Vimy Ridge in April 1917.)

STAVELEY   [14-27-W4]
~ town on the Fort Macleod-Calgary Trail.

It was named after A. Stavely Hill, Q. C., a British M.P. and Judge Advocate of the Fleet, who organized the Oxley Ranch in 1882. He is the author of *From Home to Home* (1884).
The population was 338 in 1972 and increased to 528 in 1997.

STEEN RIVER   [122-19-W5]
~ community on the Mackenzie Highway north of Meander River.

It is named after the Steen River which joins the Hay River near this isolated settlement. The name was adopted in 1950.

STEEPER   [48-22-W5]
~ former station south of Mercoal.

The railway arrived here in 1913. It is now a ghost town.

STERCO　　　　　　　　　　[47-20-W5]
~ ghost town in the Coal Branch district.

The name is a compound of the name of the nearby mine, Sterling Collieries. Previously the community had been called BASING.
(See: **COAL BRANCH**)

STERLING　　　　　　　　　[6-19-W4]
~ village northeast of Raymond.

It was named in 1899 after J. A. Stirling, a British businessman who was a large shareholder in the Alberta Railway and Coal Company.

The population was 416 in 1972 and increased to 810 in 1997.

STETTIN　　　　　　　　　　[56-1-W5]
~ former post office near Sandy Lake.

It was named in 1913 after a German Baltic port which was the former home of the first postmaster, H. Libke. It has since been closed.

STETTLER　　　　　　　　　[39-19-W4]
~ town northeast of Red Deer.

It was named after Carl Stettler, born near Berne, Switzerland, in 1861, who came to North America as a young man and settled in Alberta in 1903. Prior to 1906 the settlement was known as BLUMENAE, after a German colony in Brazil.

The population was 4,263 in 1972 and increased to 5,843 in 2008.

STEVEVILLE   [22-12-W4]
~ former post office north of Brooks.

It was named in 1910 after Stephen Hall, first postmaster. The nearby STEVEVILLE DINOSAUR PARK, was described thus by Edward McCourt in *Road Across Canada*: "It is a Dantesque nightmare, a wild eerie region of eroded hoodoos, fantastically distorted monstrous shapes of earth rising from the valley-floor between towering canyon walls. Along the valley floor, the Red Deer River runs sluggishly past dismal sage brush flats, and the stunted trees lining its banks have been twisted by the wind and floods into grotesque witch-figures fit to haunt a man's sleep if seen by moonlight."
(See: **DINOSAUR**)

STEWART   [8-21-W4]
~ former station southwest of Lethbridge.

It was named after Dr. John S. Stewart (-1972), a Lethbridge dentist and veteran of the Boer War and World War I. He rose to the rank of General. He was a member of the Legislature from 1911 to 1925 and then a member of the House of Commons from 1930 to 1935.

STEWARTFIELD   [58-4-W5]
~ former post office south of Fort Assiniboine.

It was named in 1919 after the birthplace of Earl Haig's mother, who was the daughter of Hugh Veitch of Stewartfield in Aberdeenshire, Scotland. Field Marshall Haig commanded the British and colonial troops on the Western Front.

STEWARTVILLE SETTLEMENT   [35-23-W4]
In 1908, the homesteaders in this district near Trochu, requested the grown community center be given this name. Postal officials refused and the post office was named **ELNORA**.

STOBART   [22-23-W4]
~ former station north of Gleichen.

It was named in 1906 after an early trader, F. W. Stobart.

STOLBERG [40-13-W5]
~ former station west of Alexo.

Probably named after the town of Stolberg in Saxony, Germany. There were a number of Germans among the first settlers.

STONELAW [33-18-W4]
~ former post office south of Endiang.

It was named in 1913 by John Watts, a pioneer homesteader, after his former home of Stonelaw in Scotland.

STONY PLAIN [52-1-W5]
~ town west of Edmonton.

The origin of the name is generally attributed to the region having been the former camping grounds of the Stony Indians, but Dr. James Hector, geologist and geographer to the Palliser Expedition, under the date of January 10, 1858, states that the plain "well deserves the name from being converged with boulders which are rather rare in general in this district or country".

The population was 1,686 in 1972 and increased to 12,363 in 2006.

STOWE [8-26-W4]
~ former station north of Brocket.

It was named in honor of Harriet Beecher Stowe (1811-1896), the author of *Uncle Tom's Cabin* (1852) in her anti-slavery campaign.

STRACHAN [38-8-W5]
~ former post office near Rocky Mountain House.

It was named after Major Harcus Strachan, V. C. in 1917, only a short time after this Alberta army officer had received his decoration for valor on the Western Front. Later his name disappeared from the provincial map. Major Strachan, V. C., was an unsuccessful provincial candidate in the 1921 general election. It closed in 1968.

STRANGMUIR   [22-25-W4]
~ former station west of Strathmore.

It was named in 1914 after the residence of General Thomas Bland Strange (1831-1925), of the Military Colonization Ranch, General Strange, who had served in the Indian Mutiny, commanded the Alberta field force in the Northwest Rebellion of 1885. He was in command at the engagement of Frenchman's Butte.

STRATHCONA   [53-24-W4]
~ former city on the south bank of the North Saskatchewan River opposite Edmonton, and now a suburb of Edmonton.

It was established in 1899 but was annexed to the city of Edmonton in 1911. It was named in honor of Donald Smith, Lord Strathcona and Mount Royal (1820-1914). Born in Scotland, he entered the service of the Hudson's Bay Company in 1837. While still one of the Company's traders in Labrador, Smith began to buy stock in both the Hudson's Bay Company and the Bank of Montreal. In 1869 Smith became head of the Hudson's Bay Company, Montreal department, and in 1871 a Member of Parliament.

His financial interests widening, he became a railway magnate and one of the men chiefly responsible for the building of the Canadian Pacific Railway across the continent. In 1886 he was knighted. Three years later he became governor of the Hudson's Bay Company, a post which he held until his death. In 1896 he was appointed Canada's High Commissioner in the United Kingdom, and the next year he acquired his magnificent title of Lord Strathcona and Mount Royal. An extremely wealthy man, Lord Strathcona raised a regiment, Lord Strathcona's Horse, for service in the South African War. It was also the name at one time of a federal riding.

STRATHMORE   [24-25-W4]
~ town east of Calgary.

It was named after Claude Bowes-Lyon, thirteenth Earl of Strathmore (1824-1904). His descendant, the Earl of Althone, became Governor-General of Canada in 1940.

The population was 1,220 in 1972 and increased to 11,838 in 2009.

STREAMSTOWN [51-2-W4]
~ hamlet west of Lloydminster.

It was named in 1912 by Rev. R. Smith after the Irish town of Streamstown in the county of Westmeath.

STROME [44-15-W4]
~ village south of Daysland.

It was named in 1906, probably after the Scottish village of Strome Ferry in Ross-shire, Scotland. Prior to 1906 the post office was called KNOLLTON.

The population was 239 in 1972 and increased to 252 in 2006.

STRONG CREEK [83-22-W5]
~ former post office near Peace River.

It was named after a salt stream that runs in the vicinity.

STRY [58-13-W4]
~ former post office southeast of Vilna.

It was named in 1910 after a town in the Western Ukraine which was the former home of several of the early settlers. It was closed in 1968.

STUBNO [53-10-W4]
~ former post office northwest of Mannville.

It was named in 1921 after the Polish town which was the former home of the first postmaster, M. Stepanick. It was closed in 1958.

STURGEON HEIGHTS [70-25-W5]
~ former post office west of Sturgeon Lake.

It is so named because it is located on high ground overlooking Sturgeon Lake.

STURGEON VALLEY   [54-25-W4]
~ hamlet, north of Edmonton.

It was established in 1985.

STURGEONVILLE   [56-21-W4]
~ former post office near Edmonton.

It was situated near the Sturgeon River.

STYAL   [53-8-W5]
~ former post office west of Evansburg.

It was named in 1919, probably after the English village of Styal in Chestershire. Previously the post office was called IMRIE.

SUCKER CREEK   [75-14-W5]
~ former community near Lesser Slave Lake.

There are two streams in Alberta that have this name.

The community was briefly known as SUCKER CREEK, but the residents complained because of the number of disrespectful remarks and so it was changed.

SUFFIELD   [14-9-W4]
~ hamlet north of Medicine Hat.

It was named in 1884 after Charles Harbord, fifth Baron Suffield (1830-1914), who married Cecilia Annetta, sister of Edward, first Lord Revelstoke, who assisted in financing the Canadian Pacific Railway. Revelstoke's banking house of Baring Brothers had bought fifteen million dollars worth of a Canadian Pacific bond issue and so had averted the last financial crisis during the building of the transcontinental railway line.

A laboratory of the Defense Research Board, costing millions of dollars, is in operation at Suffield for studies of biological warfare. A large area of land is in the protected area, which is also used as a military training ground.

The population of the hamlet in 1972 was 104.

SUGDEN [62-11-W4]
~ former post office near Therien.

It was named after the first postmaster, D. S. Sugden. It was in operation from 1916 to 1970.

SULLIVAN LAKE [35-13-W4]
~ former post office south of Castor.

It was named in 1909 after John W. Sullivan, secretary to the Captain John Palliser Expedition of 1857 -1859.

SUMMERVIEW [7-29-W4]
~ former post office near Pincher Creek.

It was so called in 1904 because it enjoyed a warm southern exposure at the southern end of the Porcupine Hills.

SUNALTA [24-1-W5]
~ former station near Calgary.

It was so called in 1920, the name being a compound of "Sunny" and the abbreviation for "Alberta". Alberta has more hours of sunlight in the year than any other province.

SUNDANCE [52-5-W5]
~ former post office south of Wabamun Lake.

This name has no particular meaning, but was thought to be more or less in keeping with the Indian names in the vicinity. Prior to 1923, the post office was called LITTLE VOLGA.

SUNDANCE BEACH [47-1-W5]
~ summer village on Pigeon Lake.

The Indians, in days gone by, at certain times of the year, used to hold "sun dances", at which times the young braves were initiated into the tribe.

SUNDIAL   **[13-21-W4]**
~ former hamlet north of Lethbridge.

In the neighborhood there is a cairn with concentric circles and radiating lines of stones. It must have been constructed at least two hundred years ago.

SUNDRE   **[33-5-W5]**
~ town west of Olds.

It was named after the Norwegian birthplace of N. T. Hagen, the first postmaster.

The population was 948 in 1972 and increased to 2,518 in 2006.

SUNNYBROOK   **[49-2-W5]**
~ former post office near Drayton Valley.

It was opened in 1911, but has since been closed. It was named after Sunnybrook Creek, that flows into Strawberry Creek.

SUNNYNOOK   **[27-12-W4]**
~ hamlet south of Hanna.

It was opened in 1911. The name is descriptive.

SURBITON   **[75-5-W6]**
(See: **BRAEBURN**)

SUNNYSLOPE   **[31-26-W4]**
~ hamlet south of Olds.

The post office, when opened, was on the western slope of a hill near Kneehill Creek. The name was given by Peter Giesbach, the first postmaster.

SWAN RIVER   **[73-10-W5]**
(See: **KINUSO**)

SWALWELL   [30-24-W4]
~ hamlet north of Drumheller.

It was named in 1911 after Mr. Swalwell, an auditor of the Grand Trunk Railway. Previously the community had been called RAWDONVILLE.

The population in 1972 was 53.

SWAN HILLS   [66-10-W5]
~ town south of Lesser Slave Lake.

It is a boom community connected with the Swan Hills oil field, which was discovered in 1960.

The population was 1,414 in 1972 and increased to 1,858 in 2008.

SWAN LAKE   [38-1-W5]
(See: **SYLVAN LAKE**)

SWASTIKA   [26-25-W4]
~ former station near Calgary.

It was built in 1911. *Swastika* is a Sanskrit word, signifying a primitive cross.

SWEET VALLEY   [15-19-W4]
~ former community north of Lethbridge.

The name is descriptive. It was established in 1911 but only lasted a couple of years.(See: **TRAVERS**)

SWEETGRASS LANDING   [114-12-W4]
~ hamlet north of Fort MacMurray.

An isolated northern community on the Peace River in Wood Buffalo National Park where, in olden times, herds of buffalo used to graze in large numbers. The post office was opened in 1960.

The population was 143 in 1972.

SYLVAN LAKE   [38-1-W5]
~ town west of Red Deer.

It was named in 1907 after the nearby lake, which had previously been known as SWAN LAKE. *Sylvan* comes from the Latin word for "wood" or "forest".

The population was 1,494 in 1972 and increased to 11,115 in 2008.

T

TABER   [10-16-W4]
~ town east of Lethbridge.

According to the Geographic Board of Canada, the name is derived from the first part of the word "tabernacle". The town was named in 1904 out of consideration for Mormon settlers in the vicinity. The next station of the Canadian Pacific Railway was **ELCAN** ("nacle" spelled backwards).

According to the *Encyclopedia Canadiana,* a visit from Senator Tabor of Colorado in 1904 led to the naming of the community after him, but spelling was changed on incorporation as a town in 1907".

The population was 4,694 in 1972 and increased to 7,821 in 2008.

TAIL CREEK   [38-22-W4]
~ former Metis settlement east of Red Deer.

It was named after a stream that runs into Buffalo Lake. It became a large settlement in the 1870's consisting of several hundred buffalo hunters and their families. In 1875 there was a North West Mounted Police detachment located here.

TALBOT   [38-9-W4]
~ former post office north of Coronation.

It was named after Peter Talbot (1854-1919) who was of Anglo Irish descent. For several years, he was a Fort Macleod teacher before he became a Lacombe farmer. He was a member of the Northwest Territories. Legislative Assembly from 1902 to 1904. A year later, he vacated his seat on being appointed to the Senate. He then sat in the House of Commons for two years.

It opened in 1907 and closed in 1970.

TANGENT   **[78-24-W5]**
~ hamlet northwest of Falher.

A railway station was opened here in 1906. It is the commencement of a thirty-five mile tangent or stretch of straight railway tracks.

TANNIS   **[39-28-W4]**
(See: **BRIGGS**)

TAPLOW   **[30-13-W4]**
~ former station southeast of Hanna.

It was named in 1920, probably after the village of Taplow in Buckinghamshire, England. The name means "Taeppa's burial-mound".

TAPSCOTT   **[29-25-W4]**
~ former post office at Acme.

The origin is unknown. It opened in 1905 and closed in 1909. (See: **ACME**)

TAR ISLAND   **[92-10-W4]**
~ isolated community north of Fort McMurray.

It was so named in 1892. There is an extraction plant here connected with the Athabasca tar sands.

TARVES   **[14-1-W4]**
(See: **MANY ISLAND**)

TAWATINAW   **[61-24-W4]**
~ hamlet north of Westlock.

It was so named in 1911. The word is Cree for "river which divides the hills" or "valley river". It was a village in 1929.

TAYLOR   **[27-20-W4]**
~ former station near Drumheller.

It was named after J. E. Taylor, a pioneer settler and farmer.

TAYLORVILLE [1-24-W4]
~ former village south of Cardston.

It was named after James H. Taylor, one of the original Mormon pioneer settlers and the first postmaster in 1900. He became the Bishop of the Taylorville Mormon stack.

TEEPEE CREEK [74-3-W6]
~ former post office north of Grande Prairie.

It was named in 1924 after a nearby stream. *Teepee*, or *tepee*, is the Sioux word for "tent" or "wigwam". A wigwam was made of bark, mats, or skins stretched over a frame of poles converging to and fastened together at the top.

TEES [40-24-W4]
~ hamlet northwest of Alix.

It was named in 1905 after the owner of the original townsite, W. S. Tees. Previously the community was called BROOK.

TELFORD [49-25-W4]
~ south of Edmonton.

It was named after Robert T. Telford (1860-1932) who served with Northwest Mounted Police as a young man. He became the first pioneer settler in the community named after him and served as Mayor. Robert Telford also served in the Legislature from 1905 to 1913. The name was changed in 1905. (See: **LEDUC; CALGARY-EDMONTON TRAIL STAGING POSTS,** TELFORD'S STOPPING HOUSE)

TEMPEST [9-19-W4]
~ former station northeast of Lethbridge.

It was so named in 1894 and may have been named after Marie Tempest (1864-1942), an English operetta singer and actress who was at the height of her fame at the time. It was closed in 1916.

TEMPLE   [28-15-W5]
~ *former station east of Lake Louise.*

The name is derived from nearby Mount Temple, so called in 1884 after Sir Richard Temple, leader of the British Association excursion party to the Rockies in that year. It was first ascended by S. E. E. Allen, L. F. Frissell, and W. D. Wilcox in 1894. The mountain's height is 12,626 feet.

TENNION   [11-19-W4]
~ *former station near Picture Butte.*

The origin of this name is unknown.

THELMA   [7-2-W4]
~ *post office south of Medicine Hat.*

There is a community called Thelma in the State of Georgia. It was opened in 1911 and has since been closed.

THERIEN   [60-9-W4]
~ *hamlet southwest of Bonnyville.*

It was named in honor of Rev. J. Therien, OMI, first director of the native colony of ST. PAUL DES METIS, established in 1894. The post office was opened here in 1910 and closed in 1984.

THORENSKJOLD   [48-21-W4]
~ *former station near Camrose.*

It was named after a pioneer Norwegian pioneer settler. Federal officials abolished it in 1911. It was replaced by **ARMENA**, which is said to be a shorter form of the name "Armenia".

THORHILD   [60-21-W4]
~ *village north of Smoky Lake.*

The first homesteaders in the district in 1912 included M. G. Jardy, a Finn, who became the first postmaster and gave the post office its name.

The population was 506 in 1972. It had lost four residents by 1997.

THORSBY [49-1-W5]
~ village north of Pigeon Lake.

Many of the original homesteaders in this district were Scandinavians and the community was named after "Thor", who is the god of thunder in Norse mythology. "By" is the Norse word for "village".

The population was 608 in 1972 and increased to 945 in 2006.

THREE HILLS [31-24-W4]
~ town north of Drumheller.

It owes its name to three nearby hills. An old buffalo trail crosses a stream here. It is one of the oldest trails in Alberta, having been in use long before the Edmonton-Calgary trail.

The population was 1,452 in 1972 and 3,322 in 2008.

THREE SISTERS [24-10-W5]
~ former station east of Banff.

It was named after three mountain peaks in the same ridge, resembling each other by G. M. Dawson in 1886. Previously known as THREE NUNS.

THRONE [35-9-W4]
~ hamlet south of Coronation.

It was named to commemorate the crowning of his Majesty King George V, in 1911. Previously the post office was called HAMILTON LAKE.

(See: **CORONATION, LOYALIST, THRONE** and **VETERAN**)

TIELAND [67-2-W5]
~ former station north of Fort Assiniboine.

It was the site of a large saw mill that produced railway ties for many years.

TIGER LILY   [60-6-W5]
~ *former post office south of Fort Assiniboine.*

One of the most common garden lilies is the *lilium tigrinum* or tiger lily, which is often seen growing wild, having escaped cultivation. This post office may not have been named for the flower, but after the Indian Princess "Tiger Lily" who protects Peter and his friends in Sir James Barrie's play *Peter Pan.*

TILLEY   [17-12-W4]
~ *village south of Brooks.*

It was named after Sir Samuel Leonard Tilley, Federal Minister of Finance in Mackenzie's Liberal administration, 1874-1878. He later was named Lieutenant Governor of New Brunswick. His son was the Liberal premier of New Brunswick during the 1930's.

The population was 254 in 1972 and increased to 4 0 5 in 2007.

TIMEU   [64-4-W5]
~ *former post office north of Fort Assiniboine.*

It is the Cree word for "deep".

TINCHEBRAY   [40-14-W4]
~ *former post office west of Alliance.*

It was named after Tinchebrai, France, where the Catholic missionary order, Pères de Ste. Marie-de-Tinchebrai, has a college. Six members of this order settled here in 1904. The post office was in operation from 1907 to the 1960's.

TITIAN
~ *former station.*

It was named after Titian (Tiziano Vecellio, 1477-1576), the Italian Renaissance painter. He was born at Pieve de Cadore in Northern Italy, and was the pupil of Giorgione, the Venetian master. He excelled as a painter of portraits and of sacred and mythological subjects. The station was opened in 1892, and closed the next year.

TOD CREEK   [9-3-W5]
~ former post office east of Blairmore.

It was named in 1915 after a nearby stream which, in turn, was named after a pioneer settler of the district, William Todd, who had arrived in 1886. The spelling is erroneous.

TOFIELD   [51-19-W4]
~ town southwest of Beaverhill Lake.

It was named in 1898 after Dr. James H. Tofield, one of the first physicians in the area, who had come from Edmonton. The name was first applied to a school district.

The population was 1,035 in 1972 and increased to 1,876 in 2006. (See: **LOGAN**)

TOLLAND   [48-5-W4]
~ former post office south of Vermilion.

It was named in 1913 after the former home of the first postmaster, O. H. Webber, who had come from the State of Massachusetts.

TOLMAN   [33-22-W4]
~ former post office.

It was named after J. A. Tolman, the first postmaster. It was open from 1908 to 1918.

TOMAHAWK   [51-6-W5]
~ hamlet east of Wabamun Lake.

Early homesteaders in this district came from Tomahawk in the State of Wisconsin. A "tomahawk" was an axe of the North American Indian, used as a weapon of war. It was also used as a tool and agricultural implement. The post office was opened in 1907.

TOPLAND   [62-7-W5]
~ former post office north of Fort Assiniboine.

It was named from its situation on a ridge between the Athabasca and Freeman Rivers. The post office was opened in 1914.

TORLEA   **[48-14-W4]**
~ *former station northwest of Viking.*

The name is possibly derived from "torr", the Norse word for a "hill", and "lea", an open space. Prior to 1916, the post office was called NESTOR.

TORRINGTON   **[32-26-W4]**
~ *village east of Olds.*

It may be named after Torrington in the county of Devon, England. The name means the "hill pasture homestead".

The population was 132 in 1972 and increased to 177 in 1997.

TOTHILL   **[9-4-W4]**
~ *former post office south of Medicine Hat.*

It was named after Alfred Tothill, the first postmaster. It was open from 1924 to 1959.

TOWERS   **[21-20-W4]**
~ *former station near Cluny.*

The origin of this name is unknown. It was in operation from 1912 to 1915.

TOWN LAKE   **[45-3-W5]**
~ *former station south of Pigeon Lake.*

It was named after a nearby body of water called Township Lake in 1924.

TRAVERS   **[15-19-W4]**
~ *hamlet north of Enchant.*

The railway line arrived here in 1915. The post office's name was **SWEET VALLEY** at one time.

TREFOIL   **[26-16-W4]**
~ *former station southeast of East Coulee.*

A "trefoil" is a plant of the genus *trifolium*, having triple or trifoliate leaves. It is also another name for "clover".

TRENVILLE [24-22-W4]
~ former post office near Delburne.

It was named after an early pioneer homesteaders and general store owner Trenaman. It had a post office from 1905 to 1927.

TRIANGLE [74-18-W5]
~ former post office west of High Prairie.

There is a community called Triangle in the State of Idaho.

TRING [53-3-W4]
~ former post office near Lloydminster.

It was probably named after the English town of Tring, Hertfordshire. It was opened in 1908 and closed in 1931.

TRISTRAM [42-23-W4]
~ former post office near Ponoka.

It was named after the first postmaster, Tristram F. Fry. It was opened in 1907 and closed in 1928.

TROCHU [33-23-W4]
~ town north of Drumheller.

It was named after Colonel Armand Trochu (1857-1930). He was the nephew of General Louis-Jules Trochu (1815-1896) who resigned as the Governor of Paris rather than surrender the city to the Germans in January 1871.

Colonel Trochu led a group of French Catholic army officers in establishing the St. Ann Ranch Trading Company in 1905. The community became known as TROCHU VALLEY. Then the name was shortened to Trochu in 1911.

On the outbreak of the Great War, many of the settlers returned to France to rejoin the army. They had left the army and France in protest against the government's anti-Catholic stand with regard to education.

The population was 731 in 1972 and increased to 1,113 in 2009.

TROON   [39-23-W4]
~ former station near Red Deer.

It was named in 1914 after the Scottish seaport in Ayrshire, from whence some of the early homesteaders had come. This Gaelic word means "cape" or "point".

TROUT LAKE   [86-4-W5]
~ hamlet north of Slave Lake.

It was named after the fish species.
The population in 1972 was 85.

TRUMAN   [63-8-W4]
~ former post office near St. Paul.

It was named after Harry S. Truman, president of the United States from 1945 to 1952. The post office opened in 1948 and closed in 1963.

TUDOR   [25-23-W4]
~ hamlet south of Drumheller.

It was named in 1911 after the royal house of Welsh descent who ruled England for three generations: Henry VII (1485-1509); his son Henry VIII (1509 -1547); and his three children, Edward VI (1547-1554), Mary I (1554-1558), Elizabeth I (1558-1603). On Queen Elizabeth's death the house of Tudor ceased to exist.

TULLIBY LAKE   [55-2-W4]
~ hamlet south of Frog Lake.

There is a place called Tullytown in the State of Pennsylvania. *Tully* is the Irish word for "hill" and *by* is the Norse word for "village".

TUPPER CREEK   [76-13-W6]
~ former post office near Peace River.

It was so named from its proximity to Tupper River, a tributary of the Pouce Coupe River, which in turn was named after Frank Tupper, who was the first to survey this region of northern Alberta. It was opened in 1920 but has since been closed.

TURIN [12-19-W4]
~ hamlet north of Lethbridge.

It was named after "Turin" a champion imported Percheron stallion, owned by eight farmers. It was opened in 1910.

TURNER VALLEY [20-3-W5]
~ town south of Calgary.

It was named after the two Turner brothers, Robert and James, who were pioneer Scottish settlers. They homesteaded in 1886 near Sheep Creek.

TUTTLE [37-27-W4]
~ former station south of Red Deer.

The railway line reached here in 1892, and the station was named after a pioneer rancher, W. W. Tuttle.

TWEEDIE [68-12-W4]
~ former station northeast of Lac La Biche.

It was named after Thomas Mitchell March Tweedie (1872-1944) who was the nephew of Lemuel J. Tweedie, premier of New Brunswick and later Lieutenant Governor of the province. T. M. M. Tweedie became a prominent Calgary lawyer. He sat in the Legislature from 1911 to 1917, and the House of Commons from 1917 to 1921. Acting Justice Minister named Tweedie Justice of the Alberta Supreme Court in the autumn of 1921. He served as the Chief Justice of the Trial Division.

TWIN BUTTE [4-29-W4]
~ former post office near Pincher Creek.

It was named after two neighboring hills or buttes. The post office was opened in 1905.

TWIN LAKES
~ former custom post south of Cardston.

It was named after two nearby lakes. It was opened in 1904 but was closed in 1917.

TWIN RIVER   [1-20-W4]
~ former post office west of Milk River.

It is named after a nearby river, a tribute of the Milk River which ultimately flows into the Gulf of Mexico. Prior to 1921, the post office was called HACKE.

TWINING   [31-24-W4]
~ hamlet northwest of Drumheller.

It was named in 1912, probably after Sir Philip Geoffrey Twining (1862-1920), the Canadian-born quartermaster-general of the First British Army during the Great War. He was a graduate of the Royal Military College at Kingston.

TWO CREEKS   [61-16-W5]
~ hamlet south of Iosegun Lake.

The community is located close to two streams that are tributaries of the Athabasca River.

TWO HILLS   [54-12-4]
~ town southwest of St. Paul.

The name is descriptive, there being two hills in the neighborhood. The post office was opened in 1914.
    The population was 1,133 in 1972 and 1,232 in 2007.

TYROL   [56-5-W4]
(See: LINDBERGH; MOOSWA)

U

UKALTA [57-17-W4]
~ former post office northeast of Lamont.

The name is from the two initial letters of "Ukraine" added to the abbreviation for the province of Alberta. There were many Ukrainians among the original settlers in this district. The post office was in service from 1934 to 1964.

ULLIN [39-8-W5]
~ former station near Rocky Mountain House.

It was probably named after Thomas Campbell's poem, "Lord Ullin's Daughter":
"Now who be ye, would cross Lochgyle,
This dark and stormy water?"
"O, I'm the chief of Ulva's isle,
And this Lord Ullin's daughter."

UNCAS [52-21-W4]
~ former post office east of Edmonton.

It was named in 1909 after the American town of Uncas, in the State of Oklahoma. The Nineteenth century American novelist Fenimore Cooper introduces a character "Uncas" in his novel, *Last of the Mohicans*. The post office was in service from 1925 to 1968.

UNIPOUHEOS [56-3-W4]
~ Cree Indian Reserve in Northern Alberta established in 1879.

It is named after Chief Unipauhaos, successor to Puckeechkeeheewin, who was a noted gambler. The name means "standing erect"; the chief's English name was Stanley.

USONA   [44-26-W4]
~ former post office southwest of Wetaskiwin.

It was opened in 1905, and closed after 1930. The word is formed from the initial letters of "United States of North America". There is a place in California with the same name. There were a large number of Americans among the first homesteaders in the district.

V

VAL SOUCY [58-21-W4]
~ *former post office north of Edmonton.*

It was named in 1917 after the first postmaster J. L. Soucey. The post office has since been closed.

VALE [15-3-W4]
~ *former post office north of Medicine Hat.*

It was named in 1913 after the American town of Vale in the State of Oregon, the former home of the first postmaster, John Evers.

VALHALLA [75-10-W6]
~ *former post office north of Hythe in the Peace River Country.*

The name was suggested in 1916 by Rev. Halvor N. Ronning, Lutheran pastor, who founded the settlement. His son was Chester Ronning, member of the Legislature from 1932 to 1935, then as Alberta CCF leader, who after World War II became a Canadian diplomat.

In Norse mythology, "Valhalla" is a banqueting hall of Odin, leader of the Gods, where the Valkyries bring Viking heroes after death to feast with the gods.

VALLEJO [35-7-W4]
(See: LOYALIST)

VALLEY CITY [40-24-W4]
~

It was named by early pioneers in the expectation of large population growth in 1909. The name was officially changed to CLIVE in 1912.

VALLEYVIEW   [70-22-W5]
~ town on the Edmonton to Peace River Country trail.

"This highway covers forest lands and a desolate stretch of muskey country before it hits at VALLEYVIEW, where the traveler leaves road-squeezing timber to get his first breath-taking view of the semi-open agriculture land that gives **GRANDE PRAIRIE** its name". (Liddell)

The population was 1849 in 1972 and increased to 1,884 in 2007.

VANDYNE   [24-3-W4]
~ former post office north of Medicine Hat.

The origin of the name is unknown. Van Dyne is a Dutch surname. It was opened in 1912 and closed after 1930.

VANESTI   [47-4-W4]
~ former post office near Wainwright.

The origin of this name is unknown. It was opened in 1911 and closed in 1948.

VANRENA   [81-4-W6]
~ former post office south of Fairview.

The name is derived from the names of two early settlers in the district, Van and Rooney. A post office was opened here in 1914 but has since been closed.

VAUXHALL   [13-16-w4]
~ village east of Lethbridge.

It was named in 1923 after Vauxhall, near London, England. The name is ultimately derived from Old French *vaux*, meaning "valleys". An English manor house is often referred to as a "hall". In the 1920's and 1930's, Vauxhall was a popular small British automobile, built in the industrial center.

The population was 982 in 1972 and increased by twelve in the next twenty-five years.

VEGA [62-3-W5]
~ *former post office northeast of Fort Assiniboine.*

A star of the first magnitude in the constellation Lyra is called Vega.

VEGREVILLE [52-14-W4]
~ *town east of Edmonton.*

This town was first settled in 1895 by French-speaking Catholic pioneers from the State of Kansas. The post office, which was opened that year, was named in honor of Father Valentin Végréville was taken prisoner by Louis Riel at Batoche in 1885, but was later released. He died in 1903.

The population was 3,776 in 1972 and increased to 5,834 in 2009.

VELDT [36-15-W4]
~ *former hamlet northwest of Castor.*

This community was named in 1909 after the Dutch word for "the high grassy plateau that is found in South Africa". A neighboring station is called **BOTHA**, after the famous Boer general.

VENICE [66-15-W4]
~ *former hamlet south of Lac La Biche.*

It was so named in 1916 after the former home of the first postmaster, J. O. Billos. Venice is an ancient city built on numerous small islands in the Adriatic. It was one of the most important Italian city-states during the middle ages. The hamlet has since disappeared. It had been an Italian settlement.

(See: **BILLOS**)

VERDANT VALLEY [29-18-W4]
~ *former post office southeast of Drumheller.*

The name is descriptive of this valley. The post office was opened in 1910, and closed in 1945.

VERGER   [22-15-W4]
~ former station north of Brooks.

A "verger" is a church official who serves as sacristan, caretaker, usher and general attendant.

VERMILION   [50-6-W4]
~ town west of Lloydminster.

It gets its name from the river on which it is situated. When the original settlers saw the red clay along the river banks, they named it the Vermilion River. The post office was called **BREAGUE** until 1906, after the Cornish town of the same name.

The population was 2,949 in 1972 and increased to 4,472 in 2007.

VERMILION VALLEY   [49-16-W4]
(See: HOLDEN)

VESELA   [54-9-W4]
~ former post office near Willingdon.

Vesela is the Russian word for "cheerful". It was opened in 1926, but has since been closed.

VETERAN   [35-8-W4]
~ village southeast of Coronation.

The communities of **CONSORT**, **CORONATION**, **LOYALIST**, **THRONE** and **VETERAN** are adjacent, and were named in the Coronation year, 1911. King Edward VII died that year and was succeeded by his son, George V. Formerly this village had the descriptive name of **WHEATBELT**.

The population was 264 in 1972 and increased to 293 in 2006.

VICTORIA [58-17-W4]
~ Methodist mission.

PAKAN was known as VICTORIA until 1887. In 1862, Rev. George McDougall selected it as the site of a Methodist Mission and named it in honor of Her Majesty Queen Victoria (1819-1901), who came to the throne in 1837. A Hudson's Bay trading post was established here in 1864. For years the road from EDMONTON to PAKAN was called the Victoria Trail.

VIKING [47-13-W4]
~ town south of Mannville.

It was named in 1904 by Norwegian pioneer settlers in honor of their ancestors who reached the North American continent and established settlements in Newfoundland in the tenth century. *Viking* is the Old Norse word, commonly regarded as being formed from *vik*, meaning creek, inlet, or bay, plus "ing". A Viking was thus one who frequented inlets of the sea.

The population was 1,203 in 1972 and decreased to 1,085 in 2006.

VILLENUEVE [54-26-W4]
~ hamlet north west of Edmonton.

It was named after Frederic Villeneuve, son of Senator Joseph Octave Villeneuve, who served as the St. Albert member of the N.W.T. Legislative Assembly from 1892 to 1902. He was a lawyer and publisher of a French language newspaper. The post office was in operation from 1900 to 1970. Previously known as **Saint-Pierre.**

VILNA [59-13-W4]
~ village north of St. Paul.

It was a Polish settlement, named in 1920 after the then Polish city of Vilna by settlers from there. Vilna is the ancient capital of the Lithuanian principality founded in 1322.

The population was 344 in 1972 and decreased to 274 in 2006.

VIMY [58-25-W4]

This name commemorates the struggle for Vimy Ridge in France in April, 1917. The battle was without doubt the greatest Canadian victory of the Great War. The primary objective for the Canadians was a crest 7,000 yards wide in the center of which stood the village of Vimy. The advancing troops crossed the devastating "no-man's land" to storm the strongly held German positions. The Canadians suffered 10,602 casualties in the three-day battle.

VIOLET GROVE [48-8-W5]
~ hamlet south of Drayton Valley.

The name is descriptive, but is meaningless. A grove means a group of trees, while the flowers of pink-violet hue (Epilobibicum angusta folium) are commonly called "fire-weed", a weed like plant that grows in ditches, and where there has been a prairie fire.

VOLMER [54-25-W4]
~ former hamlet west of Edmonton.

It was named after Joseph Vollmer, a pioneer German homesteader who sold land for a railway siding in 1908. The original spelling of the hamlet was VOLLMER.

VULCAN [17-24-W4]

In Roman mythology, Vulcan was the god of fire. His Greek name is Hephaestus, the son of Zeus and Hera, he is most famous as the blacksmith of the gods and their chief artificer and builder. Volcanoes are named for Vulcan. It was said that the community's twenty grain elevators was a record number for any Alberta town.

The population was 1,612 in 1972 and increased to 1,940 in 2006.

W

WABAMUN [53-4-W5]
~ hamlet on the shore of Wabamun Lake, west of Edmonton.

Captain Palliser's Map of 1865 identifies this body of water as "White Lake". *Wabamun* is the Cree word for "mirror". This deep lake is clear and blue in color.

The population was 483 in 1972 and increased to 662 in 2009.

WABASCA [80-25-W4]
~ former post office north of Athabasca.

It was opened in 1908 and called after Wabasca Lake, which is a corruption of the Cree word *wapuskau*, meaning "grassy narrows.".

It was combined to form **WABASCA-DESMARAIS** in 1982. (See: **DESMARAIS**)

WAGHORN [39-27-W4]
(See: **BLACKFALDS**)

WAGNER [73-7-W5]
~ former station south of Lesser Slave Lake.

It was so named in 1914 after the German engineer who constructed this section of the Edmonton, Dunvegan and British Columbia Railway line.

WAHSTAO [59-15-W4]
~ former post office south of Smoky Lake.

The name is a corruption of the Cree word *wahsato*, meaning "spiritual light". It was so named by Peter Erasmus. The post office was opened in 1907 and closed in 1957.

WAINWRIGHT   [44-6-W4]
~ town southeast of Edmonton.

It was named in 1908 after William Wainwright, an executive of the Grand Trunk Pacific Railway. The post office was formerly called DENWOOD.

The population was 3,735 in 1972 and increased to 5,775 in 2008.

WALROND   [8-29-W4]
~ ranch near Hanna.

It was named after Sir John Walrond (1818-1889). He leased an area of 10,000 acres in June 1884 and the ranch became one of the largest in western Canada. The operation was wound up in 1897.

WALSH   [11-1-W4]
~ hamlet east of Medicine Hat.

It was named after Major James Morrow Walsh, North West Mounted Police, who was an inspector in the force from 1873 to 1883. Major Walsh led a detachment of the North West Mounted Police to the Cypress Hills in 1875 to build Fort Walsh, Saskatchewan. This was a danger area when Sitting Bull and some 5,000 Sioux braves crossed the border into Canada following the Custer massacre of the Little Big Horn in Montana. The Sioux remained in the Cypress Hills area for five years before re-crossing the 49th parallel. Fort Walsh and **MEDICINE HAT** was in the postal district of Assiniboia West prior to 1905.

Walsh is an English word (from Old English *wealh* meaning "a foreigner"), and is what the Anglo-Saxons called Celtic peoples of the West.

WANDERING RIVER   [72-16-W4]
~ former post office north of Lac La Biche.

It was named after a stream that flows into Lac La Biche. The name is descriptive.

WANEKVILLE   [57-7-W5]
(See: **ROCHFORT BRIDGE**)

WANHAM [78-3-W6]
~ village north of Birch Hills.

The name is taken from the Cree word for "Chinook". It was so named in 1916.

The population was 294 in 1972 and decreased to 216 in 1997.

WAPITI [69-8-W6]
~ former post office south of Grande Prairie.

It was named after the Cree word for "elk". The elk was a characteristic species of the Parkland until the arrival of the fur-traders. It is now found mainly in the mountains and in the foothills of the Rockies.

WARBURG [48-3-W5]
~ village north of Pigeon Lake.

It was named in 1916 after the ancient castle of Warberg in Sweden. The change in spelling was an error. Many of the original homesteaders in the district came from Scandinavia.

The population was 453 in 1972 and increased to 696 in 2009.

WARDEN [38-20-W4]
~ former post office south of Stettler.

There is a village called Warden with a Saxon church in Northumberland, England. The name is derived from the Old English *weard dun*, meaning "watch hill".

WARDLOW [22-12-W4]
~ hamlet north of Brooks.

It was named in 1922 after a daughter of rancher J. R. Sutherland, across whose property the railway tracks were built.

WARNER   [4-17-W4]
~ *hamlet north of Lethbridge.*

It was named after A. L. Warner, an American land agent who encouraged farmers from the Dakotas to resettle in Canada in 1906. It was previously called BRUNTON.
The population was 446 in 1972 and decreased 383 in 2007.

WARPER
~ *former station near Fort McMurray.*

It was opened in 1917 and closed down a few years later.

WARRENSVILLE   [84-24-W5]
~ *former post office north of Cardinal Lake.*

It was named in 1921 after the first postmaster, E. Warren.

WARSPITE   [59-18-W4]
~ *village southwest of Smoky Lake.*

It was named after a British cruiser engaged in the Battle of Jutland, May 31, 1916. It was changed from SMOKY LAKE CENTRE in September, 1916.
    The population was 119 in 1972 and decreased to 73 in 1997.

WARWICK   [53-14-W4]
~ *hamlet north of Vegreville.*

It was named after an early pioneer of the district, S. R. Warwick. This surname is derived from Warwick, England; the first holders of it would have come from that part of England. The Anglo-Saxon name *warwick* means "dwelling by the weir". The post office was in operation from 1904 to 1970.

WASEL   [58-15-W4]
~ *former post office near Lamont.*

It was named after the first postmaster, Wasel Hawrelak. (William Hawrelak, mayor of Edmonton in the 1950's, was his son.) it was in operation from 1911 to 1969. *Wasel* is the Ukrainian for "William".

WASKATENAU   [59-19-W4]
~ village south of Smoky Lake.

This is the Cree word meaning "opening in the banks", from the cleft in the ridge though which the river of this name flows into the North Saskatchewan.

The population was 154 in 1972 and increased to 278 in 2006.

WASTINA   [31-8-W4]
~ former post office near Oyen.

It is a corruption of *miwasin*, the Cree word for "pretty place". It was opened in 1912 and closed after 1930.

WATER VALLEY   [29-5-W5]
~ former post office southwest of Cremona.

The name refers to the fact that there is an abundance of water in the vicinity. There is a city called Water Valley in the State of Mississippi.

WATERGLEN   [43-22-W4]
~ former post office near Red Deer Lake.

The name refers to the abundance of water in the vicinity. It was opened in 1908 and closed some time later.

WATERHOLE   [81-3-W6]
~ former post office south of Fairview.

It was so named in 1912 because there was a "waterhole" in a coulee on the **DUNVEGAN** to **PEACE RIVER** trail. It was a favorite camping site for homesteaders moving into the PEACE RIVER Country.

(See also: **FAIRVIEW**)

WATERTON LAKES   [1-30-W4]

~ townsite in Waterton Lakes National Park.

It was named by Blakiston in honor of Charles Waterton (1782-1865), naturalist and author of *Wandering in South America, the North West of the United States and the Antilles in 1812, '16,'20 and '24.* It is one of the most beautiful parts of the Canadian Rockies.

WATERWAYS   [89-9-W4]

~ hamlet south of Fort McMurray.

It is the terminus of the Northern Alberta Railway line. Trans-shipment from rail to the Athabasca River takes place here for heavy goods going into the north, and vice-versa, during the summer shipping season. It was so named in 1921.

WATINO   [77-24-W5]

~ hamlet west of Falher.

Watina is the Cree word for "valley". Prior to 1925 the community had been called SMOKY.

WATT LAKE   [34-10-W4]

~ former post office near Lower Therien Lake.

The name "Walter" was generally pronounced without the "L" sound and probably the surname "Watt" belongs to the personal name. It was opened in 1923 and has since been closed.

WATTSFORD   [54-13-W4]

~ former post office near Lamont.

It was named in 1914 after Thomas Watt, a pioneer rancher of the district. There is a ford across a nearby stream in the vicinity.

WAUGH   [58-23-W4]

~ former post office near Westlock.

It was named after the first postmaster, W. J. Waugh. This surname is probably Old English *wealh*, meaning "foreigner", a name given by the Anglo-Saxons to Strathclyde Celts. It was in operation from 1905 to 1970.

WAYBROOK [57-23-W4]
~ former post office north of Edmonton.

It was opened in 1910, and has since been closed down.

WAYNE [28-19-W4]
~ hamlet south of Drumheller.

It was so named in 1914. Previously the community had been called ROSEDEER. There are counties called Wayne in sixteen states of the United States as well as a city in the State of Nebraska.

WEALD [51-19-W5]
~ former station southeast of Edson.

It was named in 1912, probably after the Sussex Weald, a tract of country, formerly wooded, which lies between the north and south downs in England.

WEALTHY [52-9-W4]
~ former post office near Vermilion.

It was named in 1909 on the suggestion of hopeful young homesteaders of the district.

WEASEL CREEK [60-20-W4]
~ former post office near Smoky Lake.

It was named after a nearby stream of the same name. Weasels at that time were plentiful in the neighborhood. It was in operation from 1927 to 1970.

WEBSDALE [20-9-W4]
(See: JENNER)

WEBSTER [74-5-W6]
~ former station near Grande Prairie.

It was named after George H. Webster, Calgary businessman and railway contractor. He served as the Mayor of Calgary and was then a member of the Legislature from 1926 to 1933. It was established in 1916.

WEED CREEK   **[48-1-W5]**
~ former post office near Wetaskiwin.

A "weed" has been defined as "a plant out of place". The name was descriptive.

WELLING   **[6-21-W4]**
~ hamlet south of Lethbridge.

It was named after Horace Welling, a pioneer Mormon settler who homesteaded in 1902.

WELLSDALE   **[53-5-W4]**

(See: **CLANDONALD**)

WELLSVILLE   **[7-25-W4]**
~ former post office near Alsask, Saskatchewan.

It was named after George Wells, the first postmaster in 1910. Later it was closed.

WEMBLEY   **[71-8-W6]**
~ town southeast of Beaverlodge.

It was named after the Wembley (London) Exposition in 1924 by the Lake Saskatoon Board of Trade.

The population was 321 in 1972 and increased to 1,443 in 2006.

WENHAM VALLEY   **[47-3-W5]**
~ former post office near Drayton Valley.

It was named after Mark Wenham, the first postmaster. It opened in 1911 and closed in 1952.

WENO   **[24-9-W4]**
~ former post office near Bassano.

The name is derived from the motto of the Alberta Financial Brokers of Calgary - "We Know". It was opened in 1914 and closed some years later.

WESSEX   [29-1-W5]
~ former station south of Carstairs.

This station was opened in 1910. The part of south western Britain settled by the West Saxons in the fifth century became known as "Wessex". Alfred the Great was the King of the West Saxons in the 8th century.

WEST WINGHAM   [32-11-W4]
~ former post office near Hanna.

It was named after Wingham, Ontario, from where many of the pioneers settlers had formerly resided. It opened in 1912 and closed in 1959.

WESTCOTT   [30-3-W5]
~ former post office southwest of Didsbury.

It was given its present name in 1908. Previously it was called KANSAS. There is a Westcott in Berkshire, England.

WESTERDALE   [32-3-W5]
~ former post office near Olds.

There is a parish of this name in Yorkshire, England. The post office was opened in 1910 and closed in 1932.

WESTEROSE   [46-28-W4]
~ former post office near Wetaskiwin.

It was named after Westerose, Sweden, the former home of some of the pioneer settlers in 1907.

WESTLOCK   [60-26-W4]
~ town north of Edmonton.

In 1912, the future townsite was purchased from William Westgate and Mr. Lockhart. Prior to then, the post office was called **EDISON**.

The population was 3,314 in 1972 and increased to 4,964 in 2008.

WESTWARD HO   [32-4-W5]
~ hamlet west of Olds.

It was named after the novel *Westward Ho,* written by Charles Kingsley and published in 1855. The name was suggested by an early settler in the district, a former British officer, Captain Thomas. The post office was in operation from 1905 to 1970.

WETASKIWIN   [46-24-W4]
~ city on the old Calgary-Edmonton trail.

The eighth largest city in Alberta, it came into being about 1892 when the Calgary and Edmonton Railway was in the course of construction. The Indian name for the neighboring Peace Hills, Wetaskiwin, was adopted. The name is a translation of the Cree word *wi-ta-ski-oo-cha-ka-tin-ow.* According to C. D. Smith, the Cree and the Blackfoot made a treaty here in 1867, after an exhausting battle.

The population was 6,586 in 1972 and increased to 12,285 in 2009.

WHARRANTON   [27-11-W4]
(See: **BARACA**)

WHATCHEER   [33-11-W4]
~ former post office near Hanna.

The name is "What cheer?", a form of greeting similar to "How are you?" it was opened in 1914 and closed after 1930.

WHEATBELT   [35-8-W4]
~ former post office, southeast of Coronation.

It was named when a post office was established. The name was descriptive of the bumper crop obtained in the district. The name was changed in 1913. (See: **VETERAN**)

WHEAT CENTRE   [16-18-W4]
~ former post office near Travers.

When this post office was opened in 1910, it had every prospect of being a large grain growing district.

WHEELER [97-11-W4]
~ *former post office near Bitumount.*

It was named after A. N. Wheeler, the first postmaster. It was opened in 1926 and later closed.

WHISKEY GAP [1-23-W4]
~ *former hamlet south of Cardston.*

The only events that break the quiet of WHISKEY GAP are the bi-weekly arrival of a train and the daily visits of the mail truck. This small community near the Montana border is populated by four families and a grand total of eighteen residents.

It was once an important distributing center. The product was whiskey and it flowed back and forth across the International Border. The whiskey came by mule team and pack horse along the trail through the Milk River Ridge, as it was on the direct route to **FORT WHOOP-UP**. During the 1920's, when the United States had prohibition, the whiskey flowed in reverse into Montana, but the current of traffic changed when Alberta, in its turn, went "dry".

The name was changed to **FAREHAM** through the influence of a man who was a strong temperance supporter. But the local inhabitants agitated until they got their community's name restored. The word "whiskey" is derived from the Gaelic *visge (-beatha)*, meaning "water of life".

WHITBURN [79-8-W6]
~ *former post office east of Blueberry Hills.*

There is a Whitburn in the County of Durham, England. The name means "White's burial mound".

WHITECOURT [59-12-W5]
~ *town on the Edmonton-Peace River Trail.*

It was named in 1909 after the first postmaster, Walter L. White. The "Court" was added to conform with **GREEN COURT**, twenty-six miles distant, Mr. White's old home.

The population was 3,114 in 1972 and increased to 9,202 in 2008.

WHITECROFT   **[52-23-W4]**
~ hamlet east of Edmonton.

The Old English word *croft* means a small enclosed field, especially one with a cottage. In Scotland a crofter is a small farmer.

WHITEFISH LAKE   **[61-12-W4]**
~ Methodist mission north of Lac La Biche.

It was established in 1859 by the Canada Methodists and suffered as a result of an outbreak of smallpox some ten years later.

WHITELAW   **[82-1-W6]**
~ hamlet north of Fairview.

It was named after a car service accountant of the Edmonton, Dunvegan, and British Columbia Railway.

WHITEMUD HOUSE   **[58-16-W4]**
~ early trading post at the junction of the White Earth and North Saskatchewan Rivers.

This North West Company trading post was opened in May, 1810, and later moved to **FORT VERMILION**[1]. The chimneys of the house were standing in 1858 and ruins were still marked in 1925.

WHITFORD   **[56-15-W4]**
~ hamlet north of Lamont.

It was named after the first family to settle near the lake of the same name. In Cree, *munawanis* means "the place where eggs are always gathered". Whitford was the name of an early provincial constituency. The post office was in operation from 1893 to 1970. (See: **Calgary-Edmonton Trail Staging Posts**)

WHITLA   **[11-8-W4]**
~ hamlet south of Medicine Hat.

This community used to be a village, named after R. J. Whitla, a merchant from Winnipeg. The Canadian Pacific Railway tracks reached here in 1895.

WHITNEY **[10-22-W4]**
~ former station north of Lethbridge.

There is a Whitney in Hereford, England. The name means
"Hwita's Island" or "White Island".

WIDEWATER **[73-7-W5]**
~ hamlet south of Lesser Slave Lake.

The name is descriptive, referring to the width of the lake
opposite the community. The post office was opened in 1923. Now
it is a wide spread hamlet.

WIESVILLE **[40-28-W4]**
This name was changed to **ASPEN BEACH** in 1916.

WILD HORSE{1} **[1-2-W4]**
~ custom post on the Canadian-American border, south of Medicine Hat.

The post office, which was opened in 1913, was called
SAGE CREEK until it received its present name in 1926 to agree
with the name of the nearby border crossing. The community was
named after a nearby creek.

WILD HORSE{2} **[57-4-W5]**
(See: **BALLANTINE**)

WILDMERE **[48-6-W4]**
~ former post office near Vermilion.

The name is descriptive. *Mere* is an Old English word for
"pool" or "lake". It was opened in 1910 and has since been closed.

WILDWOOD **[53-9-W5]**
~ village east of Chip Lake.

The name is descriptive.
The population in 1972 was 403.

WILHELMINA **[34-2-W4]**
(See: **ALTORADO**)

WILLESDEN   [43-5-W5]
~ former post office near Rimbey.

It was named on the suggestion of the first postmaster in 1913 after his former home, Willesden Green, near London, England. It was closed in 1947.

WILLINGDON   [56-15-W4]
~ village north of Vegreville.

It was named in honor of Freeman-Thomas, Marquis of Willingdon, Governor-General of Canada, 1926-1931. Born in 1866, Freeman-Thomas was educated at Eton and Cambridge prior to going to Australia in 1895 as Aide-de-camp to his father-in-law, Lord Brassey, who was Governor of Victoria. He sat in the British House of Commons as a Liberal member from 1900 to 1910. He was then made Baron Willingdon of Ratton, and took his seat in the House of Lords. Lord Willingdon served as Governor of Bombay (1913-1919) and of Madras (1919-1924), and was created a Viscount.

Appointed to succeed Lord Byng as Governor-General of Canada, he assumed office in 1926. Five years later he was created an earl and appointed Viceroy of India. In the course of fifty years of public service, he proved himself an accomplished diplomat and one of the shrewdest of British negotiators. He died in 1941.

The population was 387 in 1972 and decreased to 295 in 2006.

WILLMORE WILDERNESS PROVINCIAL PARK
It is the largest provincial park in Alberta, situated north of **JASPER NATIONAL PARK**. It is named after Norman Willmore (1909-1963) an Alberta politician. Born in Fessenden in the State of North Dakota, he came to Canada as a child and was educated in **EDMONTON**. He became a shoe merchant in **EDSON**. Willmore entered provincial politics when he was elected as the Social Credit member for EDSON in 1944. He was named to Manning's cabinet nine years later as Minister of Lands and Forests, and died in office.

WILLOW CREEK **[28-19-W4]**
~ hamlet south of Drumheller.

The name is descriptive, there being willows along the banks of the nearby stream.

WILLOWLEA **[52-1-W4]**
~ former post office near Lloydminster.

The name was descriptive. The post office was opened in 1917 and closed in 1956.

WILLOWS **[13-29-W4]**
(See: **BLACKTAIL**)

WILSON **[7-20-W4]**
~ former station south of Lethbridge.

It was named after Ernest H. Wilson, an executive of the Alberta Railway and Irrigation Company in 1912.

WIMBORNE **[33-26-W4]**
~ hamlet north of Olds.

It was named in 1909, probably after the English town of Wimborne in Dorset. *Wimborne* means "a meadow with a stream or burn".

WINAGAMI **[77-19-W5]**
~ former station south of Kimiwan Lake.

Winagami is the Cree word signifying "dirty-water lake". The name is descriptive.

WINDFALL **[60-15-W5]**
~ hamlet west of Whitecourt.

The name is descriptive, a large number of trees having been blown down in the district before the area was settled.

WINDY RIDGE **[68-20-W4]**
(See: **PLEASANT VIEW**)

WINFIELD   [46-3-W5]
~ hamlet near Camrose.

It was named after V. Winfield Smith, a prominent railway contractor who after retiring became a farmer. He was a member of the Legislature from 1921 to 1952 and served as the Minister of Railways and Telephones. He married late in life. His son was Hon. J. Winfield McBraine Smith was made Justice of the Alberta Court of Queen's Bench (1997).

WINNIFRED   [11-9-W4]
~ hamlet west of Medicine Hat.

It was named after Winnifred, daughter of R. J. Whitla in 1888. It was a station on the narrow gage railway that took **LETHBRIDGE** coal to the main Canadian Pacific Railway line near **MEDICINE HAT**. Previously known as WHISTLE STOP MILE 31.

WINSTON CHURCHILL PROVINCIAL PARK
~ near Lac La Biche.

It was named after the Right Honorable Sir Winston Churchill (1874-1965), the son of Lord Randolph Churchill and an American mother. He was educated at Harrow and Sandhurst Military College. After a brief but eventful career in the army, he became a member of the Conservative governments during the first three decades of the century. After the outbreak of the Second World War he was appointed First Lord of the Admiralty, a post which he had earlier held from 1911 to 1915.

In May 1940 he became Prime Minister and remained in office until 1945. He took over the premiership again on the Conservative victory of 1951 and resigned four years later. However, Churchill remained a Member of Parliament until the general election of 1964 when he did not seek re-election. Queen Elizabeth II conferred on him the dignity of knighthood after he had refused the dukedom of London in 1953. Ten years later President Kennedy conferred on him honorary citizenship of the United States. He is the only man to be so honored.

Churchill's literary career began with campaign reports: *The Story of the Malakand Field Force* (1899), an account of the campaign in the Sudan and the Battle of Omdurman. His first major work was a biography of his father, *Lord Randolph Churchill* (1906). His other famous biography, the life of his great ancestor, the first Duke of Marlborough, was published in four volumes in the 1930's. He received the Nobel Prize for Literature in 1953. His magnificent oratory survives in a dozen volumes of speeches. He was also a gifted amateur painter.

WINTERBURN   [52-25-W4]
~ hamlet west of Edmonton.

There are numerous Winterburns in England. The post office was opened in 1903. It could have been named after the custom of winter burning of muskeg.

WISDOM   [8-5-W4]
~ former post office south of Medicine Hat.

The name expressed the opinion of early homesteaders in the district who thought they were wise to settle in this part of the province. It was opened in 1913 and closed in 1960.

WISTE   [32-7-W4]
~ former post office near Oyen.

It was named after the Swedish father-in-law of C. Leaf, the first postmaster. It was opened in 1910 and closed in 1932. It was a Swedish settlement.

WITHROW   [39-4-W5]
~ former post office near Rocky Mountain House.

It was named after William H. Withrow (1839-1908), the editor of the *Canadian Methodist Magazine* for several decades.

WITTENBURG   [41-4-W5]
(See: **LEEDALE**)

WOKING   **[76-5-W6]**
~ hamlet south of Spirit River.

It was named after B. J. Prest, a railway engineer's former English home in Surrey. It had a post office from 1932 to 1968.

WOLF CREEK   **[54-16-W5]**
~ former post office northeast of Edson.

Canis Lupus, commonly called the "timber or gray wolf", is found in large numbers in the vicinity.

WOODBEND   **[51-26-W4]**
~ former post office near Edmonton.

"Woodbine" was the name submitted in 1908, being that of a grade of flour milled here at the time. Postal officials changed the spelling.

WOOD BUFFALO NATIONAL PARK[100-13-W4]
This is the largest national park in North America. Established in 1922, it has an area of 17,300 square miles, straddling the Alberta and Northwest Territories border. It provides an ideal habitat for the wood bison, for which it is named, who freely roam across the open plains and through the vast forests.

WOOD RIVER   **[43-24-W4]**
~ former post office near Ponoka.

It was named after Wood River, Nebraska, the former home of F. J. Bullock, the first postmaster, in 1903. It closed in 1947.

WOODGLEN   **[47-16-W4]**
~ former post office near Camrose.

Residents in 1908 suggested the name of GLENWOOD after a place of that name in the State of Minnesota. However, there were communities of this name is British Columbia, New Brunswick, Nova Scotia, Ontario, and Prince Edward Island. To avoid confusion, postal officials modified the name to WOODGLEN.

WOODHOUSE [11-26-W4]
~ former hamlet on the Fort Macleod-Calgary trail.

It was named after W. E. Woodhouse, a Calgary railway official in 1909. It had a post office from 1916 to 1969.

WOODPECKER [9-17-W4]
(See: **BARNWELL**)

WOOLCHESTER [10-5-W4]
~ former post office south of Medicine Hat.

There were a number of sheep ranchers in the district when it was named. Chester comes from the Latin word, *castra*, meaning a military camp.

WOOLFORD [3-24-W4]
~ former post office east of Cardston.

The name is descriptive. Many sheep are raised in this district. There are five communities in England called "Woolford". It was opened in 1912 and closed in 1963.

WORLEY [51-27-W4]
(See: **GOLDEN SPIKE**)

WORSLEY [86-8-W6]
~ former post office south of Clear Hills.

There is a village called Worsley at the start of the Bridgewater Canal in Lancashire, England. The name means "pasture for cattle".

WOSTOK   [56-17-W4]
~ *hamlet northeast of Lamont.*

On August 29, 1898, *The Edmonton Bulletin* reported that a post office, to be called "Wostok", was to be opened on Section 22-56 in township 56, range 4, west of the 4th meridian, and to be run by Theodore Nemirsky, the first Ukrainian-Canadian to do so. Nemirsky's journal states: "It was the first post office amongst our Galician settlers in the whole of Canada that was designated by a completely Russian name. I was the postmaster of the post office and myself christened it Wostok." The meaning of this Slavic word is "east". It was formerly called RUSKA SVOBODA, while George Butler of the North West Mounted Police referred to the community in 1897 as MOLE LAKE.

WRENTHAM   [6-17-W4]
~ *former hamlet south of Lethbridge.*

It was named in 1914 after the English village of Wrentham in the county of Suffolk. Local inhabitants have another story on the origin of this name. The original homesteaders in the district were very poor. Before they went to the big town of Lethbridge, they would rent clothes from the woman running the first store. In time the community was called the place where one could "Rent 'Em".

WRITING-ON-STONE Provincial Park[1-13-W4]
~ *a 1,055 acre provincial park, situated twenty-five miles east of Milk River.*

Nearby this provincial park, cut deep into a sandstone cliff, are drawings of horses, men and implements. The petroglyphs at WRITING-ON-STONE have been described in *Album of Prehistoric Canadian Art* (issued in 1923) to be a "type of art that is found as far south as Wyoming but not on the Pacific Coast or east of the Canadian or American plains". The pictures that may have been drawn in the late eighteenth century were first recorded by James Doty, an American explorer, in 1855. The drawings are childish in form, yet there are two distinct types. Some figures are long and narrow and of straight, single lines. Others, both of people and animals, are round and have form.

(See: **MASINASIN**)

WRITING-ON-STONE   [1-13-W4]
~ former customs post near Wild Horse.

It was opened in 1904 but closed in 1917 to permit the police to enlist to go overseas and was never re-established.

WYECLIF   [52-22-W4]
~ hamlet east of Edmonton.

It was named after the Wye River in the west of England.

WYND   [45-1-W6]
~ former station south of Jasper.

The name is possibly descriptive; there are many windy days in the year in this locality.

WYNDHAM RANCH   [21-25-W4]
~ south of Calgary.

The proprietor was Colonel Alfred E. Wyndham (1837-1914) who had commanded the 12th Battalion of the York Rangers (Militia Unit) during the second Riel Rebellion in 1885. Later he, with his family, stayed in Alberta. He was one of the most prominent ranchers in the ranching community. In 1898, he was an unsuccessful **HIGH RIVER** candidate in the NWT Legislative Assembly general election.

X

~ no Alberta community whose name commences with the letter 'X', has officially been recognized.

Y

YATES [53-16-W5]
~ former station near Edson.

It was named after a railway official of the Grand Trunk Pacific in 1911. It had a post office from 1913 to 1953. There is also a railway station in Montana known as "Yates".

YELGER [50-17-W4]
~ former station near Vegreville.

The name is almost a transposition of the original name RYLEY, which it was called from 1911 until 1915, when it was changed to avoid confusion with **RYLEY** station, one mile distant.

YELLOWHEAD [45-4-W4]
~ former station west of Jasper.

It is named after the nearby pass across the Rockies. The Yellowhead Pass immortalizes the Iroquois half-breed trapper of the early nineteenth century, who was nicknamed "Tête Jaune" or "Yellowhead". He may have been François Decoigne who was employed by the Hudson's Bay Company in 1814, and cached furs in the vicinity; or Pierre Hatsinaton, who guided a party of Iroquois fur hunters in the area in 1820.
(See: **DECOIGNE**)

YEOFORD [46-3-W5]
~ former post office, west of Wetaskiwin.

It was named after the first postmaster, Charles M. Marson's former English home at Yeoford, Somerset. It was opened in 1909 and closed in 1969.

YOUNGSTOWN   **[29-9-W4]**
~ village east of Hanna.

It was named after Mrs. James M. Bickwell (née Young), the wife of the first postmaster, a pioneer settler in 1903. Early settlers expected the community would become a large city! The community never fulfilled its early promise.

The population was 357 in 1972 and has decreased to 170 in 2006.

Z

ZAMA CITY   [113-5-W6]
~ oil prospecting hamlet community in Northern Alberta.

It was named after a nearby lake which, in turn, was called after a Slave Indian Chief.

ZAWALE   [56-16-W4]
~ former post office near Lamont.

This Ukrainian settlement was established in 1910 and named after the town in Galicia, from where many of the original homesteaders came. It closed in 1949.

ZETLAND   [32-9-W4]
~ former post office near Hanna.

It was opened in 1912 and has since been closed.

Zetland is the local official name of the Shetland Islands, off the north coast of Scotland. The group contains about one hundred islands, of which twenty-three are inhabited. Most of the inhabitants are of Norse descent. The islands were acquired by Scotland in 1469. There is a hamlet in Ontario's Huron County called Zetland.

(See: **HEMARUKA**)

ZOLDOVARA   [48-9-W4]
~ former post office near Vermilion.

It was opened in 1912 and closed in 1928. The origin of this name is unknown.

Index

Bain, James (railway foreman), 19

Baintree, 19

Baker, Walter R. (railway executive), 278

Balfour (British Conservative Party leader), 42

Balkan, 281

Ballantine, 19

Ballater, 20

Ballina, 20

Balm, 20

Balzac, 20

Balzac, Honoré de (novelist): *La Comédie Humaine*, 20

Banff, **20**; railway, xvii; vicinity, 13, 21, 63, 68, 112, 119, 220, 295, 325

Banff National Park, 146; vicinity, 20, 196

Bankhead, 21

Bannerman, William (MP), 60

Bantry, 21

Baptiste River, 21

Bar K Two Ranch, 275

Bar S Ranch, 21

Bar U Ranch, 21

Baraca, 22

Bardo, 22

Bargrave, 22

Barich, 22

Baring Brothers (banking), 316

Barker's Stopping House, 61, 266

Barlow, 22

Barlow, Dr. A. E. (geologist), 22

Barnegat, 22

Barnett, Edward (NWMP), 61

Barnett's Stopping House, 61, 195

Barney, 278

Barnwell, 23

Barnwell, R.(CPR agent), 23

Barons, 23

Barr Colony, 47, 162; British settlers, xvii

Barr, Rev. Isaac, 207

Barrhead, 23; vicinity, 31, 65, 67, 105, 161, 182, 193, 206

Barrie, Sir James: *Peter Pan*, 326

Barstow, 23

Bashaw, 24; vicinity, 109, 112

Bashaw, Eugene (land owner), 24

BASING, 311

Bassano, 24; vicinity, 86, 125, 143, 151, 159, 199, 216, 220, 306, 348

Bassano, Countess of, 86

Bassano, Marquis of, 24

Bathgate, 24

Battenburg, 24, 144

Battenburg, Prince Louis of, 24

Battle, 25

Battle Bend, 25

Battle Lake, 25

Battle Ridge, 25

Battle River, 25, 26; vicinity, 135

Battle River Crossing, 25, 104; *vicinity*, 61

Battle River Prairie, 25, 245

Battleview, 26

Bawlf, 26, 230

Bawlf, Nicholas (executive), 26

Bay of Fundy, 4

Bay Tree, 26

Bayrock, 26

Bayrock, L. A. (geologist), 26

Beach Corner, 26

Beacon Corner, 27, 245

Beadle, G. J. (postmaster), 202

Bear Canyon, 27

Bear Lake, 33; vicinity, 28, 53

Bear River, 53

Bearberry, 27

bears: grizzly, 27, 154

Bearspaw, 27

Beauharnois, Charles de la Boische, Marquis de: Governor of New France, 282

Beaumont, 27

Beauvallon, 27

Beaver Crossing, 28, 80

Beaver Mines, 28

Beaver River, 28

Beaver tribe, xiii, 257; reserve, 238; words, 190

Beaverdam, 28

Beaverdam River, 68

Beaverhill, 28; vicinity, 100, 266

Beaverhill Lake: vicinity, 28, 167, 169, 205, 212, 301, 327

Beaverlodge, 28, 196; vicinity, 114, 148, 157, 171, 173, 193, 202, 213, 279, 348

beavers, 28, 68, 280

Beazer, 29

Beddington, 29

Bedson, 227

Begg, Alexander (rancher, historian): *History of the Northwest*, 104

Behan, 29

Behan, Brother (missionary, cook), 29

Beiseker, 29; Scandinavian settlers, xvii

Beiseker, Thomas L. (banker), 29

Belgian: painter, 217; settlers, 267

Belgium: Dinant, 99; Ghent, 143; settlers, 232

Bellcamp, 29

Bellcott, 30

Belle Rock, 30

Bellevue, 30, 89

Bellis, 30

BELLOW, 28

Belloy, 30

Belloy, Madame (opera singer), 30

Bellshill, 30

Belly River, 189; vicinity, 303

Belvedere, 31, 194, 259

Bemis Bag Company, 182

Bemis, Judson, (businessman), 182

Ben Nevis Coal Mine, 239

Benalto, 31

Benbow, 31

Benbow, William N. (Private), 31

Benedickson, Mr. (homesteader), 98

374   Community Names Of Alberta

Chinook Valley, 74
Chip Lake, 74, 200;
  vicinity, 118, 149, 214,
  221, 258, 353
Chipewyan, xiii; words, 115,
  235
Chipewyan Lake, 74;
  vicinity, 74
Chipman, 75
Chipman, Clarence
  Campbell (HBC
  Commissioner), 75
Chisholm, 75
Chisholm Mills, 75
Chisholm, Thomas
  (contractor), 75
Chokio, 75
Choquette, Charles
  (freighter), 136
Churchill, Sir Winston (British
  Prime Minister), 356
Churchill,Winston (Am.
  novelist), 67
Cinque Ports, 173
city, 6, 63, 103, 134, 135, 276,
  290, 308; 1882, 224; 1885,
  204; 1890, 201; 1892, 350;
  1893, 59; 1903, 207; 1912,
  150; 1930, 103; capital,
  110; defined, xxii; former;
  1899, 314; largest, 59
Clairmont, 75
Clandonald, 75
Claresholm, 76; vicinity,
  15, 38, 83, 146, 213, 255
Clarinda, 76
Clark Manor, 76
Clark, Clarinda, Mrs.
  (mother), 76
Clark, F. Miss (postmistress),
  76
Clark, J. G. (postmaster), 76
Clarkson Valley, 76
Claysmore, 76
Clear Hills, 76; vicinity, 76,
  359
Clear Prairie, 76
Clearview, 77
Clearwater River, xiii; vicinity,
  134
Clever, Martin (farmer), 69
Cleverhill, 69
Clivale, 77
Clive, 77

CLIVE, 335
Clive, Robert (British
  statesman), 77
Clover Bar, 77, 111
Clover, Thomas H. (gold
  prospector), 77
Cluny, 77; vicinity, 328
Clut, Rev. Isadore, 291
Clyde, 78
Clyde, George
  (postmaster), 78
Clymont, 78
coal, 14; aerial tramway, 5;
  deposits, 64, 110, 204,
  207, 285, 304;
  discovered, 9; industry,
  180; mines, 54, 64, 78, 79,
  81, 103; 1880's, xviii; 1901,
  137; 1904, 212; 1907, 30,
  64; 1917, 51; 1929, 167;
  Beaver, 28; Ben Nevis,
  239; Black Diamond
  Mine, 37, 98; Brazeau
  Collieries, 243; Canadian
  Dominion, 57; Galt Coal
  Mine, 159; Newcastle,
  241; North American
  Collieries, 236; Reliance
  Coal Company, 275,
  278; Rosedale Colliery,
  285; Star Mine, 5;
  Sterling Collieries, 311;
  mining communities, 35,
  72, 78, 79, 103, 166, 204,
  243, 265; 1913, 57;
  Scotland, 6; railway, 356
Coal Branch District, xviii, 12,
  57, 78, 79, 100, 124, 127,
  184, 204, 211, 212, 225,
  248, 275, 281, 299, 311
Coal Valley, 78; ghost town,
  xviii
Coalbanks, 14, 78, 79, 86,
  204; coal, xviii
Coalbanks, Red Deer
  River, 78
Coaldale, 79
Coalhurst, 79, 81; coal, xviii
Coalspur, 78, 79; ghost town,
  xviii
Cochrane, 79, 222;
  vicinity, 71, 143, 230, 272
Cochrane Lake: vicinity, 208
Cochrane Ranch, 80, 222

Cochrane, Admiral Sir
  Thomas, 230
Cochrane, Lady Adela, 230
Cochrane, M. H.
  (Senator), 79, 80
Cochrane, T. B. H. (ranch
  owner), 230
Codesa, 80, 155
Codner, 80
Coghill, 80
Cold Lake, 28, 80, 150; Metis,
  xvii
Cold Lake House, 80
Coldwater Lake, 80
Coleman, 81, 89; vicinity,
  266, 298
Coleman Lake: vicinity, 69,
  83, 173
Coleridge, 104
Colinton, 81
College Heights, 81
Colles, 188
Collicutt, 81
Collicutt, Dr. Frank
  (rancher), 81
Colliery, 79, 81
Collins, E. (railway official),
  80
Collins, George H.
  (postmaster), 184
Colorado: Senator, 321
Columbia River, xiv, 164
Columbine, 81
La Comédie Humaine
  (Balzac), 20
COMMEMORATIVE NAME -
  defined, xvi
Commerce, 82
community, xxii; 1892, 322;
  1909, 333; former, 6, 10,
  36, 70, 94, 253, 254, 288,
  299, 316; 1899, 160; 1907,
  253; 1908, 252; 1910, 291;
  1911, 319
Compeer, 82
Comrey, 82
Condor, 82
Conjuring Creek, 82
Conklin, 82
Conklin, John (railway
  official), 82
Connacher, Mr (real estate
  promoter), 83
Connaught, Duke of, 256

Darling River, 92

Darwell, 92

Darwin, Charles: *The Origin of the Species*, 173

Dauntless, 93

Davidson, Abraham (postmaster), 52

Davidson, Sir Charles Peers (judge), 258

Davidson, William (postmaster), 198

Dawson, Captain (colony manager), 270

Dawson, G. M., 325

Day, Egerton W. (businessman), 93

Day, Tony (rancher), 88

Daysland, 93; vicinity, 270, 307, 315

De Winton, 93

De Winton Ranch, 93

De Winton, General Sir Francis (rancher), 93

Deadwood, 93

Deaver, 93

Deaver, G. C. (postmaster), 93

Debney, 262

Debney, Philip, (railway engineer), 262

Debolt, 94

DeBolt, Henry E. (MLA), 94

Decoigne, 94, 180

DECOIGNE, 363

Decoigne, François (fur trader), 94, 180, 363

Decrene, 94

Decrene, Mr. (contractor), 94

Deep Creek, 94

deer, 122, 305; black tailed, 38, 94; caribou, xiii, 17; elk, 113, 343; horns, 52; Indian words, 266; moose, xiii, 231, 305

Deer Hill, 94

Deer Mound, 94

Defense Research Board, laboratory, 316

Del Bonita, 95

Delacour, 95

Delburne, **95**, 140; vicinity, 14, 211, 329

Delia, 95

Delnorte, 175

Delph, 96

Demay, 96

Demers, Fr. Modeste (missionary), xiv

Demmitt, 96

Demmitt, Chelsea (pioneer), 96

Denhart, 96

Denis, Saint, 293

Denisville, 293

Denmark: Dalum, 92

Dennis, 96

Dennis, John Stoughton (surveyor, civil servant), 96

Denny, Cecil (NWMP), 91

DENWOOD, 342

Department of Energy, Mines and Resources: Toponymy Division, xi

Department of the Interior: map 1883, 224

Derwent, 97

Desa, J. (railway official), 80

DESCRIPTIVE NAME - defined, xv

Desjarlais, 97

Desjarlais, David (postmaster), 97

Desmarais, 97, 341

Desmarais, Rev. Alphonse Desmarais (OMI), 97

Devenish, 97

Devenish, Gwen, 97

Deville, 97

Deville, Dr. E. G. (Surveyor General), 97

Devon, 97

Devona, 98

Devonshire, Cavendish, Victor Christian William (9th Duke of), 68

Dewberry, 98

Dewdney, 248

Dewdney, Edgar (MP), 248

Diamond City, **98**; coal, xviii

Diana, 155

Dickens, Captain Francis J. (son, NWMP), 60

Dickens, Charles (novelist): *Tale of Two Cities*, 60

DICKENSON STOPPING HOUSE, 60

Dickson, 98

Dickson Creek, 98

Dictionnaire de la Langue des Cris, (Fr. Lacombe), 195

Didsbury, **98**; vicinity, 88, 229, 293, 349

Dimsdale, 99

Dimsdale, Henry G. (railway official), 99

Dina, 99

Dinant, 99, 267

Dinosaur, 99, 312

Dinosaur Provincial Park and Museum, 99

Dinton, 99

Dinwoodie, 99, 199

Dinwoodie, Mr. (postmaster), 99

Direlton, 100

Diss, 100

Dixon, James, (Stony Chief), 179

Dixon, Roy (merchant, postmaster), 100

Dixonville, 100

Dobson, 100

Dodds, 100

Dodds, John (settlers), 100

Dog's Rump, 293

Dogpound, 100

Domesday Book (1086), 29, 111

Dominion Experimental Farm, 7

Donalda, 100, 112

Donatville, 101

Dongray, 101

Donley, A. B. (lumberman), 3

Donnelly, 101, 155

Doran, 9

Dore, W. O. (postmaster), 101

Dorenlee, 101

Dorothy, 101

Doty, James (explorer), 72, 360

Dover, white cliffs of, 7

Dovercourt, 101

Dowling, 102

Dowling, Dr. D. B. (surveyor), 102

Dozois, Rev. Nazaire (OMI), 292

24; missionaries, 195;
newspaper, 288;
Northwest Rebellion of
1885, xiv; settlement, 292;
1870's, 321
Metiskow, 226
Mewassin, 226
Mexican: Mennonite
settlements, 40
Mexico, Gulf of, 227
Michichi, 226
Michigan, 226; Brutus, 51;
settlers, 265
Michigan Centre, 226
Middle Creek, 226
Middleton, 200
Midland Coal Mine, 227
Midland Securities, 248
Midlandvale, 227
Midnapore, 227
Miette, 227
Miette River, 164
Military Colonization Ranch,
314
military fort, 131, 134
military training ground, 316
Milk River, 95, 220, 222, **227**;
tributary, 332; vicinity,
332, 360
Milk River Ridge, 351
Mill Creek, 233
Millar, Malcolm (settler), 228
Millarville, 228
Miller, John M. (postmaster),
228
Miller, R. J. (postmaster), 279
Millerfield, 228
Millet, 228
Millet, Jean Francois
(painter), 228
Millicent, 103, **228**, 286
Milne, J. M., 81
Milo, 216, **228**
Milton, Viscount, 71
Minaret, 229
Minburn, 229
Minehead, 281
minerals, 110
miners, xviii; early, 61
mines: anthracite, 13; coal.
See under coal, mines;
copper, 284; disasters,
166, 167; Federal Dept.,
xi; towns; 1905, 21; silver,
301; Sweden, 121

Minister of Railways and
Canals, 39
Ministik Lake, 229
Minnesota: Glenwood,
358; settlers, 64
Mintlaw, 229
Mirror, 229
Missawawi Lake, 111
Mission Beach, 229
missionaries, xiv; 102; 1894,
292; 1905, 292; Alberta's
first, xiv; Catholic, xiv, 16,
29, 35, 50, 57, 58, 97, 121,
150, 154, 181, 195, 200,
201, 202, 229, 234, 244,
252, 324; 1844, 195; 1904,
326; conference, 232;
French, 48; massacred,
139; Methodist, 140, 352;
Our Lady of Assumption
school, 16; Protestant, xiv
Mississippi: Prentiss, 267;
Water Valley, 345
Mississippi River, 95, 227
Missouri: Louisiana, 211;
Sedalia, 297
Missouri River, xiv, 32, 227
Mitford, 230
Mitford, Mrs. Percy, 230
Mitsue, 230
Mitzpah, 230
Moberly, H. J. (HBC Factor),
134
Mole Lake, 360
Molstad, 26, **230**
Molstad, O.
(postmaster), 26
Monaghan, Edward
(homesteader), 144
Monarch, 230
Monday, Garrington, 142
Monday, H. C. (postmaster),
142
Monitor, 230, 305
Monkman, 231
Monkman, P. J.
(postmaster), 231
Montana: Babb, 67; border,
351; Chief Mountain, 72;
Fort Benton, 32, 78, 131,
136; gold prospectors,
197; Helena, 186;
Kessler, 186; Little Big
Horn, 342; Milk River,

227; Ronan, 284; Yates,
363
Montgomery, 231
Montgomery, Hugh John
(MLA), 231
Monvel, 231
Moon Lake, 231
moose, 231, 232. *See* deer
Moose Lake, 43, 133
Moose Portage, 231
Moose Ridge, 231
Mooswa, 232
Moravian settlement, 51
More (or Moore) (railway
contractor), 39
Morin, Abbé, 232; *Le nord-
ouest Canadian et ses
Resources Agricole*, 232
Morinville, **232**, 265; French
districts, xvii; vicinity, 15,
55, 294
Morley, **232**, 301; mission, xiv;
vicinity, 253
Mormons: Colorado, 10;
communities, 23, 64, 112,
251; ecclesiastical
districts, 5, 29, 323;
leaders, xx, 64; names,
168; ranches, 80, 275;
region, xvii; settlers, 58,
188, 201, 275, 321, 323,
348
Morningside, 232
Morrin, 233
Morrison, J.C. (postmaster),
24
Mosquito Creek: vicinity, 21
Mosside, 233
Mound, 233
Mount Geikie, 143
Mountain House, 231
Mountain Mill, 233
Mountain Park, 78; ghost
town, xviii; vicinity, 184
Mountain View, 233
Mudge, 127
Muirhead, 234
Mulga, 234
Mulhurst, 234
Mulligan, G. (postmaster),
234
Mundare, **234**; Ukrainian
settlements, xvii; vicinity,
24, 240, 307

S

The map reference numbers
start in the north west, and
winds down to the southeast.

Alphabetic list

Lamont	47.
Langdon	92.
Leslieville	64.
Lomond	107.
MacKay	87.
Magrath	118.
Manning	7.
Mannville	42.
Mayerthorpe	25.
McLennan	19.
Meander River	2.
Milk River	120.
Morley	89.
Mundare	45.
Myrnam	41.
Nanton	102.
Niton Junction	57.
Olds	83.
Peers	58.
Picture Butte	106.
Provost	71.
Raymond	119.
Redcliff	111.
Redwater	32.
Retlaw	109.
Rich Lake	23.
Rimbey	65.
Rumsey	77.
Rycroft	12.
Sangudo	26.
Saunders	62.
Sexsmith	13.
Sherwood Park	48.
Smoky Lake	33.
Standard	95.
Sterco	61.
Strathmore	93.
Sylvan Lake	66.
Therien	37.
Thorhild	31.
Thorsby	49.
Three Hills	80.
Tofield	46.
Trochu	79.
Turner Valley	90.
Two Hills	44.
Vauxhall	110.
Vilna	35.
Vulcan	103.
Wabamun	50.
Wandering River	21.
Warburg	51.
Waterton Park	117.
Wembley	17.
Westlock	30.
Whitefish Lake	34.
Wild Horse	122.
Zama Lake	1.